PAULINE LETTERS

Texts@Contexts

Series Editors
Athalya Brenner-Idan
Archie C. C. Lee
Gale A. Yee

PAULINE LETTERS

Texts@Contexts

Edited by
Menghun Goh

t&tclark
LONDON • NEW YORK • OXFORD • NEW DELHI • SYDNEY

T&T CLARK

Bloomsbury Publishing Plc, 50 Bedford Square, London, WC1B 3DP, UK
Bloomsbury Publishing Inc, 1359 Broadway, New York, NY 10018, USA
Bloomsbury Publishing Ireland, 29 Earlsfort Terrace, Dublin 2, D02 AY28, Ireland

BLOOMSBURY, T&T CLARK and the T&T Clark logo are trademarks of Bloomsbury Publishing Plc

First published in Great Britain 2024
Paperback edition published in 2025

Copyright © Menghun Goh and contributors 2024

Menghun Goh has asserted her right under the Copyright, Designs and Patents Act, 1988, to be identified as Editor of this work.

All rights reserved. No part of this publication may be: i) reproduced or transmitted in any form, electronic or mechanical, including photocopying, recording or by means of any information storage or retrieval system without prior permission in writing from the publishers; or ii) used or reproduced in any way for the training, development or operation of artificial intelligence (AI) technologies, including generative AI technologies. The rights holders expressly reserve this publication from the text and data mining exception as per Article 4(3) of the Digital Single Market Directive (EU) 2019/790.

Bloomsbury Publishing Plc does not have any control over, or responsibility for, any third-party websites referred to or in this book. All internet addresses given in this book were correct at the time of going to press. The author and publisher regret any inconvenience caused if addresses have changed or sites have ceased to exist, but can accept no responsibility for any such changes.

A catalogue record for this book is available from the British Library.

A catalog record for this book is available from the Library of Congress.

ISBN: HB: 978-0-5677-1178-6
PB: 978-0-5677-1182-3
ePDF: 978-0-5677-1179-3
eBook: 978-0-5677-1181-6

Series: Texts@Contexts

Typeset by Newgen KnowledgeWorks Pvt. Ltd., Chennai, India

For product safety related questions contact productsafety@bloomsbury.com.

To find out more about our authors and books visit www.bloomsbury.com and sign up for our newsletters.

CONTENTS

Series Preface	vii
List of Abbreviations	xiii
List of Contributors	xv
INTRODUCTION Menghun Goh	1

Part I
CONTEXTUAL CONCERN

Chapter 1
WAS PAUL HAPPY? A CONTEXTUAL READING OF PHILIPPIANS 3.1–4.1 IN CONVERSATION WITH NORTH AMERICAN PSYCHOLOGY AND ITS LIMITATIONS   11
    Greg Carey

Chapter 2
FROM 'G'DAY' TO 'BLESS YOU': AN AUSTRALIAN-AMERICAN REFLECTION ON PAUL'S 'FAREWELLS' OF PHILIPPIANS 3.1 AND 4.4   19
    Bruce A. Lowe and Marshall Findlay

Chapter 3
PAUL OF TARSUS AND MARY OF MAGDALA: VIRTUAL HISTORY, POLITICS OF IDENTITY, POSTMODERN ENCOUNTERS   45
    Ingrid Rosa Kitzberger

Part II
HERMENEUTICAL LENS

Chapter 4
PAUL AND THE 'MOMMY WARS': READING PAUL'S MATERNAL METAPHORS IN CONTEMPORARY AMERICAN CONTEXT   69
    Jennifer Houston McNeel

Chapter 5
'GOD'S WORK. OUR HANDS.': A LUTHERAN READING OF ROMANS
7.15–8.13   84
   Amy Lindeman Allen

Part III
ETHICS OF INTERPRETATION

Chapter 6
WHEN ALLEGORIES ATTACK: HAGAR AND SARAH IN GALATIANS
4.21-31   103
   Sid D. Sudiacal

Chapter 7
THE PERSECUTOR AND THE PERSECUTED: AN INTERPRETATION OF
GALATIANS 4.30 FROM A TAIWANESE CONTEXT   119
   Menghun Goh

Index of Scripture   135
Index of Ancient Sources   139
Index of Authors   141

SERIES PREFACE

Myth cannot be defined but as an empty screen, a structure ... A myth is but an empty screen for transference.

Mieke Bal (1993)

'לתורה פנים שבעים' (The Torah has seventy faces')[1]

The discipline of biblical studies emerged from a particular cultural context; it is profoundly influenced by the assumptions and values of the Western European and North Atlantic, male-dominated and largely Protestant environment in which it was born. Yet like the religions with which it is involved, the critical study of the Bible has travelled beyond its original context. Its presence in a diversity of academic settings around the globe has been experienced as both liberative and imperialist, sometimes simultaneously. Like many travellers, biblical scholars become aware of their own cultural rootedness only in contact with, and through the eyes of, people in other cultures.

The way any one of us closes a door seems in Philadelphia nothing at all remarkable, but in Chiang Mai, it seems overly loud and emphatic – so very typically American. In the same way, Western biblical interpretation did not seem tied to any specific context when only Westerners were reading and writing it. Since so much economic, military and consequently cultural power has been vested in the West, the West has had the privilege of maintaining this cultural closure for two centuries. Those who engaged in biblical studies – even when they were women or men from Africa, Asia and Latin America – nevertheless had to take on the Western context along with the discipline.

But much of recent Bible scholarship has moved towards the recognition that considerations of not only the contexts of assumed, or implied, biblical authors

---

1. This saying indicates, through its usage of the stereotypic number 70, that the Torah – and, by extension, the whole Bible – intrinsically has many meanings. It is therefore often used to indicate the multivalence and variability of biblical interpretation and does not appear in this formulation in traditional Jewish biblical interpretation before the middle of the first millennium CE. Its most known appearances are in the medieval commentator Ibn Ezra's introduction to his commentary on the Torah, towards the introduction's end (as in printed versions), in Midrash Numbers Rabbah (13.15-16) and in later Jewish mystical literature.

but also the contexts of the interpreters are valid and legitimate in an inquiry into biblical literature. We use contexts here as an umbrella term covering a wide range of issues: on the one hand, social factors (such as location, economic situation, gender, age, class, ethnicity, colour and things pertaining to personal biography) and, on the other hand, ideological factors (such as faith, beliefs, practiced norms and personal politics).

Contextual readings of the Bible are an attempt to redress the previous long-standing and grave imbalance that says that there is a kind of 'plain' unaligned biblical criticism that is somehow 'normative', and that there is another, distinct kind of biblical criticism aligned with some social location: the writing of Latina/o scholars advocating liberation, the writing of feminist scholars emphasizing gender as a cultural factor, the writings of African scholars pointing out the text's and the readers' imperialism, the writing of Jews and Muslims, and so on. The project of recognizing and emphasizing the role of context in reading freely admits that we all come from somewhere: no one is native to the biblical text, and no one reads only in the interests of the text itself. North Atlantic and Western European scholarship has focused on the Bible's characters as individuals, has read past its miracles and stories of spiritual manifestations or 'translated' them into other categories. These results of Euro-American contextual reading would be no problem if they were seen as such; but they have become a chain to be broken when they have been held up as the one and only 'objective', plain truth of the text itself.

The biblical text, as we have come to understand in the postmodern world and as pre-Enlightenment interpreters perhaps understood more clearly, does not speak in its own voice. It cannot read itself. We must read it, and in reading it, we must acknowledge that our own voice's particular pitch, timbre and inflection affect the meaning that emerges. Biblical scholars usually read the text in the voice of a Western Protestant male. When interpreters in the Southern Hemisphere and in Asia have assumed ownership of the Bible, it has meant a recognition that this Euro-American male voice is not the voice of the text itself; it is only one reader's voice, or rather, the voice of one context – however familiar and authoritative it may seem to all who have been affected by Western political and economic power. Needless to say, it is not a voice suited to bring out the best meaning for every reading community. Indeed, as biblical studies tended for so long to speak in this one particular voice, it may be the case that that voice has outlived its meaning producing usefulness: we may have heard all that this voice has to say, at least for now. Nevertheless, we have included that voice in this series, in part in an effort to hear it as emerging from its specific context, in order to put that previously authoritative voice quite literally in its place.

The trend of acknowledging readers' contexts as meaningful is already, inter alia, recognizable in the pioneering volumes of *Reading from This Place* (Segovia and Tolbert 1995, 2000, 2004), which indeed move from the centre to the margins and back, and from the United States to the rest of the world. More recent publications along this line also include *Her Master's Tools?* (Stichele and Penner 2005), *From Every People and Nation: The Book of Revelation in Intercultural Perspective* (Rhoads et al. 2005), *From Every People and Nation: A Biblical Theology of Race* (Hays and Carson 2003) and *The Global Bible Commentary* (GBC; Patte et al. 2004).

The editors of the GBC have gone a long way towards this shift by soliciting and admitting contributions from so-called Third, Fourth and Fifth World scholars alongside First and Second World scholars, thus attempting to usher the former and their perspectives into the centre of biblical discussion. Contributors to the GBC were asked to begin by clearly stating their context before proceeding. The result was a collection of short introductions to the books of the Bible (Hebrew Bible/ Old Testament and New Testament), each introduction from one specific context and, perforce, limited in scope. At the Society of Biblical Literature's (SBL's) annual meeting in Philadelphia in 2005, during the two GBC sessions and especially in the session devoted to pedagogical implications, it became clear that this project should be continued, albeit articulated further and redirected.

On methodological grounds, the paradox of a deliberately inclusive policy that foregrounds differences in the interpretation of the Bible could not be addressed in a single- or double-volume format because, in most instances, those formats would allow for only one viewpoint for each biblical issue or passage (as in previous publications) or biblical book (as in the GBC) to be articulated. The acceptance of such a limit may indeed lead to a decentring of traditional scholarship, but it would definitely not usher in multivocality on any single topic. It is true that, for pedagogical reasons, a teacher might achieve multivocality of scholarship by using various specialized scholarship types together; for instance, the GBC has been used side by side on a course with historical introductions to the Bible and other focused introductions, such as *The Women's Bible Commentary* (Newsom and Ringe 1998). But research and classes focused on a single biblical book or biblical corpus need another kind of resource: volumes exemplifying a broad multivocality in themselves, varied enough in contexts from various shades of the confessional to various degrees of the secular, especially since in most previous publications the contexts of communities of faith overrode all other contexts.

On the practical level, then, we found that we could address some of these methodological, pedagogical and representational limitations evident in previous projects in contextual interpretation through a book series in which each volume introduces multiple contextual readings of the same biblical texts. This is what the SBL's Contextual Biblical Interpretation Consultation has already been promoting since 2005 during the American Annual Meeting, and since 2011 also at the annual International SBL conference. The Consultation serves as a testing ground for a multiplicity of readings of the same biblical texts by scholars from different contexts.[2]

---

2. Since 2010, when this book series was started and the first volume published with this Preface, interest in contextual interpretation has grown considerably. Worth noting is the SBL Press series International Voices in Biblical Studies (IVBS). As can be seen from the website (http://www.sbl-site.org/publications/Books_IVBS.aspx), seven volumes have been published since 2010. However, the IVBS mission is different from ours, although two of

These considerations led us to believe that a book series focusing specifically on contextual multiple readings for specific topics, of specific biblical books, would be timely. We decided to construct a series, including at least eight to ten volumes, divided between the Hebrew Bible (HB/OT) and the New Testament (NT). Each of the planned volumes would focus on one or two biblical books: Genesis, Exodus and Deuteronomy, Leviticus and Numbers, Joshua and Judges, the so-called History books and later books for the HB/OT; Mark, Luke–Acts, John and Paul's letters for the NT.[3] The general HB/OT editor is Athalya Brenner-Idan, with Archie Lee and Gale Yee as associate editors. The first general NT editor was Nicole Duran; presently it is James Grimshaw, with Daniel Patte and Teresa Okure as associate editors. Other colleagues have joined as editors for specific volumes.

Each volume focuses on clusters of contexts and of issues or themes, as determined by the editors in consultation with potential contributors. A combination of topics or themes, texts and interpretive contexts seems better for our purpose than a text-only focus. In this way, more viewpoints on specific issues will be presented, with the hope of gaining a grid of interests and understanding. The interpreters' contexts will be allowed to play a central role in choosing a theme: we do not want to impose our choice of themes upon others, but as the contributions emerge, we will collect themes for each volume under several headings.

While we were soliciting articles for the first volumes (and continue to solicit contributions for future volumes), each contributor was and is asked to foreground her/his own multiple 'contexts' while presenting her/his interpretation of a given issue pertaining to the relevant biblical book(s). We asked that the interpretation be firmly grounded in those contexts and sharply focused on the specific theme, as well as in dialogue with 'classical' informed biblical scholarship. Finally, we asked for a concluding assessment of the significance of this interpretation for the contributor's contexts (whether secular or in the framework of a faith community).

Our main interest in this series is to examine how formulating the content-specific ideological and thematic questions from life contexts will focus the reading of the biblical texts. The result is a two-way process of reading that (1) considers the contemporary life context from the perspective of the chosen themes in the given biblical book as corrective lenses, pointing out specific problems and issues in that context as highlighted by the themes in the biblical book; and (2) conversely,

---

the volumes (Vaka'uta 2011 on Ezra–Nehemiah 9–10 and Havea and Lau 2015 on Ruth) do discuss specific texts against contextual, geographical-cultural perspectives. Worth noting too in this connection is the SBL series Global Perspectives on Biblical Scholarship (https://www.sbl-site.org/publications/Books_GPBS.aspx) and especially the 2012 volume on postcolonial African interpretation, edited by Musa W. Dube, Andrew M. Mbuvi and Dora R. Mbuwayesango.

3. At this time, no volume on Revelation is planned, since Rhoads's volume, *From Every People and Nation: The Book of Revelation in Intercultural Perspective* (2005) is readily available, with a concept similar to ours.

considers the given biblical book and the chosen theme from the perspective of the life context.

The word *contexts*, like *identity*, is a blanket term covering many components. For some, their geographical context is uppermost; for others, the dominant factor may be gender, faith, membership in a certain community, class and so forth. The balance is personal and not always conscious; it does, however, dictate choices of interpretation. One of our interests as editors is to present the personal beyond the autobiographical as pertinent to the wider scholarly endeavour, especially but not only when *grids of consent* emerge that supersede divergence. Consent is no guarantee of Truth speak; neither does it necessarily point at a sure recognition of the biblical authors' elusive contexts and intentions. It does, however, have cultural and political implications.

Globalization promotes uniformity but also diversity, by shortening distances, enabling dissemination of information and exchanging resources. This is an opportunity for modifying traditional power hierarchies and reallocating knowledge, for upsetting hegemonies and for combining the old with the new, the familiar with the unknown – in short, for a fresh mutuality. This series, then, consciously promotes the revision of biblical myths into new reread and rewritten versions that hang on many threads of welcome transference. Our contributors were asked, decidedly, to be responsibly non-objective and to represent only themselves on the biblical screen. Paradoxically, we hope, the readings here offered will form a new tapestry or, changing the metaphor, new metaphorical screens on which contemporary life contexts and the life of biblical texts in those contexts may be reflected and refracted.

The Editors

References

Bal, Mieke (1993), 'Myth à la Lettre: Freud, Mann, Genesis and Rembrandt, and the Story of the Son', repr. in *A Feminist Companion to Genesis*, ed. A. Brenner-Idan, 343–78, Sheffield: Sheffield Academic Press; originally in *Discourse in Psychoanalysis and Literature*, ed. S. Rimon-Kenan, 57–89 (London: Methuen, 1987).

Dube, Musa W., Andrew M. Mbuvi and Dora R. Mbuwayesango, eds (2012), *Postcolonial Perspectives in African Biblical Interpretations*, Global Perspectives on Biblical Scholarship, 13, Atlanta: SBL Press.

Havea, Jione, and Peter H. W. Lau, eds (2015), *Reading Ruth in Asia*, IVBS, Atlanta: SBL Press.

Hays, J. Daniel, and Donald A. Carson (2003), *From Every People and Nation: A Biblical Theology of Race*, New Studies in Biblical Theology, Downers Grove, IL: InterVarsity Press.

Newsom, Carol A., and Sharon H. Ringe, eds ([1992] 1998), *The Women's Bible Commentary*, Louisville: Westminster/John Knox Press.

Patte, Daniel, J. Severino Cratto, Nicole Wilkinson Duran, Teresa Okure and Archie Chi Chung Lee, eds (2004), *The Global Bible Commentary*, Nashville: Abingdon Press.

Penner, Todd, and Caroline Vander Stichele, eds (2005), *Her Master's Tools? Feminist and Postcolonial Engagements of Historical-Critical Discourse*, Global Perspectives on Biblical Scholarship, Atlanta: SBL Press.

Rhoads, David, ed. (2005), *From Every People and Nation: The Book of Revelation in Intercultural Perspective*, Minneapolis: Augsburg Fortress Press.

Segovia, Fernando F., and Mary Ann Tolbert eds (1995), *Reading from This Place. Vol. 1, Social Location and Biblical Interpretation in the United States*, Minneapolis: Augsburg Fortress Press.

Segovia, Fernando F., and Mary Ann Tolbert, eds (2000), *Reading from This Place. Vol. 2, Social Location and Biblical Interpretation in Global Perspective*, repr., Minneapolis: Augsburg Fortress Press (originally published 1995).

Segovia, Fernando F., and Mary Ann Tolbert, eds (2004), *Teaching the Bible: The Discourses and Politics of Biblical Pedagogy*, repr., Eugene, OR: Wipf & Stock (originally published 1997).

Vaka'uta, Nasili (2011) *Reading Ezra 9–10 Tu'a-Wise: Rethinking Biblical Interpretation in Oceania*, IVBS, Atlanta: SBL Press.

ABBREVIATIONS

BDAG	*A Greek-English Lexicon of the New Testament and Early Christian Literature*, Frederick W. Danker, Walter Bauer
BDF	*A Greek Grammar of the New Testament and Early Christian Literature*
EDNT	*Exegetical Dictionary of the New Testament*
LSJ	*Liddell and Scott Greek-English Lexicon*
P. Oxy II	Papyrus Oxyrynchus II
TDNT	*Theological Dictionary of the New Testament*
ELCA	Evangelical Lutheran Church of America

Translations/Versions of the Bible:

ASV	Authorized Standard Version
CEV	Contemporary English Version
GNT	Good News Translation
KJV	King James Version
NEB	New English Bible
NIV	New International Version
NIRV	New International Readers' Version
NRSV	New Revised Standard Version
RSV	Revised Standard Version
TMB	Third Millenium Bible
TYN	Tyndale Bible

CONTRIBUTORS

Amy Lindeman Allen is Indiana Christian Church Associate Professor of New Testament at Christian Theological Seminary in Indianapolis, Indiana. She is an ordained minister in the Evangelical Lutheran Church in America and, at the time of writing her essay for this collection, served as co-lead pastor of the Lutheran Church of the Good Shepherd in Reno, Nevada. Her two monographs, *For Theirs Is the Kingdom* (2019) and *The Gifts They Bring* (2023) focus on the contextual relationships between children in the gospels and today.

Greg Carey is Professor of New Testament at Lancaster Theological Seminary. His most recent publications include *Death, the End of History, and Beyond: Eschatology in the Bible* and *Using Our Outside Voice: Public Biblical Interpretation*.

Marshall Findlay grew up in New England, where he also studied. After living for two years in China, he completed a Master of Biblical Studies at Reformed Theological Seminary in Atlanta, Georgia. Marshall now lives with his family in Guatemala, serving the community there and teaching at Seminario Teológico Centroamericano.

Menghun Goh is a Chinese Malaysian teaching New Testament studies, semiotics and post-colonial studies at Taiwan Graduate School of Theology. Goh received his PhD from Vanderbilt University. His latest publication in Chinese is entitled *Trial and Temptation: Biblical Interpretation and Semiotics*.

Ingrid Rosa Kitzberger is an independent scholar in Münster, Germany. A native from Linz, Austria, she studied Catholic Theology and English, and American Language and Literature at the University of Salzburg (Dr. theol. 1985; Mag. theol., Mag. phil. 1978). Her main research areas are reader response criticism and (post-)feminist interpretation. She is the author of *Interfigural Readings of the Gospel of John* (2019) and the editor of *The Personal Voice in Biblical Interpretation* (1999), *Transformative Encounters. Jesus and Women Re-viewed* (2000) and *Autobiographical Biblical Criticism. Between Text and Self* (2002).

Bruce A. Lowe grew up in rural Australia on a farm and now lives in Atlanta, Georgia, where he serves as Associate Professor of New Testament at Reformed Theological Seminary. Bruce has a PhD in analytical chemistry (University of Queensland) and a PhD in ancient history (Macquarie University).

Jennifer Houston McNeel is a core faculty member in Biblical Studies at St. Mary's Ecumenical Institute in Baltimore, Maryland. McNeel received her PhD from Union Presbyterian Seminary and specializes in Pauline letters and women in the New Testament. She is the author of *Paul as Infant and Nursing Mother: Metaphor, Rhetoric, and Identity in 1 Thessalonians 2:5–8*.

Sid D. Sudiacal (he/him/siya) is a Filipino-Canadian scholar living in Hamilton, Ontario. He received his PhD in Christian Theology from McMaster Divinity College. His dissertation examines Augustine's treatment of the Donatists during the Donatist Controversy through the lens of Disgust Psychology. His research interests include Roman North African Christianity, religious violence, pop culture and the intersection between history, theology and psychology.

INTRODUCTION

Menghun Goh

Texts by definition being semiotic constructs, necessitating the active participation of readers or listeners for their existence, the textual object is dynamic, unstable, elusive ... It is naive to believe that we can analyze without interpreting, that we can work and live without lending meaning to the world around us.

Bal (1988: 135–6)

Texts and Contexts

This volume has seven essays. Coming from different social locations and perspectives (such as gender, motherhood, 'race'/'ethnic', religious traditions, language, culture, etc.), the contributors make explicit how their context and hermeneutical framework help them notice and highlight certain textual features of the biblical texts. Like the editors in the ten volumes of Romans through History and Cultures series (Campell, Hawkins and Schildgen 2007; Ehrensperger and Holder 2008; Gaca and Welborn 2005; Grenholm and Patte 2000, 2005; Odell-Scott 2007; Patte and Grenholm 2013; Patte and Mihoc 2013; Patte and Teselle 2003; Yeo 2004), these editors, in one way or another, highlight that biblical interpretations entail three interpretive poles: (1) textual, (2) hermeneutical and (3) contextual. The textual pole refers to the textual features, materials and signification systems of the text. The hermeneutical pole refers to our world view, whether religious, theological or secular, that renders certain conceptual frameworks and practices plausible. The contextual pole refers to the pragmatic concerns or concrete life-situation issues that we encounter in our social location. Within each pole, we also make choices, prioritizing a certain aspect over others. Let me elucidate.

In terms of the contextual pole, a person's context may involve the issues of gender, 'race'/'ethnic', social status, religion, culture and so forth, but it does not mean that s/he tackles them all at once in her/his contextual problems. S/he will only foreground a certain issue while bracketing out others. Such is the case in

Sid Sudiacal's interpretation, where the issue of skin colour and nationality is his entry point into addressing the issue of authority in Gal. 4.21-31. In terms of the hermeneutical pole, Amy L. Allen shows how an individual-centred, community-centred or an apocalyptic approach can render the notion of 'sin' in Rom. 7.14–8.13 very differently. It can go from individual and structural problem to the power of the evil force. With each perception of 'sin', we will then have a corresponding solution. Similarly, in addressing the so-called mommy wars in the United States that debate on what counts as an ideal motherhood, Jennifer H. McNeel shows that Paul's maternal metaphors can be approached ideologically or apocalyptically. As such, McNeel speaks of a balance between 'authority' and 'nurture' in a mother and child relationship. While other contributors may not accentuate the hermeneutical framework as much, the contextual and textual poles are clearly brought into play with each other in all the essays.

What these three intertwining poles bring to the fore is that we do not just interpret the biblical texts, as if they are mere objects waiting to be parsed out and analysed. Rather, we are also interpreting our context and our world view or hermeneutical/theological framework that help us make sense of our living conditions and existence (Grenholm and Patte 2000: 14–34). Hence, in interpreting the text, we are also being interpreted, if not also drawn by the text to engage it, as Mieke Bal points out in the epigraph.

Having said this, a contextual interpretation does not seek to privilege our context at the expense of other contexts. It certainly does not imply absolutizing one's context, as if it cannot be critiqued or only people in that context can understand its ins and outs. To do so is the opposite of practicing contextual interpretation. It reifies context and denies its potential fluidity. A contextual interpretation readily admits the intersectionality and overlapping of contexts. There is no isolated context. All contexts are necessarily intercontextual, as the pandemic has repeatedly taught us, in case we have not learned in the past that we are all interconnected.

However, in trying to make explicit our process of interpretation, the practice of contextual interpretation can be risky. It can make the interpreter vulnerable to unwarranted criticisms, since, traditionally, a critical interpretation is required to be scientific and objective; that is, without a context. Context pollutes. It is unstable and emotional. Some may even opine that to say one's interpretation is contextual is to suggest that it lacks academic rigour. However, as embodied beings, how can we be without context? How can we get rid of our context? We are the products of our context as we produce our context.

Hence, to do contextual interpretation takes patience, courage and trust. We trust that as we make explicit the reasoning behind our contextual, hermeneutical and textual choices, others too may join in the endeavours and conversations. Such will be the spirit of conversation, as Hans-Georg Gadamer reminds us that we do not conduct, but 'fall into', conversations, since in a genuine conversation, we do not know how the conversation will turn out (2006: 385). What we can do is to be open minded and willing to be transformed by our conversations with the biblical texts and each other. Finally, this making explicit of our interpretive process embodies an ethics of interpretation. It exhorts us to be responsible for our interpretation so that our readers, in turn, may be empowered to respond to our interpretation. Indeed, if our interpretation can minister to the life and death of our readers, in particular those who take the Christian Scripture as the Word to live by, we are obliged to make explicit the contextual character of our interpretive process.

Part I: Contextual Concern

This volume has three parts. All the essays reflect the interplay of text, hermeneutics and context. But the three essays in Part I highlight more how the interpreter's context leads her/him to notice certain textual features that may otherwise be easily overlooked. The two essays in Part II focus more on the hermeneutical framework in interpretation, and the two essays in Part III address the issues of ethics of interpretation.

In Part I, Greg Carey's essay in Chapter 1 pays attention to Paul's language of joy in Phil. 3.1–4.1 as he engages the 'happiness research' conducted by Martin E. P. Seligman at the University of Pennsylvania's Positive Psychology Center, as well as by Jonathan Haidt, Ellen T. Charry and so forth. While Paul's notion of joy bears similarities and differences with that of the Greek and Roman philosophers and of contemporary happiness researches, Carey notes that 'the experience of happiness or joy [that] requires a reorientation of the self' is common among them. Moreover, the importance of 'relationships, vocation, growth, and contributions' to happiness highlighted by positive psychology can shed light on how the joy exhortation in Philippians is tied to Paul's identity, suffering and experience of union with Christ. For Carey, Paul's notion of joy can in turn provide contemporary happiness researches a different understanding of joy and happiness.

What Carey briefly points out is significant when we consider the detailed analysis and argument of Bruce A. Lowe and Marshall Findlay in Chapter 2 in determining the meanings of 'the common epistolary *charein greeting* ('A [wishes] B *to rejoice*')' in Phil. 3.1 and 4.4. Taking note of sociocultural and linguistic difference between Australia and Southern United States in greetings and farewells, Lowe and Findlay demonstrate that the *charein greeting* is not just formulaic and without content and context, as scholars generally maintain. On the contrary, the mood-free infinitive form of *charein* conveys a sense of exhortation and wish, as indicated by its forms in the imperatival and optative moods. The great advantage of a mood-free greeting is that 'any sender who was uncertain about whether to praise or blame the recipient, could leave it to the reader to decide which boot may best fit'. In the light of Paul's concerns for the Philippian believers to rely on God in Jesus in the immediate verses of Phil. 3.1 and 4.4, Lowe and Findlay point out that the 'joy-farewells seem consistently reserved for *ultimate* (e.g. deathbed) departures, sometimes with strong irony'. This finding of Lowe and Findlay, triggered and intrigued by the sociocultural differences in Australia and Southern United States, can certainly bring much impact to the studies of Philippians.

The third essay in Part I demonstrates a counterfactual interpretation as Ingrid R. Kitzberger entertains the possibility of 'What if Paul and Mary Magdalene had met?' As a scholar who has worked extensively on Paul and Mary Magdalene, Kitzberger finds J. Cheryl Exum's notions of 'virtual history' or 'counterfactual' helpful to her interpretation of 1 Cor. 15.3-6. For Exum, in asking 'what could have been', counterfactual works as a heuristic device, illustrating 'how biblical historians work to synthesize and evaluate evidence, posit theories, and test historical reconstructions' (2000: 3). As counterfactual can help us ask and frame different questions, it is a 'serious scholarly inquiry into alternative historical possibilities, not simply fiction or fantasy' (Exum 2000: 2). Kitzberger goes on to list 'What If Paul Had Travelled East Rather Than West?' by Richard Bauckham, *Paul the Accused* by Marie-Eloise Rosenblatt and *Paul between Damascus and Antioch: The Unknown Years* by Martin Hengel and Anna Amaria Schwemer as examples of what counterfactuals can offer to scholarly investigation. For Kitzberger, even though Paul might not know about the risen Christ appearing to Mary Magdalene – 1 Cor. 15.6 says that Christ 'had appeared to more than five hundred brothers and sisters at one time' (NRSV) – the implication that had Paul met Mary is great. It can have an impact on the dynamics of authority in both the Early Church and contemporary churches. In the age of artificial intelligence, such a virtual history (or reality?) is timely. Here Kitzberger's focus on *adelphoi* as a literary figure in 1 Cor. 15.6 can take us to McNeel's 'Paul and the "Mommy Wars": Reading Paul's Maternal Metaphors in Contemporary American Context' in Part II.

Part II: Hermeneutical Lens

The two essays in Part II underscore the hermeneutical framework that the interpreter employs in her/his interpretation. In Chapter 4, as McNeel speaks of Paul's maternal metaphor, which necessarily entails a tensive and creative chemistry between two fields of meaning potentials, she shows the comparison and contrast among three contexts: Paul's, the Roman Empire's and the United States's. This critical juxtaposition is important because it can underline the pertinent values in Paul's notion of mother. Undoubtedly, Paul shares some of the ancient Graeco-Roman understanding and practice of motherhood. For many contemporary Americans from the United States, they may also think that Paul speaks to their notion of motherhood. Yet, as McNeel argues, the apocalyptic and cosmic image of mother in Romans 8 not only speaks of Paul's emphasis on God's intervention but also foregrounds the importance of solidarity. That is, in McNeel's context, the different American ideal images of motherhood – that is, 'working or staying at home, breastfeeding or bottle-feeding, crib sleeping or co-sleeping, cloth or disposable diapers, baby-wearing or stroller-pushing and so forth' – should work together, instead of against one another. A functional metaphor should be able to allow and accommodate differences as it creates new meanings out of the existing meanings.

This both-and emphasis also comes to the fore in Chapter 5, '"God's Work. Our Hands.": A Lutheran Reading of Romans 7.15–8.13' by Allen. As a scholar and a pastor of the Evangelical Lutheran Church in America, Allen finds it problematic for churches to tout themselves as either a 'Bible' church or a 'liturgical' church, as if the two are, and can be, separated. Equally troubling is churches treating the proclamation of the gospel and the work of justice as two separate kinds of worship. In her 'Lutheran, liturgical reading of Rom. 7.14–8.13' that stresses liturgy as a public service – in which God serves people and in response people are inspired to proclaim gospel and justice in the world – Allen highlights the 'dual character of liturgy as both a source of spiritual nourishment and an impetus for mission'. Using the Lutheran liturgy of baptism as an example, Allen speaks of the experience of confession and forgiveness and goes beyond the individualistic to the corporate as well as an apocalyptic understanding of 'sin', 'forgiveness' and freedom. In conversation with Brendan Byrne and Daniel Patte, Allen views 'sin' as a structural and spiritual evil force that can 'warp the good intentions of humanity (such as service to God, the good, etc.) into idol worship'. The intense struggle of the 'I' in Romans 7 is a case in point. For Allen, such 'infestation of absolutizing idolatries' can be addressed 'by giving a central place to the crucified and resurrected Christ'. This problem of absolutizing one's understanding is also the focus of the two essays in Part III, which, by chance, both tackle the ethics in how we interpret Gal. 4.21-31.

Part III: Ethics of Interpretation

In Chapter 6, Sudiacal points out how Paul's allegory in Galatians 4 was used by Augustine in 408 CE to attack the Donatists for the sake of religious unity, even though Augustine was initially against 'religious coercion'. Then Sudiacal reviews the debates on whether Paul's allegory should be taken as a typology that underlines the importance of history. While Sudiacal is inclined to treat Paul's allegory as a typology, his emphasis on Henri De Lubac's notion of allegory not 'found in history as narrative, but in history as event' blurs the distinction between allegory and typology. In referring to the work of Letty Russell that offers an ideological critique of Paul's allegory, Sudiacal then foregrounds the strengths and limitations of allegory. Following Anne Davis's argument that allegory can provide 'a statement that either explicitly or implicitly counters conventional understanding about a text, a character, or an event' (2004: 165), Sudiacal claims that Paul's allegory 'shocks his audience and forces them to re-imagine the Old Testament in novel and *nouvelle* (new) ways'. Yet, the devastating effects of the same allegory from the Early Church to the present cannot be overlooked. Here, the concrete context of how Paul's allegory is interpreted and used in response to certain contextual problems must be made explicit. Without it, the value and validity of diverse interpretations are hard to be discussed and determined.

The ethical concern regarding the effect of our interpretation is rather prominent in my essay (Chapter 7). I am concerned with the implementation of transitional justice in Taiwan that continues to polarize Taiwanese. Interpreting Gal. 4.30 in such a context, I highlight the apocalyptic features of Galatians and the ambivalences caused by God's intervention. As such, the 'driving out' command in Gal. 4.30 is the prerogative of God, as Paul also transforms Sarah's command in Gen. 21.10 into what the Scripture says in Gal. 4.30. Taking hints from Daniel Patte's (structural) semiotic analysis that foregrounds six systems of convictions in Galatians, which can also engender ambivalences – just as the ambivalences in Taiwan's society is complicated by the highly contested history of modern Taiwan – I agree that ambivalences can not only be used to divide people but also conscientize us to perceive otherwise so that we do not absolutize our viewpoints. With the help from the works of David Dawson, Stephen Greenblatt, Fredric Jameson and Margaret Hillenbrand, I argue that Paul's allegory that is marked by ambivalences can actually deconstruct the one-to-one correspondence and dualistic appearance in allegory. But why do scholars generally claim that Paul in Gal. 4.30 commands the Galatian churches to cast out the Judaizing troublemakers? Context matters! In a Taiwanese context that constantly deals with the issue of oppression, I find that it is unlikely for Paul to take the matter into his own hands, as he once did before he encountered Jesus Christ. To do so will exacerbate the existing situation. To do so will be a knee-jerk reaction. There is no freedom in such an eye-for-an-eye response. 'Driving out' is not a small matter. As interpreters of the biblical texts, we need to be extremely careful with our interpretations when we come across such texts, as our interpretations can minister to the life or death of our readers. And if Scripture aims to bring life to people, may our interpretations contribute to such a goal.

Conclusion

Ulrich Luz has reminded us that 'the history of the interpretation and influence of the text is not an appendage but is an integral part of the interpretation' (2007: 65). Paul Ricoeur has shown that 'to read is, on any hypothesis, to conjoin a new discourse to the discourse of the text ... Interpretation is the concrete outcome of conjunction and renewal' (1983: 158). This volume hopes that the seven essays will further demonstrate that the Christian Scripture, if it can be interpreted, is indeed a dynamic construction, constituted by old and new discourses. And in engaging the Scripture, may we be more critical of the effects and impacts of our interpretations. We do not interpret the Scripture in a vacuum. Nor do we interpret it only for ourselves. As Paul corrects himself in Rom. 1.11-12 ('For I am longing to see you so that I may share with you some spiritual gift to strengthen you – or rather so that we may be mutually encouraged by each other's faith, both yours and mine'), may our interpretations of the Scripture be critiqued and enriched by our different experiences, perspectives and contexts. We do not just address others in our interpretations; we also need to be addressed by one another and by the Scripture.

References

Bal, Mieke (1988), *Murder and Difference: Gender, Genre, and Scholarship on Sisera's Death*, trans. Matthew Gumpert, Bloomington: Indiana University Press.
Campbell, William S., Peter S. Hawkins and Brenda Deen Schildgen, eds (2007), *Medieval Readings of Romans*, Romans through History and Cultures Series 6, London: T&T Clark.
Davis, Anne (2004), 'Allegorically Speaking in Galatians 4:21–5:1', *Bulletin for Biblical Research* 14 (2): 161–74.
Ehrensperger, Kathy, and R. Ward Holder, eds (2008), *Reformation Readings of Romans*, Romans through History and Cultures Series 4, London: T&T Clark.
Exum, J. Cheryl (2000), 'Why Virtual History? Alternatives, Counterfactuals, and the Bible', in J. Cheryl Exum (ed.), *Virtual History and the Bible*, Leiden: Brill.
Gaça, Kathy, and L. L. Welborn, eds (2005), *Early Patristic Readings of Romans*, Romans through History and Cultures Series 4, London: T&T Clark.
Gadamer, Hans-Georg (2006), *Truth and Method*, 2nd rev. edn, trans. Joel Weinsheimer and Donald G. Marshall, London: Continuum.
Grenholm, Cristina, and Daniel Patte (2000), 'Overture: Receptions, Critical Interpretations, and Scriptural Criticism', in Cristina Grenholm and Daniel Patte (eds), *Reading Israel in Romans: Legitimacy and Plausibility of Divergent Interpretations*, 1–54, Romans through History and Cultures Series 1, Harrisburg: Trinity Press International.
Grenholm, Cristina, and Daniel Patte, eds (2005), *Gender, Tradition and Romans: Shared Ground, Uncertain Borders*, Romans through History and Cultures Series 5, London: T&T Clark.
Luz, Ulrich (2007), *Matthew 1–7: A Commentary*, Hermeneia, trans. James E. Crouch, Minneapolis: Fortress.
Odell-Scott, David W. ed (2007), *Readings Romans with Contemporary Philosophers and Theologians*, Romans through History and Cultures Series 7, London: T&T Clark.
Patte, Daniel, and Cristina Grenholm, eds (2013), *Modern Interpretations of Romans: Tracking Their Hermeneutical/Theological Trajectory*, Romans through History and Cultures Series 10, London: T&T Clark.
Patte, Daniel, and Eugene Teselle, eds (2003), *Engaging Augustine on Romans: Self, Context, and Theology in Interpretation*, Romans through History and Cultures Series 2, Harrisburg: Trinity Press International.
Patte, Daniel, and Vasile Mihoc, eds (2013), *Greek Patristic and Eastern Orthodox Interpretations of Romans*, Romans through History and Cultures Series 9, London: T&T Clark.
Ricoeur, Paul (1983), 'What Is a Text? Explanation and Understanding', in John B. Thompson (ed. and trans.), *Hermeneutics and the Human Sciences: Essays on Language, Action and Interpretation*, 145–64, Cambridge: Cambridge University Press.
Yeo, Khiok-khng (K. K.), ed. (2004), *Navigating Romans Through Culture: Challenging Readings by Charting a New Course*, Romans through History and Cultures Series 3, London: T&T Clark.

Part I

CONTEXTUAL CONCERN

Chapter 1

WAS PAUL HAPPY? A CONTEXTUAL READING OF PHILIPPIANS 3.1–4.1 IN CONVERSATION WITH NORTH AMERICAN PSYCHOLOGY AND ITS LIMITATIONS

Greg Carey

In an age when self-help books sell better than any other genre, the social sciences and the world of popular publishing have witnessed a flurry of publications related to happiness.[1] The University of Pennsylvania's Positive Psychology Center,[2] founded and led by Martin E. P. Seligman, boasts a robust website full of helpful resources, including an Authentic Happiness page that offers questionnaires and links to myriad sources of other information.[3] And don't forget the Center's Facebook page. So influential is this movement that it exerts serious influence in the realm of public education. Many educators now believe that 'grit', rather than raw intelligence, is the key to educational success. Angela Ducksworth, a Seligman student, showed 'that measures of self-control can be a more reliable indicator of students' grade-point averages than their I.Q.'s'.[4] It remains to be seen how much this research affects educational policy, but bestsellers like Seligman's *Learned Optimism: How to Change Your Mind and Life* (1998) and Jonathan Haidt's *The Happiness Hypothesis* (2006) are finding rich audiences and broad applications. Happiness research has attracted renewed interest in moral philosophy, including

---

1. This essay takes on the same subject as one by Shantz (2012: 187–201), where Colleen Shantz employs Phil. 3.4b-8a as one of two case studies. Here I avoid overlapping with or critiquing Shantz's conclusions, which stand on their own. This essay foregrounds the question of contextual hermeneutics, pursuing it through the ways in which Paul expresses value. The result is a related but somewhat different take on Paul. An essential study was published days prior to the copyediting process for this piece: Joshua W. Jipp, *Pauline Theology as a Way of Life: A Vision of Human Flourishing in Christ* (Grand Rapids: Baker, 2023).

2. Available online: http://www.positivepsychology.org.

3. Available online: https://www.authentichappiness.sas.upenn.edu.

4. Paul Tough, "What If the Secret to Success Is Failure?" *New York Times Magazine*, 14 September 2011. Available online: http://www.nytimes.com/2011/09/18/magazine/what-if-the-secret-to-success-is-failure.html. On grit, see Seligman (2011: 101–25).

historical approaches (e.g. Cahn and Vitrano 2008; Haybron 2008, 2013; McMahon 2006; Vitrano 2014).

Naturally, the movement has attracted critics, so many that a *Harvard Business Review* piece describes 'The Happiness Backlash' (Beard 2015). Critics have replied that happiness makes a very poor end in itself (more on this later); that a fixation on happiness leads to selfishness and shallowness; that a happiness culture inevitably shames people who struggle with difficult times and temperaments; and that unhappiness often leads to new sensitivity and wisdom (Ehrenreich 2009; Wilson 2008). On the other hand, happiness research has found its advocates within theology, albeit in tempered forms. Theologian Ellen T. Charry undertook a major project on *God and the Art of Happiness* (2010), while a larger Emory University Center for the Study of Law and Religion project on happiness generated a consultation followed by a major publication to which I contributed (Carey 2012: 203–24), *The Bible and the Pursuit of Happiness* (Strawn 2012). According to Charry, Western theology has tended to reserve happiness for the afterlife, when believers dwell beyond the effects of sin and reside in the full presence of God (2012: 232). This emphasis, she argues, overlooks God's own joy, which occurs when God's creatures flourish, as a ground for a doctrine of happiness (Charry 2012: 246). Instead of happiness, some theologians, including Mary Clark Moschella and Miroslav Wolf, are pursuing the question of joy and human flourishing (Volf and Crisp 2015).[5]

One criticism against the happiness movement, if we may call it so, is particularly relevant for our conversation about contextual biblical hermeneutics. Happiness research often draws upon Indian and Buddhist wisdom, with a particular emphasis on the positive power of mindfulness. However, the current search for happiness makes most sense in the context of a consumerist, individualistic Western culture such as our own late capitalist moment in the United States. Having called America 'a nation of true consumers', Eric G. Wilson writes, 'We are beginning to see that this American quest for happiness is not merely a pastime, an occasional undertaking. We are starting to realize that this push for earthly bliss is at the core of the American soul' (2008: 20–1).

My own stance is somewhat pragmatic. As one who reads theologically, I turn to happiness research as a conversation partner. Attending to this research brings out dimensions of the texts that may otherwise escape our attention. Sometimes the research challenges the biblical text. In some cases, the biblical texts complement or challenge the research. I read with all these possibilities in mind.

Framing Paul with Happiness?

Setting aside for the moment debates concerning happiness as a pursuit, we also face the question of whether Paul would recognize our concerns over happiness. To some degree, this is an old-fashioned cultural and historical question. Surely

---

5. Moschella is pursuing a long-term research project on the topic.

contemporary readers may apply our own concerns to Paul; there's no trouble in that. But we also find it useful to ask whether our conversations reflect Paul's own interests.

What do we mean by happiness? Although people commonly associate happiness with a positive emotional state, philosophers and psychologists have tended to interpret happiness in terms of more enduring human flourishing. In my own thinking, this essay represents a small turn back to the common view. Following Daniel M. Haybron, I posit happiness 'as a kind of emotional evaluation of your life' (2013: 19). Notice that Haybron considers happiness an emotional state, but he qualifies that emotional state with the language of evaluation. This understanding of happiness integrates the emotive dimension with a kind of enduring wisdom. Emotional states come and go, especially when they are tethered to fleeting realities. What conditions lead us to a positive evaluation of life, and does it make sense to bring this question to Paul?

Surely one might construct a Paul who counters contemporary Western individualism and self-indulgence. Such a construction might well lead to the sense that happiness fits poorly upon Paul, at least in any sense that means something to contemporary residents of the post-industrialized North. Paul was no disaffected hipster. But joy? Paul drank deeply from Stoic wisdom, a tradition that valued happiness (*eudaimonia*) as the proper end of life and elevated joy over pleasure (Engberg-Pedersen 2000: 47; Irvine 2008; Kim 2013: 20; Pereboom 1994: 592–625). That's the language of Paul, who defines the kingdom of God as justice and peace and joy in the Holy Spirit (Rom. 14.17), and who rejoices even in his misfortune (Phil. 2.17; 2 Cor. 6.10). It is the particular language of Philippians, for whom Paul prays with joy (1.4). Paul does not hesitate to command joy (2.18; 3.1; 4.4; see Rom. 12.12, 15; 2 Cor. 13.11; 1 Thess. 5.16). He expresses the joy that can occur in response to fortunate turns of events, but he also exhorts joy in the midst of suffering. That kind of joy, a well-being that flourishes despite circumstances, runs very close to contemporary happiness literature and in my view holds relevance for the topic.

Stoic influence bears upon Paul's letters in other ways that relate to the question of happiness. Recognizing that life, or Fate, can turn on us in an instant, the Stoics pursued happiness through training in equanimity. We typically associate the Stoics with self-control, the discipline of desire, but their true aspiration resided with virtue or excellence, the only assured path to happiness (McMahon 2006: 55). A happy thing, the Stoics argued, lives according to its nature. Living the fullness of human excellence, then, defines the happy human. Cicero, for example, critiques the view that pain is evil by imagining a person who remains happy under torture (*On Moral Ends* 3.42). Paul approaches this remarkable standard on a couple of occasions. He affirms life despite a catalogue of sufferings (2 Cor. 4.7-12), and he turns this suffering, even instances of torture, into boasting (11.16-32). Paul never employs the language of virtue (*aretē*), but he cares greatly about faithfulness and righteousness.[6] Persecution or suffering, Paul maintains, nourish a host of virtues (Rom. 5.3-5).

---

6. Rather than virtue, righteousness occurs in five of Paul's seven undisputed letters.

Troels Engberg-Pedersen argues that happiness did not concern Paul (2000: 47). I am not sure I agree. Admittedly, Paul's vocabulary only scarcely includes the standard terms for happiness. Scholars often identify two Greek words, *eudaimonia* and *makaria*, with the language of happiness. As far as happiness is concerned, *eudaimonia* reflects Aristotle's notion of happiness as virtue in action (Shantz 2012: 189). *Eudaimonia* never occurs in the New Testament. *Makarios*, conventionally translated as 'blessed', often connotes acts of blessing, often from God but also among people. When Leah bears Asher, she cries, 'Happy am I! For the women will call me happy' (Gen. 30.13). Is Leah simply describing herself as happy or even fortunate, or should we read into her exclamation gratitude that God has blessed her? Ps. 1.2 declares happy, or blessed, the one who delights in the law. Personally, I find it difficult to read the Beatitudes in terms of simple happiness. 'Blessed are the poor in spirit' only makes sense to me if one imagines God as the one doing the blessing. Paul's undisputed letters use *makarios* language infrequently. When he does use it, it is not quite clear whether he refers to divine blessing or to general well-being. He apparently employs both senses. Rom. 4.6-9 involves a discussion of who inherits Abraham's blessing. Rom. 14.22 pronounces happy those who do not condemn themselves by acting contrary to their convictions, as 1 Cor. 7.40 proclaims happy is the widow who remains unmarried. The NRSV translates *makarismos* as 'goodwill' in Gal. 4.15, a reading that makes sense to me. In short, a lexical approach does not resolve the question.

With respect to happiness and joy, Paul, the Stoics and contemporary happiness researchers all agree on one basic point. We all tend to seek happiness in counterproductive ways. We cannot acquire happiness. If happiness is an end in itself, it will slip through our fingers. The experience of happiness or joy requires a reorientation of the self.

Philippians 3.1–4.1

Identifying Phil. 3.1–4.1 as an object for analysis is arbitrary. Indeed, a major transition from one part (or fragment) of the letter to another occurs within Phil. 3.1 itself. Phil. 3.1 begins with a 'final' call to rejoice in the Lord, which then gives way to a self-conscious reflection on why Paul must write. Phil. 4.1 closes the discussion regarding the 'dogs' who promote circumcision, which begins in the second sentence of 3.1. Source critics have long noticed that it makes little sense for Paul 'finally' to call the Philippians to rejoice, only to then launch an extensive attack against the 'dogs'. In other words, the passage I have chosen – more precisely, excised – from Philippians transitions from a call to joy towards an admonition to avoid the dogs.

A paper on happiness in Philippians might well turn to more obvious passages. Elsewhere, Paul rejoices in his imprisonment (1.18), calls the Philippians to rejoice and abandon anxiety, and celebrates his own capacity to find contentment regardless of circumstances (4.10-13). Such sentiments would warm the Stoic heart. Colleen Shantz (2012) has already provided a most helpful reading of them.

According to the social psychologists, meaningful relationships provide one key determinant of happiness (Haidt 2006: 94; Seligman 2011: 20-6). The Stoics did write about friendship, but their understanding of friendship differs from the relationships Paul implies. For Stoics, friendship is possible only when both parties share a basic detachment from external things, including relationships (Kreitner 2012). Stoic ethics possesses a certain solitariness, or individualism. In isolation, Phil. 3.1-4.1 participates in that solitary ethos. However, other sections of Philippians call attention to the close, if sometimes frayed, social networks that tie Paul with the Philippians, who themselves provide a source of joy (1.4, 18, 25; 2.2, 17-18, 25-30; 4.1).

According to Shantz (2012), Paul offers his congregations both story and identity. Researchers have documented a relationship between constructing a meaningful story of one's life and happiness, particularly in recovering from trauma (Haidt 2006: 147-9). Haybron perceives a direct correlation between narrative and identity with well-being. 'How well the narrative of one's life goes depends, at least in part, on how things go with respect to the commitments that shape one's identity' (Haybron 2008: 193). In Phil. 3.4-15, Paul spells out a narrative identity, one identity that he has left behind and a new one he embraces. Shantz keenly observes that Paul's 'former' life includes values the positive psychology movement would embrace: markers of belonging and purpose (Shantz 2012: 195). Paul has lost these goods.

However, it is critical that Paul *chooses* these losses and replaces them with other goods. Paul has a *telos*, or purpose, which involves a union with Christ. The positive psychology movement posits a sense of purpose or contribution as a key contributor to happiness. Three among Seligman's five elements of well-being – engagement, meaning and accomplishment – relate to Paul's story (Seligman 2011: 16-20). Paul's language indicates agency: he chooses this path. It points to striving: he has not yet achieved and strains ahead (indeed, it seems that progress contributes more to happiness than does achievement; Haidt 2006: 82-4). And Paul points to a greater *telos*, participation in Christ at multiple levels.

Paul's *telos* speaks back to positive psychology. Paul invokes the language of vocation. From his perspective, he is pursuing not just any meaning, but the meaning to which he is called, a *klēsis*. He has rejected one set of standards for another. We ought not, I think, underestimate the importance of calling. If we're talking about emotional health, Mother Teresa was not happy, but she had a calling. One wonders whether Dietrich Bonhoeffer or Martin Luther King Jr. would have called themselves happy. Bonhoeffer and King were known for their ability to enjoy laughter and good company, but each carried enormous burdens. Mother Teresa, Bonhoeffer and King all carried a sense of calling.

Paul also steps beyond the Stoics, if not the social psychologists (Haidt 2006: 87-106), by embracing attachment. This point seems critical to me. Christine Vitrano questions Stoic indifference, wondering 'whether such fierce control over our emotions does not also inhibit or limit the experience of happiness' (Vitrano 2014: 52). Despite Paul's boast that he endures all circumstances in Christ, most readers perceive Paul as quite attached to his network of relationships. In

Philippians 3, this attachment takes the form of exhorting the Philippians to imitate his pattern of life.[7] This pattern reflects the *kenōsis* modelled by Jesus, who abandoned heavenly status for servitude, humiliation and death, and, in the end, resurrection and glory. Paul indeed abandons his former marks of identity, but he embraces new ones and an eschatological hope. In the larger context of Philippians, Paul longs for community and seeks to build it. Like the Stoics, Paul seeks a community founded on common aspirations; unlike the Stoics, Paul knows this community will not attain an ideal state.

Finally, Paul employs the language of mystical experience, a dimension for which neither the Stoics nor the psychologists make room. Social psychology does attempt to engage people's claims to religious experience, but by definition it cannot posit an objective referent for those reports. As a theologically inclined reader, I simply note Paul's language of knowing and being known by Christ, along with the intense language of participation in the power and suffering marked by Christ's resurrection and death.[8] I stand among those who regard Paul's cross and resurrection language as mystical and participatory (Bassler 2007: 35–47).[9] Whenever Paul refers to 'power' or to the Holy Spirit, mystical participation in Jesus's resurrection lies close at hand. In Philippians, Paul aspires to 'know' Christ and the *power* of his resurrection (3.10), even to the point of death. Athletes who inscribe 'Phil. 4.13' on their bodies may miss Paul's particular point concerning endurance and suffering, but they seem to grasp how Paul's sufficient strength relates to 'the one who empowers' him. That language points to mystical participation in the resurrection. I offer this point not as special pleading, and certainly not as a criticism of positive psychology research, but simply to point out what would have been obvious to Paul. Not just any pursuit would do.

In our post-industrial, nearly post-capitalist context, positive psychology emphasizes posits that happiness largely relies upon factors Paul recognizes: relationships, vocation, growth and contributions. Indeed, this contemporary research calls our attention to aspects of Paul's letters we might otherwise neglect. I find it remarkable that a contemporary happiness researcher might such as Jonathan Haidt turns to Stoicism (along with classical Buddhism), the same philosophical stream that seems to have shaped Paul's personal ethic (Haidt 2006: 81–7). I propose that Paul may also inform our grasp of psychology. He pursues *particular* sets of relationships, vocational aims and aspirations, all shaped by the cross and resurrection of Jesus. And where social psychology struggles to quantify religious experience, Paul traces his peace of mind precisely to that point, mystical participation in the resurrection.

---

7. In contrast to Elizabeth Castelli (1991), I see Paul's *mimēsis* language as restricted to the pattern of cruciform sacrifice. See Gorman (2004: 444).

8. Oddly, Paul moves from resurrection to death in Phil. 3.11.

9. Jouette M. Bassler surveys the range of opinions regarding mystical participation in Paul's letters (2007: 35–47).

References

Bassler, Jouette M. (2007), *Navigating Paul: An Introduction to Key Theological Concepts*, Louisville: Westminster John Knox.
Beard, Alison (2015), 'The Happiness Backlash', *Harvard Business Review*, July–August: 130–31. Available online: https://hbr.org/2015/07/the-happiness-backlash.
Cahn, Steven M., and Christine Vitrano (2008), *Happiness: Classic and Contemporary Readings in Philosophy*, New York: Oxford University Press.
Carey, Greg (2012), 'Finding Happiness in Apocalyptic Literature', in Brent A. Strawn (ed.), *The Bible and the Pursuit of Happiness: What the Old and New Testaments Teach Us about the Good Life*, 203–24, Oxford: Oxford University Press.
Castelli, Elizabeth (1991), *Imitating Paul: A Discourse of Power*, Literary Currents in Biblical Interpretation, Louisville: Westminster John Knox.
Charry, Ellen T. (2010), *God and the Art of Happiness*, Grand Rapids: Eerdmans.
Charry, Ellen T. (2012), 'The Necessity of Divine Happiness: A Response from Systematic Theology', in Brent A. Strawn (ed.), *The Bible and the Pursuit of Happiness: What the Old and New Testaments Teach Us about the Good Life*, 229–47, Oxford: Oxford University Press.
Ehrenreich, Barbara (2009), *Bright-Sided: How Positive Thinking Is Undermining America*, New York: Picador.
Engberg-Pedersen, Troels (2000), *Paul and the Stoics*, Louisville: Westminster John Knox.
Gorman, Michael J. (2004), *Apostle of the Crucified Lord: A Theological Introduction to Paul and His Letters*, Grand Rapids: Eerdmans.
Haidt, Jonathan (2006), *The Happiness Hypothesis: Finding Modern Truth in Ancient Wisdom*, New York: Basic Books.
Haybron, Daniel M. (2008), *The Pursuit of Unhappiness: The Elusive Psychology of Well-Being*, New York: Oxford University Press.
Haybron, Daniel M. (2013), *Happiness: A Very Short Introduction*, New York: Oxford University Press.
Irvine, William B. (2008), *A Guide to the Good Life: The Ancient Art of Stoic Joy*, New York: Oxford University Press.
Jipp, Joshua W. (2023), *Pauline Theology as a Way of Life: A Vision of Human Flourishing in Christ*, Grand Rapids: Baker.
Kim, Yung Suk (2013), *A Transformative Reading of the Bible: Explorations of Holistic Human Transformation*, Eugene: Cascade.
Kreitner, Richard (2012), 'The Stoics and the Epicureans on Friendship, Sex, and Love', *Montréal Review*, January. Available online: http://www.themontrealreview.com/2009/The-Stoics-and-the-Epicureans-on-Friendship-Sex-and-Love.php.
McMahon, Darrin M. (2006), *Happiness: A History*, New York: Grove.
Pereboom, Derk (1994), 'Stoic Psychotherapy in Descartes and Spinoza', *Faith and Philosophy*, 11: 592–625.
Seligman, Martin E. P. (1998), *Learned Optimism: How to Change Your Mind and Life*, New York: Free.
Seligman, Martin E. P. (2011), *Flourish: A Visionary New Understanding of Happiness and Well-Being*, New York: Simon & Schuster.
Shantz, Colleen (2012), '"I Have Learned to Be Content": Happiness According to St. Paul', in Brent A. Strawn (ed.), *The Bible and the Pursuit of Happiness: What the Old and New Testaments Teach Us about the Good Life*, 187–201, Oxford: Oxford University Press.

Strawn, Brent A., ed. (2012), *The Bible and the Pursuit of Happiness: What the Old and New Testaments Teach Us about the Good Life*, Oxford: Oxford University Press.
Vitrano, Christine (2014), *The Nature and Value of Happiness*, Boulder: Westview.
Volf, Miroslav, and Justin E. Crisp, eds (2015), *Joy and Human Flourishing: Essays on Theology, Culture, and the Good Life*, Minneapolis: Fortress.
Wilson, Eric G. (2008), *Against Happiness: In Praise of Melancholy*, New York: Sarah Crichton Books.

Chapter 2

FROM 'G'DAY' TO 'BLESS YOU': AN AUSTRALIAN-AMERICAN REFLECTION ON PAUL'S 'FAREWELLS' OF PHILIPPIANS 3.1 AND 4.4

Bruce A. Lowe and Marshall Findlay

Introduction

At the beginning of J. R. R. Tolkien's *The Hobbit*, Gandalf the wizard is greeted by Bilbo Baggins with the words 'Good morning!', and to this Tolkien adds, 'and he meant it'.

> The sun was shining, and the grass was very green. But Gandalf looked at him from under long bushy eyebrows that stuck out further than the brim of his shady hat. 'What do you mean?' be said. 'Do you wish me a good morning, or mean that it is a good morning whether I want it or not; or that you feel good this morning; or that it is a morning to be good on?' 'All of them at once,' said Bilbo. (Tolkien 2012: 5)

What Tolkien is wrestling with here is a question that may have occurred to many of us, at different times and places in our lives. It may be a question that arises when we are not feeling very well and someone asks how we are doing. We may be struck at this moment how 'superficial', often, greetings and farewells can be. Or it may happen in other ways and at other times.

Sometimes words are even meant one way, but heard another. This was well illustrated to me growing up in Australia when World Expo '88 visited a city near to our farming community. A friend took a position at an international pavilion, working beside several non-Australians, each with profoundly different educational expectations to hers. As one such girl got to know my friend, she confided feelings of inferiority at having only two higher degrees. My friend (same age, but with no degrees) smiled and said, 'Ah, you half-wit!' Sadly, her jocular irony was lost on the girl. Her tongue-in-cheek response was taken all the wrong ways. This girl never spoke to my friend again.[1]

---

1. Irony is a large part of Australian culture. Note the irony of Australia's more conservative party taking the label 'Liberal' (Collopy 2010).

Half a century ago, A. R. Radcliffe-Brown noted that in many cultures across Africa, Asia, Oceania and North America, there exists a relational dynamic, wherein 'one is by custom permitted, and in some instances required, to tease or make fun of the other, who in turn is required to take no offence' (1952: 90). Almost inevitably, he notes, this happens as people enter privileged relations. By contrast, Australians (with a certain contempt for privileged relations) adopt such behaviour almost immediately. M. Haugh, in studies of introductions between Anglo-Australian strangers, found such behaviour happening moments after people first met (2011: 165–84). Anecdotally, a similar contempt for privileged relational expectations is evidenced in bizarre demonstrations of 'larrikinism'. Captain Robert Edward Armstrong, in an official public address on 6 August 1945, relinquished command of the warship *Australia* by concluding with the words, 'Goodbye, you pack of bastards' (Swift 2009: 32).

Precise analysis of these elements has been a subject of recent study (Goddard 2006: 65–97; Goddard 2009: 29–53). But without moving to deduce any full explanation, I wish to simply add a somewhat complementary aspect to this cultural tendency. In addition to loving relational shock-value in responding to others, there is also pushback from Australians – in the form of litotes – when overly 'nice' things are said to them.[2] We may deduce, therefore, a fascinating combination, wherein both a love of shocking overstatement is present alongside a discomfort and dismissiveness when 'nice' compliments are offered.

When I first moved from my native Australia to the southern United States sixteen years ago, the absence of some of these elements and the presence of others became intriguing.[3] In terms of the above, the absence of ready 'offense' and the overwhelming presence of 'nice' Southern language created tension for both when it might be appropriate for me (if at all!) to express shocking irony and how to receive compliments from others.

On a completely different note, perhaps, I was struck by differences in greetings and farewells. Prior to moving, I would never think of signing off an email with 'Blessings' or say 'The Lord bless you' when concluding. Yet this was what I began to experience. I even had a devout Christian insist on greeting me every Sunday,

---

2. Anna Wierzbicka observes that litotes (ironical understatement) is far more common in Australian English than in British English, and more common in both cultures than for Americans (1991: 277). For example, if an Australian is asked how they are, the answer is more regularly 'Not bad', meaning 'Good'. According to Wierzbicka, understatement appears in other situations too (1991: 276–7). A common Australian response when thanked for assistance is 'That's all right', meaning positively, 'I was glad to help'. Recently, an American friend whose mother-in-law is Australian heard my wife respond this way and had an epiphany. For the longest time, she felt brushed aside by her mother-in-law's responses. 'Now I realize,' she said, 'it's cultural.'

3. For a more general discussion on distinctives of current Australian culture, see Craven and Purdie (2005).

'Grace and peace to you'.[4] Are such greetings and farewells genuine wishes/prayers that God might favour me? Or are they simply content-less responses, much like an Australian 'G'Day'?[5] Perhaps even deeper social dynamics are at work.[6] Yet for my part, I never perceived a religious wish or prayer that God, Nature or Fate might grant a 'good day' when a fellow Australian said 'G'Day' to me, growing up.[7] So I wondered what the case might be within my newly adopted home of the southern United States.

The latter set of observations led me to ponder greetings and farewells in ancient times, and whether as modern scholars we may be guilty of superimposing secular ideals onto situations and cultures more religious/superstitious than our own. In particular, I wondered whether greetings and farewells in ancient letter might have been perceived as genuine wishes/prayers.[8] If this were so, it would more obviously explain why the first Christ-followers felt freedom to change the common epistolary χαίρειν greeting ('A [wishes] B *to rejoice*') (Lanham 1975: 14–15) into something more Christian (χάρις ὑμῖν καὶ εἰρήνη; Rom. 1.7; 1 Cor. 1.3; 2 Cor. 1.2; Gal. 1.3; Eph. 1.2; Phil. 1.2; Col. 1.2; 1 Thess. 1.1; 2 Thess. 1.2; Phlm. 3; 1 Pet. 1.2; 2 Pet. 1.2; Rev. 1.4) and why, in a similar way, Paul shaped his farewells to align with the same grace and peace combination.[9]

In what follows, I will begin by putting the study of ancient greetings and farewells into context, combining observations from modern scholarship with evidence from the ancient world. A trend among modern Western scholars (across disciplines) is to find no word-content in greetings/farewells. They have become simple social cues of (dis)engagement. By contrast, even a cursory reading of ancient Greek speakers suggests the expectation of word-content in almost every situation. Having discussed evidence for this, my Australian-American context will then be brought to the table further, in the form of tension over knowing

---

4. Cf. χάρις ὑμῖν καὶ εἰρήνη (cf. Rom. 1.7; Rev. 1.4). The placement of *hymin* with grace alone, however, is likely significant (Fee 1995: 70–1).

5. In favour of my friend seeing content in his grace-/peace-wish is the fact that he seems offended by my reluctance to reply 'And to you'. The entire practice seems quite socially forced to me, which leads me to not wish to comply.

6. There are a great number of philosophical questions tied up in the way language use relates to social acceptance and position. This will not be discussed here, but see the numerous essays found in Blot (2003).

7. My use of 'Nature' and 'Fate' here is intended to reflect strong religious pluralism that exists today among Australians. For a recent discussion on extent and limits of secularization in Australia, see Hilliard (2010: 75–92).

8. I use 'farewell' because as we move beyond letter openings in ancient papyri, conventions become looser and more difficult to define, cf. White (1984: 1738).

9. On Paul's modification of common 'farewells', see Weima (1994: 78–104). But on the issue of making too much of closing conventions, see Reed (1997: 280–2). As will be noted below, Reed, among others, assumes that the NT authors radically modified the practice of the day by infusing meaning back into greetings where there was none.

when and how abrupt versus 'nice' words ought to be used. In the ancient world, Greek speakers seemed to use greetings to either express a pleasant kind wish/prayer for the good of the hearer, or a command (imperatively) to urge them. Depending on the religiosity of the author, or more likely what 'boot' might be perceived as fitting, a given grammatical mood was used or implied. This put me in mind that perhaps the common infinitive epistolary χαίρειν greeting may have predominated over the centuries, because it was mood-free – allowing any sender, who was uncertain about whether to praise or blame the recipient, to leave it to the reader to decide which boot may fit best ('A [wishes/commands] B *to rejoice*'). I will conclude this section by noting that joy-farewells seem consistently reserved for *ultimate* (e.g. deathbed) departures, sometimes with strong irony.

In bringing such thoughts to bear on NT greetings and farewells, it was quickly realized that a number of current epistolary debates are impinged upon.[10] Yet it

---

10. 1. It should contribute to the Arzt/Reed debate over whether the Thanksgiving was part of the common epistolary form, because under this alternative, 'Thanksgiving' becomes an extension (like other health-wishes), supplementing the initial prayer/wish for joy, grace, peace and so forth. Cf. Arzt-Grabner (1994: 29–46); Reed (1996a: 87–99). The present significance of this debate can be seen in its centrality in S. E. Porter and S. A. Adam's volume on Paul's letters: Arzt-Grabner (2010: 129–58); Collins (2010: 159–84); Pao (2010: 101–28).

2. Further, Paul's standard use of χάρις in his opening 'greeting' could then be seen as more connected to the cognate εὐχαριστέω in his 'Thanksgivings' (e.g. Rom. 1.7-8; 1 Cor. 1.3-4; Phil. 1.2-3; 1 Thess. 1.1-2), representing two sides of a single prayer concerning the receiving of and responding to God's favour. We have only just begun to consider the cultural reciprocity surrounding χάρις and its cognates in greater detail: Harrison (2003). For an earlier mention of the reciprocal response of thanks for benefaction, see *TDNT*, 9.374. For signs of a growing concern about loading theological terms with more content than context, see Schumacher (2009: 487–501). Note also Reed's evidence from papyri that χάρις might be connected to the idea of thanks from readers (1997: 193).

3. This would then go some way to clarifying the origins of Paul's use of χάρις against the more Jewish ἔλεος, in a way that might help determine whether this was his own creation or something borrowed from Christian liturgy. For a summary of debate surrounding the origins of Paul's use of χάρις, see Lieu (1985: 161–78). The origins of liturgical suggestions are somewhat older: Friedrich (1955: 272–4).

4. If this larger rereading is true, it would also dramatically change the terms of reference for discussing the supposed absence of Thanksgiving in Galatians, since in 1.5 the climactic ἀμήν is immediately proceeded by the reciprocation of honour for what God has given Christians in Christ: ᾧ ἡ δόξα εἰς τοὺς αἰῶνας τῶν αἰώνων, ἀμήν (cf. Rev. 1.4-6). For a recent re-engagement of this long standing discussion, see van Voorst (2010: 153–72).

5. Turning to the non-Pauline Jas 1.1 (the only place where we find the standard χαίρειν greeting in a non-embedded NT letter), the above idea should compel reconsideration of whether 'joy' in 1.2 (Πᾶσαν χαρὰν ἡγήσασθε, ἀδελφοί μου) is more than a pun, in ways that impinge on the sometimes disputed letter-character of this text (Exler 1923). On the χαρά

was difficult to imagine, within limited space, how any discussion of greetings could be entertained without addressing them all.[11] Thus, I decided to focus on farewells, and more particularly Paul's much-debated 'farewells' of Phil. 3.1 and 4.4 (χαίρετε ἐν κυρίῳ; 'farewell/rejoice in the Lord'), particularly since my Australian-American sensitivities may prove helpful here.[12] Would Paul's audience be offended by a 'Farewell' in 3.1, when in 1.18-26 he assured them he would soon return? What would be their response to being provoked (imperativally) to 'rejoice in the Lord' (3.1, 4.4), if indeed this is Paul's sense?

Through my eyes, χαίρετε in Phil. 3.1 appears as a dual wish, that is, as both a somewhat ironic 'Farewell' in light of Paul's uncertainty of his life (to wean them from confidence in him) as well as a bold command to look to God instead. Phil. 4.4 is then (through my eyes) an extension of the same, albeit with development. Both verses, I submit, read (from my context) as part of a linear trajectory tracing from 1.18-26 through 2.17-18, wherein Paul writes to shore up their future by

---

as 'pun' in 1.2, cf. Hartin (2003: 57); Johnson (1995: 176–7); Martin (1988: 13); Mussner (1975: 62). But note the more agreeable comments of Vouga: "*La salutation que Jc adresse à ses lecteurs, pour conventionnelle qu'elle soit, n'est pas pour lui qu'une formule: χαίρειν, que l'on doit traduire couramment par salut, signifie littéralement se réjouir. C'est la première exhortation de l'épître: que les croyants trouvent toute joie (πᾶσαν χαρὰν, V. 2), au sin même des épreuves multiples auxquelles ils sont en butte*" (1984: 39). On the debate over the letter character of James, see Llewelyn (1997: 385–93). There are two examples of embedded letters where the standard χαίρειν letter-greeting is found: Acts 15.23-29 and 23.26-30.

11. Jas 1.1 is more restricted. Because it contains the standard χαίρειν letter-greeting, it also stands out as a way to make immediate comparisons with non-biblical papyri. I suspect, in fact, that James may be being culturally subversive in 1.1, even as he defines joy in 1.2 quite differently from the way it would be understood in Mediterranean culture. In this sense, though James has superficial overlap with non-biblical papyri, he may actually have more in common with the other NT letters where a more overt subversion of the greeting of the day is to be found.

12. Since at least J. B. Lightfoot, it has been argued that in line with common ancient practice, χαίρετε in these verses should be translated 'farewell' (Lightfoot 1868: 126–7, 159–60). Cf. Goodspeed (1922); Goodspeed (1945: 174–5). 'The word group appears 16 times, equally divided between Paul's joy and theirs' (Fee 1995: 405). Cf. 1.4, 18, 25; 2.2, 17-18, 25, 28-29; 4.10. For an excellent and immediately accessible summary of the history of debate over the unity of Philippians, see Martin (1980: 14–22). It is somewhat unfortunate that Paul's use of 'joy' in 3.1 has taken on additional layers of controversy. This makes the joy/farewell in 3.1 highly significant indeed:

> The interpretive watershed in the debate over the literary integrity of Philippians has been and continues to be the beginning of chap. 3 ... Even those who maintain a single-letter theory recognize the difficulty of this transformation in textual timbre. Some might argue that if this issue could be resolved, the debate over the literary integrity of Philippians would be resolved. There are other issues at stake, of course, but non with as much importance as this one. (Reed 1996b: 63)

replacing trust in him with community cohesion and trust in God. The abruptness of the proposed irony in 3.1 would then match the abrupt warning in 3.2 (an otherwise problematic shift).

There is also (I tend to see) a continuity of ideas. Judaizers, Paul feared, might present themselves as alternative partners after he is gone (cf. 2 Cor. 11.5; Gal. 5.10-12). Paul wishes to protect the Philippians by essentially scuttling his role and focusing the Philippians' minds on their own resources (cf. 1.1), including shoring up relations with God – cf. Paul modelling relational priorities towards God in 3.7-16. This reading offers a way of nuancing Phil. 3.1 and 4.4 as connected to the larger argument of the letter. It also suggests a way of harmonizing 3.2–4.1 and 4.10-20, without requiring the strongly 'anti-farewell' approach that has often characterized recent discussions of 3.1 and 4.4.[13]

Greetings and Farewells in Ancient Context

In terms of cultural influences on interpretation, it has always been a challenge for scholars to know how much of themselves might profitably be read into ancient texts and practices.[14] One example of a potential issue is when modern scholars superimpose an overly secular perspectives onto cultures that were far more superstitious/religious. John North writes of the 'comforting assumption' of some modern Western scholars wherein 'all too often books have been constructed on the assumption that religion was a marginal part of life, interesting perhaps in an antiquarian way, but scarcely needing to be placed at the centre of our understanding' (2000: 1). North writes of Roman society being far more religious than many assume today.[15]

This issue of overly secularized readings shows up elsewhere too. E. Fredricksmeyer notes how for certain aspects of Alexander the Great's religion, 'the ancient sources provide more information about it than on any other person in antiquity' (2003: 253). Yet in terms of scholarly interest, 'there exists no comprehensive treatment of this subject' (Fredricksmeyer 2003: 253).[16] When

---

13. These two sections have been central in debate over whether Philippians was originally a single letter or not.

14. One of the most famous exposures of this issues is found in Schweitzer (2005). In this author's opinion, one of the best attempts at balancing of the hermeneutical importance of the reader is Gadamer (1989).

15. North and others oppose a modern assumption that paganism from the late Republic onwards was *so* politicized that the average Roman was disillusioned with organized religion. Cf. Beard, North and Price (1998: 1–73, 167–9); North (2000: 13–17); Scheid (2003).

16. For indications that Alexander was highly superstitious, even in contrast to his more settled Aristotelian upbringing, see Plutarch, *Alex.* 73; Diod. *Bibliotheca historica* 17.114.4-5; 17.116.

it comes to modern secular scholars interpreting ancient societies, there are illustrated dangers of minimizing the importance of religion/superstition.

How is this relevant to greetings and farewells? Studies of modern cultural greetings and farewells inevitably seem to emphasize how such language is quickly ritualized, so that it only ever plays the role of social marker (Malinowski 1923: 315–16; Sacks 1975: 57–80; Youssouf, Grimshaw and Bird 1976: 797–824). Time and again, modern greetings and farewells are discussed this way (Duranti 1997: 66).[17] So, for example, M. Saville-Troike recently reiterates the idea that greetings and leave-takings are drummed into children from an early age (when meaning apparently cannot be grasped), such that members of modern society never comprehend the real content of social (dis)engagement beyond a generation or so (2003: 231–2).[18] In studies as diverse as how people answer telephones, researchers now simply assume that the words used in greeting are lexically meaningless. Attention shifts instead to elements like 'response time' as a measure for understanding psychological intent (Schegloff 1986: 111–51; Hooper and Koleilat-Doany 1989: 157–79). With few exceptions, lexical content is the farthest thing from modern researchers' minds when studying modern greetings and farewells.[19] Even in cases where in modern cultures religion is clearly a central factor, mention is rarely made of retained religious/superstitious content in greetings and farewells (Hopkins 1931: 369–83). More often, this possibility is pushed aside in favour of reinforcing the sociological mantra of (dis)engagement.[20]

The problem here is not that we are misguided to think that greeting and farewells (in any era) are social cues for (dis)engagement, or that today many cultures have emptied greetings and farewells of any lexical content. Clearly, greetings and farewells do mark moments of social (dis)connection. The problem, as A. Duranti points out, is that in emphasizing this aspect we may ignore cases where lexical content remains:

---

17. Where debate has existed, it is often at a deeper and more technical linguistic level, cf. Coulmas (1979: 239–66).

18. But in the case of a word like 'joy' being used as a greeting/farewell, the tendency of children to attribute only one meaning to each word would speak strongly in the opposite direction. Children would be inclined to hear such a greeting/farewell quite literally, keeping alive the actual meaning of the word in spite of ritualizing tendencies, cf. Aitchison (2012: 209–21).

19. One of the strongest evidence-based bellwethers that I have been able to find, sounded against those who would completely dismiss content from greetings and farewells, is a study by Duranti on the Samoan people (1997: 63–97).

20. On the one hand, W. E. Hopkins can speak of 'the ritual connected with the reception of a guest [being] rigid and of *almost* religious significance', but, on the other hand, he can relegate the actual word-content of greetings and farewells to "more or less stereotyped formulas' (1931: 378–79, emphasis mine). Hopkins pays close attention to physical gestures and their significance for social homage, but then when it comes to words and their religious/superstitious meaning, his comments are extremely guarded.

Contrary to what is assumed by most existing studies of greetings, greetings are not necessarily devoid of propositional content; they can be used to gather information about a person's identity or whereabouts. The Samoan 'What are you going?' greeting, for example is seeking information about the addressee and, unlike what is argued by Sacks (1975) about the English 'How are you?', in answering the Samoan greeting, a lie is not the 'preferred' answer. (1997: 89)

All this becomes potentially important, as we turn to greetings and farewells among ancient Greek speakers, because in this case, too, it has been common for researchers to assume that ancient Mediterranean society used them with little or no lexical content. Francis Exler, for example, when approaching greetings in letters, constantly pushes away from χαίρειν ('joy') retaining any lexical content. This is especially striking in light of his willingness to give significance to words immediately following (i.e. 'health-wishes') (Exler 1923: 107). The same perspective is articulated by Carol Dana Lanham's study on the *salutatio* in Latin letters:

These parts of a letter, the outer framework that characterizes it as a letter and not as a conversation, are all *formulas*, polite expressions chosen from a narrow range of conventional phrases established by repeated use and normally devoid of real meaning. So too with oral greetings: to query 'How are you?' only the doctor in his office expects a reply other than 'I'm fine, thanks', and the person who instead answers 'I feel terrible' is deliberately breaking convention. (1975: 1)

One apparent exception to this trend is found in Michael Trapp's recent anthology of Greek and Latin letters. Trapp speaks of ancient letter-greetings and farewells having content, just like the health-wishes commonly following χαίρειν: 'Correspondents are compelled by convention to begin by wishing each other joy, courage, or well-being, and to end by wishing each other health and strength' (Trapp 2003: 40). Yet in a strange irony, Trapp then translates χαίρειν with the content-less 'Greetings' throughout his book, even while giving substance to the other elements just mentioned, that is, courage, health, strength and so forth (e.g. Trapp 2003: 50–3). In spite of certain tacit admissions, therefore, the idea that ancient letter-greetings had meaning seems to be the last thing on modern scholars' minds.

The same assumption is found among NT specialists – albeit with a peculiar willingness to have NT authors alone infuse meaning into their greetings. Judith Lieu attributes to the NT authors the greatest content in their letter-greetings, while at the same time assuming this to be an anomaly: 'We see that the [NT epistolary] greeting ... expresses far more than the conventional formalities' (1985: 178, emphasis mine). Jeffrey Reed similarly speaks in sociological terms of the salutations of the surrounding Graeco-Roman world as merely 'establishing the immediate interpersonal relationship between sender and recipient' (1997: 192). Then, on the other hand, Reed writes of 'Paul's modification; his formula was not a ritualistic "hello" but a means of drawing the reading into a letter with different aims than those to which they were accustomed' (1997: 193). Intriguingly, however, such authors rarely pursue this line of inquiry further. Reed's analysis of Paul's 'Thanksgivings' shows no evidence that he has thought about how the grace wish/prayer might flow naturally into a thanksgiving prayer (cf. Lanham 1975: 14–15).

Again, there are some exceptions among NT specialists to this trend. Jeffrey Weima, for example, is willing to acknowledge that farewells in ancient papyri may have had retained real word-content:

> The health wish in Greek letter *closings* also underwent certain discernible stages of development. In the third and second century BC, it occurred in letter closings less frequently than in letter openings. This may be due to the fact that the farewell wish during this period, ἔρρωσο or εὔτυχει, retained its literal meaning ('Be Strong!'; 'Prosper!'), with some writers therefore considering it redundant to close a letter with an additional health wish. (1994: 37)

But as in the case of Trapp, Weima neither develops this, nor does he speak of Paul's greetings differently.[21]

What this information shows is a tendency among classicists, historians and NT specialists alike to fall into line with modern social research on greetings and farewells. There is an overwhelming tendency to see greetings and farewells as having no real lexical content. Ironically, NT scholars can be credited with entertaining possible content in NT greetings and farewells. But this, then, has had no further impact, either on their interpretation of the NT or other papyri. More ironically, authors will sometimes indicate a belief that greetings and farewells had content (e.g. Trapp, Weima) but then continue as if they themselves had not suggested such an idea.

With these things in mind, we turn to inquire after the ancient extant evidence and what it suggests about lexical content in ancient Greek greetings and farewells.

To begin very broadly, I wish to first note evidence of people having superstitious beliefs about lexical content when it came to pronouncements, to demonstrate how superstition/religion may have driven Graeco-Roman society to retaining meaning in other words and pronouncement such as greetings/farewells. Numerous curse tablets have been discovered near public baths, where people's cloths were often stolen while relaxing. Here we find examples of the way people viewed pronouncements:

> These texts illustrate two important features of pleas for justice in particular and of the *defixiones* in general: first, they indicate how deeply rooted was the belief in their effectiveness; and second, they tell us that the commissioning of a *defixio* was not, indeed could not be, an entirely private affair. In other words,

---

21. A real problem with his analysis is the fluidity of 'farewells' in letters, which might make him and others question whether these endings were ever so formulaic anyway. Cf. discussion in Reed (1997: 280–2).

> the effectiveness of the process was dependent to a certain degree on public knowledge that 'a fix' had been placed on a particular suspect. (Gager 1992: 176)

The publishing of words had power in these people's minds, and John Gager highlights this further by noting how such words were often sufficient to force a thief to confess. In other instances, a wrongly accused person took the prayer/wish pronouncement seriously enough to seek vindication (Gager 1992: 177). What this seems to establish is that many people in the Graeco-Roman world believed that the pronouncement of a word was significant in so far as bringing responses from the divine realm.

In a philosophical sense, this bridging of the seen and unseen world, in terms of words pronounced, finds resonance in the thinking of Plato. From Plato came the idea that words (like everything) had a true and ideal form in the world of the forms. From this, there seemed to emerge an emphasis on etymology as the go-to strategy for clarifying the meaning of otherwise confusing words (cf. Lowe 2013: 179–202). For those of us living in the shadow of Ferdinand de Saussure, this sounds strange (de Saussure 1974). We no longer believe that words have intrinsic content. Yet there are reasons to believe that for some ancients, words (in general) were seen as having a metaphysical connection to an unseen realm both in their maintenance of content and in what they might achieve when pronounced.

Turning specifically to greetings, we find Plato himself interpreting greetings as retaining lexical content. In one particular passage (*Charm.* 164b-165d), he discusses the exhortatory words carved at the entrance of the Delphi temple ('know yourself') as a greeting from the gods:

> For I would almost say that this very thing, self-knowledge, is temperance, and I am at one with him who put up the inscription of those words at Delphi. For the purpose of that inscription on the temple, as it seems to me, is to serve as the god's salutation to those who enter it, instead of 'Hail!' – this is a wrong form of greeting, and they should rather *exhort* one another with the words, 'Be temperate!' And thus the god addresses those who are entering his temple in a mode which differs from that of men; such was the intention of the dedicator of the inscription in putting it up, I believe; and that he says to each man who enters, in reality, 'Be temperate!' But he says it in a rather riddling fashion, as a prophet would; for 'Know thyself!' and 'Be temperate!' are the same, as the inscription and I declare, though one is likely enough to think them different – an error into which I consider the dedicators of the later inscriptions fell when they put up 'Nothing overmuch' and 'A pledge, and thereupon perdition'. For they supposed that 'Know thyself!' was a piece of advice, and not the god's salutation of those who were entering; and so, in order that their dedications too might equally give pieces of useful advice, they wrote these words and dedicated them. (164d–165a)

This text clarifies Plato's belief that greetings were not simply haphazard and content-less social cues.

But further, Plato clearly thought of greetings in letters as retaining word-content. Commonly, his letters opened with the greeting εὖ πράττειν ('do well'; cf. *Ep.* 309a, 310b, 320a, 321c, 322c, 323d, etc.), something not unknown in other ancient letters.[22] But in *Ep.* 315a–319e, he subverts this by starting more typically, Πλάτων Διονυσίῳ χαίρειν, before explaining to Dionysius why he prefers εὖ πράττειν:

> If I [typically] wrote thus, should I be hitting on the best mode of address? Or rather, by writing, according to my custom, 'well-doing' [εὖ πράττειν]? You, indeed – as was reported by the spectators then present – addressed even God at Delphi in this same flattering phrase, and wrote, as they say, this verse – 'Joy!' ... But as for me, I would not call upon a man, and much less a god, and bid him enjoy himself. (315a-b)

Here is specific evidence for the standard opening letter-greetings (whether χαίρειν or εὖ πράττειν) being seen as having lexical content in the eyes of this formative philosopher. He believed that his recipient would be attentive to the kind of greeting offered and what it actually meant, and take this to heart when (s)he heard it.

But could it be that Plato was largely alone in such thinking? In his landmark study of 1923, Francis Exler reproduced many of the opening and closing lines from the extant papyri of his time. Exler's evidence suggests otherwise (1923: 34).[23] Briefly, there are examples in the papyri he presents where <A – to B – χαίρειν> stands alone, suggesting (to Exler) that this is the base form for beginning a letter, and that as such it became ritualized. But there are cases, Exler also includes, like P. Oxy II 269 (23 CE) and P. Oxy. II 260 (59 CE), which begin <A – to B> with no χαίρειν greeting. If χαίρειν was ritualized, might it be so easily excluded (1923: 25,

---

22. Πράττειν is an Attic form of πράσσω. Interestingly, cf. Acts 15.29, where the description of what will make them do well is followed by the farewell wish to 'do well': ἐξ ὧν διατηροῦντες ἑαυτοὺς εὖ πράξετε. Ἔρρωσθε.

23. As noted above, Exler does not always present his evidence in ways conducive to seeing letter-greetings maintaining their word-content. He does demonstrate, among other things, that 'throughout the Ptolemaic and Roman periods the formula: A – to B – χαίρειν is by far the most common' letter opening (1923: 62). But in distinguishing these and similar 'Opening Formulas' (1923: 23) from what immediately followed, that is, 'Conventional Phrases in the Body of the Letter' (1923: 101), Exler may have produced a misleading impression. Instead of discussing what immediately followed the <A – to B – χαίρειν> formula in connection with this formula, he largely relegates analysis of these phrases to the penultimate chapter, under the heading 'Initial Phrases' (1923: 103–13). This gives the distinct impression that such words bore minimal relation to <A – to B – χαίρειν>. When viewed in a different light, however, Exler's evidence suggests that χαίρειν was not so formularized but was often connected to what follows as part of a broader *wish* for good. In what follows, we will highlight different ways of combining Exler's evidence.

26)? More pointedly, Exler's work contains numerous examples where words of degree were added before χαίρειν to express 'many' or 'heartiest' joy to the recipient (<A – to B- πολλὰ / πλεῖστα χαίρειν>) (1923: 27–34, 54, 63). This would seem to gravitate away from a lexical vacuum. In numerous other cases, we find 'to be joyous *and* strong/healthy' (<A – to B- χαίρειν καὶ ἐρρῶσθαι / ὑγιαίνειν>) where the joy-wish and health-wish are both in the infinitive and both connected in a way suggesting they were seen together. This is the point that Trapp acknowledges but then does not highlight in his actual translations (2003: 34–5).

Further to this, Exler shows there was regularly a combining of elements, wherein we find elaborate variations like 'to be heartily joyous and healthy' (<A – to B- πλεῖστα χαίρειν καὶ ὑγιαίνειν>) and 'to be heartily joyous and through everything healthy' (<A – to B- πλεῖστα χαίρειν καὶ διὰ παντὸς ὑγιαίνειν>) (1923: 32–3). This simply does not read like χαίρειν standing as part of the ritual introduction, having no lexical content. The second category just noted (<A – to B- πλεῖστα χαίρειν καὶ διὰ παντὸς ὑγιαίνειν>) is particularly striking, in the way we find a superlative comment about health on top of the wish for joy, indicating comparison where the second clause is emphasized by way of contrast and on the basis of some measurable content in the first. This gives further strong indication of a belief in retained lexical content for the joy-wish.[24]

The kinds of patters just mentioned span, in almost every case, several centuries of practice, including the first century CE, and yet with the kind of ebb and flow suggesting a deliberate avoidance of ritualizing (Exler 1923: 61). It will not do, therefore, to argue that somewhere after Plato, greetings were quickly ritualized. The evidence suggests the opposite. The joy-greeting (like many other words in the ancient world) was seen as retaining genuine lexical content.

One last example may be added, suggesting this trajectory of retained meaning across the NT era. Satirist Lucian (b. 125 CE), recounts a story where in the morning an afternoon greeting was accidently offered to a patron. The 'offending party' saw this as no small issue and so felt compelled to write and explain himself:

> I am in both predicaments at once; coming to make you my morning salutation, which should have taken the orthodox form of Rejoice, I bade you, in a very choice fit of absent-mindedness, Be healthy – a good enough wish in its way, but a little untimely and unconnected with that early hour. (Fowler and Fowler 1905: 2:34)

---

24. Interestingly, Exler at one point admits that χαίρειν sometimes combines with the health-wish to form a single unit. But here, it is only by way of the health-wish *losing content* and being absorbed into his content-less opening formula. Exler (like scholars that follow) seems to find it impossible to entertain the idea that χαίρειν may actually have had content (cf. 1923: 106). But as just noted, Exler's evidence reads differently. The wide variation on how <A – to B – χαίρειν> letters were suggests, instead, that χαίρειν was viewed as a call/wish for joy.

Lieu sees this text 'vividly characteriz[ing] the beliefs and conventions of the society of his time', meaning, for her, that it was a satire on the pedantic nature of social cues (1985: 161). But while it is likely that some social satire is being offered, it may be wondered whether Lucian was simply critiquing the pedantic nature of his culture in general. In order for such a critique to have any bite, it must also be addressing a real phenomenon. As we read on, the majority of the text dwells on justifying the *content* of different word-greetings and their appropriateness. What might instead be argued is that Lucian was satirizing his culture's obsession with superstition about wishes/prayers – the very subject we are addressing in this essay.

Before moving from this discussion, it is important to return for a moment to Plato to note how in the case of both the Delphi inscription and his discussion of letter-greetings, the communicated content was not about wish so much as imperatival command. This raises the important additional issue of communicative mood in greetings.

Even if we acknowledge that ancient Greek speakers saw retained content in greetings and farewells, what content did they see? What was being communicated? Was it simply, like the curse tablets, a prayer pronouncement wishing/praying for something to happen to the recipient or (with Plato) a piece of social instruction? At one level we might say that the matter will be difficult to decipher in the NT period, since the imperative seemed to have absorbed the optative mood: there was a 'strong tendency to use the imperative instead of the optative, not only in requests, for which the imperative has a place in classical too, but also in imprecations which in classical take the optative: ἀνάθεμα ἔστω G 1:8f' (BDF 1961: §384). Perhaps this shift explains why Liddel and Scott, in their entry on χαῖρε/χαίρετε, make no mention of the optative form χαίροις, being used in greetings or farewells – even though their work purports to span ancient Greek history.[25]

In fact, we know from Sophocles's fifth-century BCE Greek tragedy *Electra* that in former times the optative χαίροις was used as a greeting. This play provides a dark comic moment that highlights how this was an accepted greeting wishing/praying for joy towards its recipient.[26] So there is every indication that Plato's exhortation must be balanced against clear indications of a wish/prayer for joy.

25. The same is true of the relevant entries in Spicq, *EDNT*, *TDNT* and *BDAG*.

26. The girl Electra speaks to her hated stepfather Aegisthus (responsible for her father's death) about the body of her supposedly dead brother (the rightful heir), arriving home after a chariot accident in a distant land. Aegisthus speaks down to the girl as he seeks details, before sarcastically referring to her response as an uncommonly pleasant greeting (ἦ πολλὰ χαίρειν μ᾽ εἶπας οὐκ εἰωθότως; 1455). To this she replies, 'May joy be yours, if joy is what you find in these things' (χαίροις ἄν, εἴ σοι χαρτὰ τυγχάνοι τάδε; 1455). Again, the indication here is that the joy-greeting/farewell had content. But the intense irony in her words, must also be noted, because she knows that in reality her brother's (living) body will soon return (he had not died) to spell Aegisthus's downfall. So Aegisthus's 'joy' in news of his supposed death will really be no joy at all. Here we find the optative present as a sarcastic wish/prayer for future joy, which would only work as comical irony if Aegisthus is left in the dark by this response, that is, if this was an acceptable social greeting.

At the same time, a certain ambiguity is present in the use of the imperative in the NT era due to general absorption of the optative mood. Revealingly, we frequently find in the papyri the words 'but before all I wish you to be healthy' (πρὸ δὲ πάντων εὔχομαί ὑγιαίνειν), follows directly after <A – to B – χαίρειν>, often in combination with εὔχομαί ('I wish/pray') and with direct reference to θεός (Exler 1923: 107–10).[27] This highlights how some authors saw the need to clarify (perhaps) that they were offering a wish rather than commanding something even present in their use of the mood-less infinitive χαίρειν (cf. Plato).

What is further revealing though, is that from the first century CE onwards, letter writers were at times leaving the infinitive in favour of a specific imperative in their opening greeting <Χαῖρε B from A>, or a specific optative <Χαίροις B from A> (Exler 1923: 35–6, 67–8).[28] What this somewhat neat piece of evidence suggests is that people were indeed wrestling with the question of the ambiguity between prayer/wish and social command in the joy-greeting. All of which goes to show further that they most certainly intended lexical content. But more than this, it suggests there was a struggle to properly communicate desired context, in light of *how* the recipient was to rejoice.

It is here that I would like to reintroduce my Australian context into this discussion and the tendencies of Australians to both enjoy shocking words as well as being hypersensitive to 'nice' things offered to them. I find myself drawn in part towards reading the infinitive χαίρειν greeting as an abrupt kind of command for the recipients to 'Joy-up!' My Australian context likes this because it also avoids an option that might be overly 'nice', that is, reading this as a sincere and openhearted prayer/wish for good. But then as one now living in the southern United States, I also feel a pull in the opposite direction.[29] Might it not be better to see χαίρειν as a pleasant prayer/wish on someone's behalf?

What this does is make me wonder whether the populace at the time felt any similar tensions over whether to praise or blame a hearer and how it might be received. The fact is that the <Χαῖρε B from A>/ <Χαίροις B from A> imperative/ optative clarification did not catch on. The ambiguous infinitive χαίρειν maintained popularity over time.[30] Given distance and uncertainty in knowing the mood (literally) a letter would find its recipient in, might it not have seemed best for a writer (knowing audiences saw words as meaningful) to use the mood-less

---

27. Note that if the δέ is taken as adversative, here is yet another piece of evidence for a kind of superlative extension beyond 'joy', indicating the joy-χαίρειν was read with lexical content.

28. Exler himself rejects Ziemann's suggestion that these letters reflect different social classes of writers (1923: 68).

29. Saying and receiving 'nice words' of compliment is very much part of my adopted culture.

30. For discussion of how it originally began as part of the verbal greeting of the one who delivered the letter, see Lanham (1975: 11, 14).

infinitive, allowing them to imply their *own* content, <A [commands/wishes/prayers] B to be joyful> and thereby avoiding the possibility of relational offence?[31]

A final comment is necessary concerning the use of χαῖρε/χαίρετε as a *farewell*. Our attention until now has focused on joy-greetings, not farewell, and with good reason. It was far more commonly used as a greeting. Yet in terms of its use as farewell, something has not commonly been noted, that is, the χαῖρε/χαίρετε wish/command to joy seemed reserved for *ultimate* goodbyes where the person speaking believed departure was essentially permanent.[32] When Odysseus gives permanent leave to Arete, he says, 'My farewell, oh queen' (χαῖρέ μοι, ὦ βασίλεια; *Od*. 13.59). When Heracles is about to go off to the world of the dead, he says to his brother, 'And farewell my brother' (καὶ χαῖρε πόλλ' ὦδελφέ; *Theoc*. 1.144). What reason can be offered for this particular farewell at this moment? Whatever else, one observation is that sorrow would be a predictable feeling on occasions of ultimate farewell. So, a call/wish for joy makes sense as a corrective response to the expected opposite. The specificity of apparently reserving χαῖρε/χαίρετε for an ultimate farewell stands as a mirror image of the anticipated emotion on such an occasion.

One further example must be added both by way of suggesting that lexical content is retained and because of its special relevance to what will soon be said about Paul's Philippian letter. Earlier in *The Odyssey*, before Odysseus bids leave to Queen Arete, the nymph Calypso (who has taken him for her own) is trying to persuade Odysseus that he would do better staying with her than taking a perilous voyage home. She speaks of the dangers of the sea and of her own superior beauty compared with Penelope, Odysseus's wife. In the midst of this attempted seduction, Calypso bids him 'Farewell' (χαῖρε; *Od*. 5.206). The way she speaks directly after this about the issues of safety and her own beauty suggests lexical content and also a strong sense of irony: 'Will you really find joy if you take permanent leave of me? Will you be happier if you go, once and for all?' This speaks to the likelihood of lexical content being expected, but her pointed double-meaning will also have relevance when I return to consider Australian-American reflections on Phil. 3.1 and 4.4.

Reflecting on the 'Farewells' of Philippians

We now take the above information, alongside self-awareness of my Australian-American context, into reconsidering the 'farewells' of Philippians. In the minds of some, seeing χαίρετε as 'farewell' in Phil. 3.1 (Τὸ λοιπόν, ἀδελφοί μου, χαίρετε ἐν κυρίῳ) and 4.4 (Χαίρετε ἐν κυρίῳ πάντοτε· πάλιν ἐρῶ, χαίρετε) 'is in fact impossible

---

31. This possibility that a letter might wrongly disrupt relations by coming across the wrong way is a theme important in light of the relational nature of letters (Trapp 2003: 35).

32. This is what appears to be true for all examples listed in LSJ χαίρω, A III. 2.

... Nothing is in its favor, and everything is against it' (Fee 1995: 291n25).[33] One thing in its favour is the parallel with 2 Cor. 13.11 (Λοιπόν, ἀδελφοί, χαίρετε), which is essentially the same and is found only two verses before 2 Corinthians concludes (Harrison 2003: 392).[34] This certainly offers *some* evidence for 'farewell' being reasonable in Phil. 3.1. Yet for those seeking to read Philippians as a unified letter, this raises more questions than answers, such that λοιπός must necessarily be read without a sense of 'Finally …'[35] Then comes a barrage of arguments against χαίρετε ever possibly meaning 'farewell' in either Philippians or 2 Corinthians:[36]

1. Whatever is true for Phil. 3.1 should be true for 4.4, and in the case of the latter, it is nonsense to think that Paul would be taken to mean 'farewell in the Lord *always*, again I say, farewell'.
2. It makes the imperative χαίρετε mean something radically different from what it means in the rest of Philippians, 2 Corinthians and elsewhere in the NT.
3. Particularly in Philippians, joy/rejoicing is such a keynote for the epistle that it is difficult to imagine how the audience would take it any other way in 3.1 or 4.4.

---

33. Cf. Marvin R. Vincent: 'Not … "farewell", for which there is no sufficient ground' (1911: 91); L. Alexander: 'Almost certainly, then, Paul is not saying "farewell" but repeating the exhortation to "rejoice" which is so much a feature of this letter' (1989: 97); B. B. Thurston: 'In my view there is no real evidence for translating it "farewell", as some have suggested' (Thurston and Ryan 2009: 112). For an adamant statement in favour of 'farewell', see Beare (1959: 100). There are, in fact, recent (worrying) signs that authors are done with this discussion, in favour seeing only 'rejoice' in Paul's use of this word. In Charles Cousar's succinct but scholarly treatment of Philippians, he feels no need to even mention the issue (2009: 67, 84–5; cf. Heil 2010: 116, 148–9). Many English versions have translated Corinthians, 'Finally, brothers, farewell/good-bye', even if they do not follow suite for Philippians: RSV, NRSV, NEB, TYN, KJV, NKJV, NIV, ASV, CEV, NIRV, GNT and TMB. In terms of the argument from λοιπόν, see Craddock (1985: 47, 71). Those who oppose this argument merely point to other possible translations for λοιπόν. In must surely be admitted, however, that in the case of 2 Cor. 13.11, it clearly indicates a conclusion.

34. As mentioned earlier, this is one of the problems which has almost blacklisted a reading of 'finally' as meaning anything approaching a conclusion: 'Several scholars have taken Paul's remarks at the beginning of ch. 3 to indicate that Paul is closing off his letter. This, then, has led to various questions about the letter's unity' (Fowl 2005: 143).

35. 'As is well known, the crux in the analysis of Philippians comes at 3.1, where Paul, after apparently winding down towards the close, takes off again into a polemical passage' (Alexander 1989: 89). Reading Τὸ λοιπόν as 'finally' only serves to further exacerbate this winding down/taking off problem. Not surprisingly then, Fee thinks it is 'a purely gratuitous translation' (1995: 290).

36. This list was compiled primarily from comments found in Alexander (1989: 97); Fee (1995: 291); Harris (2005: 932); Moule (1893: 85, 111); and Reed (1996b: 80–2).

4. Χαίρετε is grouped together with other imperatives in Phil. 3.1, 4.4 and 2 Cor. 13.11, meaning it should better be taken in all cases as an injunction to rejoice among other injunctions.
5. There is no lexical justification for χαίρετε meaning 'farewell' in papyri. Though a few letters use it as part of the opening greeting, it is never used as a wish near the end.
6. NT parallels for χαῖρε/χαίρετε as a farewell are completely lacking. In all six occurrences where either is used, they are initial greetings (Mt. 26.49, 27.29, 28.9; Mk 15.18; Lk. 1.28; Jn 19.3).
7. If χαίρετε really meant 'farewell', it might be expected at the absolute end of the letter.

As overwhelming as this list first appears, it must be noted that the first four points lose traction when we remove the dichotomy between χαῖρε/χαίρετε only ever having word-content ('rejoice') and never at the same time functioning as a social cue ('Farewell'). All four points assume this dichotomy, which as we saw above is more a modern construct than an ancient reality. Ancient Greek speakers used χαῖρε/χαίρετε as part of social (dis)engagement, while simultaneously retaining its lexical content. In this sense, the first four complaints are now immaterial.

This leaves only the last three. In response to the fifth and sixth, whenever χαῖρε/χαίρετε was used as a farewell, it was an *ultimate* farewell, that is, anticipating the finish of a relationship (see above). Since ancient letters most regularly functioned in 'creating and sustaining friendships' (Trapp 2003: 40; cf. Koskenniemi 1956: 35–7), and because in the vast majority of extant cases they are either business transactions or short and superficial, it is unremarkable that no other extant letter might be found with the agenda of a final farewell. Neither should we wonder that there are few (if any) narrative examples of χαιρ- farewells in the NT.[37] Other arguments could be added.[38] But moving to the seventh and

---

37. Interestingly, it might be argued that in Jn 19.3, the soldiers are not greeting Jesus so much as farewelling him in anticipation of his imminent death – as a point of rubbing salt into the wounds of his suffering. They are already with him, so how does it make sense that they would greet him at this point? In the end, however, their greeting is in response to him suddenly being 'dressed as king', and so their words do in fact make more sense as a greeting. What is cutting in their words is that they do not simply greet him in a more neutral way (ἀσπάζομαι) but chose instead to command him to rejoice.

38. Our examples of χαίρετε as a letter-greeting in papyri, demonstrate the possibility that verbal greetings/farewells being validly employed in letters. Complaint 5, in particular, comes from a form-critical perspective where greetings and farewells are view as stereotyped words. As noted above, it is this kind of thinking that has led to our modern diminishing of content in greetings/farewells in the first place. The popularity of χαίρειν in letters may have been less about fixed forms and more about the desire to keep an open mood (see above).

final complaint, we need only say that this is a weak argument, which cannot possibly bear the weight of the case when left alone.[39]

But what can be said (more positively) in favour of χαίρετε having an added nuance of 'farewell' in 3.1 or 4.4? Note carefully the words 'added nuance'. The lexical content of 'joy' (as I have suggested) is never lost even when this was used as a social cue of impending departure. This must be said again. Never in the ancient world (evidence suggests) was a greeting or farewell suggested to have no content. So when we speak of χαίρετε in 3.1 or 4.4 meaning 'farewell', we are not thereby eliminating the content 'joy' from it.

But regarding whether χαίρετε has this kind of dual sense in Phil. 3.1, there is almost a mandate to at least consider this, given the extreme difficulties that have followed this verse. B. Weiss says, 'The hypotheses which have gathered around the message of 3.1 furnish a sad illustration of how matters stand in the exegesis of Philippians' (1897: 389; quoted in Reed 1997: 239). More pointedly, L. E. Keck says of Phil. 3.1, 'No one really knows what to make of it' (1971: 846). Reed adds, 'There is perhaps no other verse in Philippians with so many grammatical and lexical interpretive difficulties' (1996b: 72). So does a dual reading of χαίρετε help these dilemmas? I will argue it may.[40]

From my Australian context, Phil. 3.1 raises expectations, almost a hope, of shock-value and ironic twist here, especially when in the next verse there is the delightfully shocking rhetoric of 'dogs ... evil-doers ... mutilators' (3.2). The reader may remember the delight of one Australian in offering a shocking farewell: 'Goodbye, you pack of bastards.' From an Australian perspective, there is reason to have Paul saying something ironic and provocative. But is this at all illuminating or suggestive in the current case?

In the second half of Phil. 3.1, the apostle claims, 'To write the same things to you is no problem, but is a safeguard for you' (τὰ αὐτὰ γράφειν ὑμῖν ἐμοὶ μὲν οὐκ ὀκνηρόν, ὑμῖν δὲ ἀσφαλές). What are these 'same things' (plural)? It would be appropriate if his reference were to 'rejoice in the Lord' (since it immediately proceeds these words).[41] But the problem is that he speaks of 'things', plural (τὰ

---

39. In the instance of 2 Corinthians, χαίρετε is essentially a final item in the letter. And given the jury being out on whether Philippians was originally multiple letters, any assertion about the original location of 3.1 is precarious. As will soon be seen, I am not suggesting that my re-reading of Phil. 3.1 points towards Philippians as a composite letter. I am merely suggesting that this argument (which, to be fair, came from Harris's analysis of 2 Cor. 13.11) cannot be reasonably applied to Philippians. In general, commentators feel no stress in suggesting that Paul is wrapping up his argument in Phil. 3.1, only to kick on to further discussion, cf. Fee (1995: 288n12).

40. For the value of arguments based on utility, see Wright (1992: 99–104) and, more foundationally, Latta and Macbeath (1929: 348–74).

41. For a more recent summary of debate, see O'Brien (1991: 350-2). In my opinion, it would still be best to read it as a reference to what immediately precedes if possible – is Paul trying to confuse us? The only reason this is not adopted is that it seemed untenable, cf. Fee (1995: 292-3).

αὐτὰ) (Moule 1893: 94). What 'things' (plural) are conveyed by 'rejoice in the Lord'? What if Paul has in mind the sort of dual meaning discussed above (i.e. seeing χαίρετε as 'rejoice'/'farewell' together)? Through χαίρετε, Paul would then (1) be announcing a dramatic goodbye and, at the same time, in light of this, (2) be offing a challenge to be happy (in the Lord). This would account for the plural.

The challenge with such a reading is to find where before this he has said these same things, and, preferably, we might find this evidence together since his comment in 3.1 is that this is a repeat idea (τὰ αὐτὰ γράφειν ὑμῖν; 3.1).

It is noteworthy that difficulties in finding such a parallel antecedent (under any readings) have led to a great diversity of suggestions.[42] But one suggestion that stands out as helpful is Reed's. He argues that Phil. 2.17-18 is the logical antecedent, since it is the immediate previous time Paul has used χαίρετε and because of the general abundance of joy language elsewhere in these verses (1996b: 79–80). But if we take 2.17-18 as Paul's reference point, what immediately emerges is that both the elements just mentioned are found here, right next to each other: (1) 'Even if I am to be poured out on the sacrifice and service of your faith, I rejoice, and rejoice together with you all' (Ἀλλὰ εἰ καὶ σπένδομαι ἐπὶ τῇ θυσίᾳ καὶ λειτουργίᾳ τῆς πίστεως ὑμῶν χαίρω καὶ συγχαίρω πᾶσιν ὑμῖν·) and (2) 'so you also must rejoice and rejoice together with me' (τὸ δὲ αὐτὸ καὶ ὑμεῖς χαίρετε καὶ συγχαίρετέ μοι).

The first part is an admission (somewhat shockingly in light of 1.18-26) that Paul may soon die. This draws attention to 'farewell' and of the need for them to potentially shift their gaze beyond him. But then, in the second part, there is a command (in light of this) that they must rejoice.[43] What Paul would then be saying in 2.17-18 is that with the possibility of his imminent death, they must have a joy that reflects submission to God's [implied] will – even as 1.18-26 is filled with explicit discussion of God's will for everyone.[44] The dual elements I suggested as present in Paul's use of χαίρετε as 'rejoice'/ 'farewell' in Phil. 3.1 could be dual elements implied by τὰ αὐτὰ in 3.1b, which then are stated together in what seems

---

42. Debate over the reference point has a long history: 'The reference is probably to a former letter, or to former letters' (Vincent 1911: 91). But he then admits, 'Out conclusion rest rather on the antecedent probability of lost letters.' Lightfoot says, 'If the epistle itself supplies the requisite allusion, it is much more naturally sought here' (1868: 125). According to William Kelly, 'joy in the Lord is the truest safeguard against the religious snares of the enemy' (1869: 69).

43. It is true that there is no rejoicing in the Lord here. But we must leave room for development. Since 1.18-26 suggests he will not be dying and 2.17-18 now shifts this position a little, it ought not to be surprising that 3.1 should also have some elements of further shift. In its essentials, however, we find a striking presence of the same ideas that are to be repeated in 3.1, particularly the theme of 'rejoicing' which is of course the key issue surrounding χαίρετε in 3.1.

44. This definition of 'rejoicing in the Lord' as essentially a God-ward perspective on life is most fully clarified (I will suggest) in 4.4-20 first through instruction and then through Paul's own example.

like the most logical antecedent 2.17-18, as expected from reference to 'the same'. If χαίρετε means both 'rejoice' and 'farewell' in Phil. 3.1, sense emerges in this otherwise obscure verse.

Such an approach also offers clarity on the otherwise peculiar idea that 'joy' is their safeguard (ὑμῖν δὲ ἀσφαλές; 3.1b).[45] Joy per se is not the safeguard. It is rather their breaking with Paul (as a traveling missionary; cf. 3.2-3) and subsequent shift in confidence to the Lord that makes them safe. 'Safe' is them owning up to Paul's possible departure, which must lead them to replacing the subsequent relational vacuum with confidence in the Lord, rather than in other (potentially dangerous) individuals. More will be said on this below.

Already the theme of dependence on Paul for spiritual well-being has appeared in the midst of questions over his departure: 'But to remain in the flesh is more necessary on your account. Convinced of this, I know that I shall remain and continue with you all, for your progress and joy in the faith, so that in me you may have ample cause to glory in Christ Jesus, because of my coming to you again' (Phil. 1.24-26). He speaks here of his optimism of release *based on* their *need* for him, that is, for their 'progress and joy from faith' (εἰς τὴν ὑμῶν προκοπὴν καὶ χαρὰν τῆς πίστεως).[46] His personal choice would be departure (1.23). But staying is better for them. I therefore submit that one role Phil. 1.27–2.29 could perform is beginning the process of weaning the Philippians from confidence in him and to instead direct their confidence towards the Lord. Already in 1.27 (the first verse of this unfolding discussion), Paul says 'whatever happens' (μόνον), before he points them to God and Christ (1.27-30).

I also take 4.1 to be an important summary of this goal in the letter: 'Therefore, my brethren, whom I love and long for, my joy and crown, stand firm, in this way, in the Lord beloved (οὕτως στήκετε ἐν κυρίῳ, ἀγαπητοί).' Here is intimate language affirming that he does not mean to abandon them (a logical corrective clarifying 3.1) but also demonstrating a move to have them established in the Lord.

So, a progression from measured optimism of return in 1.18-26, to 'if' in 2.17-18, to 'farewell' in 3.1 and further (as will soon be argued) to a complete call to look to the Lord in 4.4 produces a kind of steady rhetorical unfolding from Paul.

But what this also does clarifies Paul's shift to otherwise strange topics in both 3.2–4.1 and 4.10-20, with otherwise surprising emotional moods accompanying them. These two sections have caused the greatest trouble for exegetes wishing to see Philippians as a unified letter.[47] But note how even J.-F. Collange, a scholar decidedly against a unified Philippians, labels 3.1b–4.1 'To Know Christ'

---

45. 'In what cogent sense would it be *safe* (ἀσφαλές) to urge the readers to rejoice' (O'Brien 1991: 351), though cf. Caird (1976: 132).

46. I translate the genitive as derivative ('from') because of what follows. Their faith will be increased by his release, 'so that in me you may have ample cause to glory in Christ Jesus, because of my coming to you again' (1.26).

47. 'There are no real problems with the structure of the letter up until 3.1' (Engberg-Pedersen 2000: 83).

(1979: 122–3). If Paul has just spoken (in 3.1) in the clearest terms about his own pastoral use-by date – something he has not done overtly before (cf. 'if' in 2.17-18) – an element of drama has entered, which reads well for an Australian. Indeed, the call to 'joy' in this kind of farewell stands in contrast to their anticipation of sorrow. Paul is now (for the first time) 'admitting' he could leave. In light of this drama, it becomes reasonable that he will continue being dramatic (cf. 'dogs', 'mutilators'; 3.2) about … who?[48] About those who have a track record of filling pastoral voids with destructive alternative partnerships (cf. Gal. 4.17). Not only the dramatic mood but also the topic of false teachers becomes reasonable if Paul is pronouncing his own departure and calling them to embark on a new kind of leadership model in their midst.[49]

What could be more reasonable than that he would here point them most fully to *knowing Christ* as the true alternative to dangerous partnerships?[50] And this, of course, is what 3.7-8 is filled with. No sooner has the apostle warned of false teachers than he turns to reflect on 'the surpassing greatness of *knowing* Christ Jesus my Lord' (3.8).

But even as he models for them a life that is looking to the Lord in 3.7–4.1, so 4.10-20 appears to have the same purpose. There has been a long-standing debate over why Paul adds a 'thankless thanks' especially here in 4.10-20 rather than in the beginning of the letter (Peterman 1991: 261–70). Could it be that thanks is absent because this is not really his primary purpose? Could we not say, instead, that Paul is again modelling the relational hope ἐν κυρίῳ that he has been arguing for (cf. Ἐχάρην δὲ ἐν κυρίῳ μεγάλως ὅτι ἤδη ποτὲ ἀνεθάλετε τὸ ὑπὲρ ἐμοῦ φρονεῖν; 4.10) in the midst of his present difficulties?

Phil. 3.7–4.1 has been quite general; now in 4.10-20 he gets specific again about his own current situation. But again, the point is to model a life that rejoices in the Lord. This section would then be included so that everything may ultimately contribute to their relationship with the Lord (4.17). Paul will be glad if they continue partnership with him, but either way, *his* hope is not in them but in the Lord (4.11-13, 19-20). He is modelling the kind of Christian maturity that he has just called them to – one which is God-centred and faith-centred. In this way, it is fitting that this section should also begin with 'I rejoice greatly in the Lord' (4.10). It is not that he does not wish their partnership – his hope is to continue with them

---

48. This is no small point in favour of reading χαίρετε as I am suggesting. The entire complaint against 3.2–4.1 being part of the same letter as what has come before is that the mood has significantly swung. But if Paul is building his own moment of emotional crisis in the Philippians by announcing his farewell, the dramatics of 3.2-3 make much more sense. J. P. Sampley sidesteps, to some degree, the otherwise severe mood swing from 3.1 to 3.2-3 in his discussion of frank speech (Sampley 2003: 310–12).

49. In this regard, I would suggest that this is not a real present group of opponents, but rather those who would present themselves as an alternative to Paul and the other friends they currently have, see esp. Fowl (2005: 146–7).

50. For the importance of friendship in Philippians, see esp. Stowers (1991: 105–21).

(1.18-26). It is just that, more than anything, he desires (as a true pastor) to leave them secure in this world, whatever happens, that is, in a stronger relationship with the Lord.

This only leaves 4.4 to comment upon, that is, the second place where debate has surrounded the issue of whether χαίρετε means 'farewell'. Paul has repeated the theme of inner unity among them in 4.2-3 (an important part of their strengthening, cf. 1.27-29) before emphatically furthering the call of 3.1 in 4.4: 'Rejoice in the Lord always, I say it again, Rejoice!' (Χαίρετε ἐν κυρίῳ πάντοτε· πάλιν ἐρῶ, χαίρετε). In light of a 'progression-towards-confidence-in-God-not-him' from 1.27-29 to 2.16-17 to 3.1, 4.4 then stands as a kind of final step, even as Paul is about to illustrate his desires for them with his own life of trust (4.10-20). But now the emphasis is *all* on the Lord and finding joy in him. It is 'rejoice in the Lord always' together with a repeat 'rejoice!' This reading is immediately reinforced by what follows in 4.4b-9.[51]

But in so far as the argument has moved on in a progression, it becomes difficult to say explicitly whether there is now any intended sense of 'farewell' in the χαίρετε of 4.4. There may very well be a kind of 'if the boot fits'. It may almost be like what I proposed above with the 'mood swings' embedded in the infinitive letter-use of χαίρειν. If a hearer is still struggling to let go of their spiritual father's coat-tails (1.24-25), Paul would have them hear 'farewell' one last time and be commanded to 'rejoice' – could this even explain his repetition (πάλιν ἐρῶ, χαίρετε; 4.4b)? But if a hearer has gotten Paul's point, then his χαίρετε appeal becomes a last emphatic wish/prayer, which as a wish/prayer would be received by this religious society as moderns like us may not otherwise see it, that is, as a summary prayer to God: 'Finally brothers I pray you might rejoice in the Lord always, again I pray you would rejoice.' The multivalence here, with the possibility of both a harsh word but also a 'nice' word, is most pleasing for me within an Australian-American context.

References

Aitchison, J. (2012), *Words in the Mind: An Introduction to the Mental Lexicon*, 4th edn, Malden: Wiley-Blackwell.

Alexander, L. (1989), 'Hellenistic Letter-Forms and the Structure of Philippians', *JSNT*, 37: 87–101.

Arzt-Grabner, P. (1994), 'The "Epistolary Introductory Thanksgiving" in the Papyri and in Paul', *NovT*, 36: 29–46.

Arzt-Grabner, P. (2010), 'Paul's Letter Thanksgiving', in S. E. Porter and S. A. Adams (eds), *Paul and the Ancient Letter Form*, 129–58, Pauline Studies 6, Leiden: Brill.

Beard, M., J. A. North and S. R. F Price (1998), *Religions of Rome, Volume 1: A History*, Cambridge: Cambridge University Press.

---

51. Note the intriguing suggestions that 4.4-7 is put together so 'as to imply that their whole ethical behavior should issue from the disposition of "joy in the Lord"' (Morrice 1985: 129–30; cf. Fowl 2005: 180–9).

Beare, F. W. (1959), *A Commentary on the Epistle to the Philippians*, HNTC, New York: Harper.
Blot, R. K., ed. (2003), *Language and Social Identity*, Westport: Praeger.
Caird, G. B. (1976), *Paul's Letters from Prison: Ephesians, Philippians, Colossians, Philemon, in the Revised Standard Version*, The New Clarendon Bible, Oxford: Oxford University Press.
Collange, J.-F. (1979), *The Epistle of Paul to the Philippians*, trans. A. W. Heathcote, London: Epworth.
Collins, R. F. (2010), 'A Significant Decade: The Trajectory of the Hellenistic Epistolary Thanksgiving', in S. E. Porter and S. A. Adams (eds), *Paul and the Ancient Letter Form*, 159–84, Pauline Studies 6, Leiden: Brill.
Collopy, B. (2010), 'How We Like Our Irony Served Down Under: Well Done', *Sydney Morning Herald*, 18 May.
Coulmas, F. (1979), 'On the Sociolinguistic Relevance of Routine Formulae', *Journal of Pragmatics*, 3: 239–66.
Cousar, C. B. (2009), *Philippians and Philemon: A Commentary*, New Testament Library, Louisville: Westminster/John Knox.
Craddock, F. B. (1985), *Philippians, Interpretation*, Louisville: Westminster/John Knox.
Craven, R., and N. Purdie (2005), 'What Does It Mean to Be an Australian?: The Perceptions of Students, Senior and Prominent Australians', *Annual Conference of the Australian Association for Research in Education (AARE - 2005)*, UWS Parramatta Campus. Available online: http://www.researchgate.net/publication/228810945_What_does_it_mean_to_be_an_Australian_the_perceptions_of_students_senior_and_prominent_Australians.
de Saussure, F. (1974), *Course in General Linguistics*, ed. C. Bally and A. Sechehaye, trans. W. Baskin, rev. edn, London: Fontana.
Duranti, A. (1997), 'Universal and Culture-Specific Properties of Greetings', *Journal of Linguistic Anthropology*, 7: 63–97.
Engberg-Pedersen, T. (2000), *Paul and the Stoics*, Edinburgh: T&T Clark.
Exler, F. X. J. (1923), *The Form of the Ancient Greek Letter of the Epistolary Papyri: 3rd C. B. C.–3rd C. A. D.*, Washington, DC: ARES.
Fee, G. D. (1995), *Paul's Letter to the Philippians*, NICNT, Grand Rapids: Eerdmans.
Fowl, S. E. (2005), *Philippians*, Grand Rapids: Eerdmans.
Fowler, H. W., and F. G. Fowler, trans. (1905), *The Works of Lucian of Samosata, Complete with Exceptions Specified in the Preface*, 4 volumes, Oxford: Clarendon, 1905.
Fredricksmeyer, E. (2003), 'Alexander's Religion and Divinity', in J. Roisman (ed.), *Brill's Companion to Alexander the Great*, 25–378, Leiden; Boston: Brill.
Friedrich, G. (1955), 'Lohmezer's Theses Über "Das Paulinische Briefpräskript" Kristisch Beleuchtet', *ZNW*, 46: 272–4.
Gadamer, H.-G. (1989), *Truth and Method*, trans. J. Weinsheimer and D. G. Marshall, 2nd edn, London: Sheed & Ward.
Gager, J. G. (1992), *Curse Tablets and Binding Spells from the Ancient World*, New York: Oxford University Press.
Goddard, C. (2006), '"Lift Your Game, Martina!" – Deadpan Jocular Irony and the Ethnopragmatics of Australian English', in C. Goddard (ed.), *Ethnopragmatics: Understanding Discourse in Cultural Context*, 65–97, Berlin: De Gruyter.
Goddard, C. (2009), 'Not Taking Yourself Too Seriously in Australian English: Semantic Explications, Cultural Scripts, Corpus Evidence', *Intercultural Pragmatics*, 6: 29–53.

Goodspeed, E. J. (1922), *The New Testament: An American Translation*, Chicago: University of Chicago Press.
Goodspeed, E. J. (1945), *Problems of New Testament Translation*, Chicago: University of Chicago Press.
Harris, M. J. (2005), *The Second Epistle to the Corinthians: A Commentary on the Greek Text*, NIGTC, Grand Rapids: Eerdmans.
Harrison, J. R. (2003), *Paul's Language of Grace in Its Graeco-Roman Context*, WUNT 172, Tübingen: Mohr Siebeck.
Hartin, P. J. (2003), *James*, Collegeville: Liturgical.
Haugh, M. (2011), 'Humour, Face and Im/politeness in Getting Acquainted', in D. Bethan, M. Haugh and A. J. Merrison (eds), *Situated Politeness*, 165–84, New York: Continuum.
Heil, J. P. (2010), *Philippians: Let Us Rejoice in Being Conformed to Christ*, SBLECL 3, Atlanta: Society of Biblical Literature.
Hilliard, D. (2010), 'Australia: Towards Secularisation and One Step Back', in C. G. Brown and M. Snape (eds), *Secularisation in the Christian World: Essays in Honour of Hugh McLeod*, 75–92, Farnham: Ashgate.
Hooper, R., and N. Koleilat-Doany, 'Telephone Openings and Conversational Universals: A Study in Three Languages', in S. Ting-Toomey and F. Korzenny (eds), *Language, Communication and Culture*, 157–79, Newbury Park: Sage.
Hopkins, W. E. (1931), 'Hindu Salutations', *Bulletin of the School of Oriental Studies, University of London*, 6: 369–83.
Johnson, L. T. (1995), *The Letter of James: A New Translation with Introduction and Commentary*, New York: Doubleday.
Keck, L. E. (1971), 'Philippians', in *Interpreter's One Volume Commentary on the Bible*, 845–55, Nashville: Abingdon.
Kelly, W. (1869), *Lectures on the Epistle of Paul the Apostle to the Philippians with a New Translation*, London: Paternoster.
Koskenniemi, H. (1956), *Studien Zur Idee Und Phraseologie Des Griechischen Briefes Bis 400 n.Chr*, Suomalaisen Tiedeakatemian toimituksia, Saraja B 102.2, Helsinki: Suomalainen Tiedeakatemia.
Lanham, C. D. (1975), *Salutatio Formulas in Latin Letters to 1200: Syntax, Style, and Theory*, MBMRF 22, München: Arbeo-Gesellschaft.
Latta, R., and A. Macbeath (1929), *The Elements of Logic*, London: Macmillian.
Lieu, J. M. (1985), '"Grace to You and Peace": The Apostolic Greeting', *BJRL*, 68: 161–78.
Lightfoot, J. B. (1868), *Saint Paul's Epistle to the Philippians*, London: Macmillan.
Llewelyn, S. R. (1997), 'The Prescript of James', *NovT*, 39: 385–93.
Lowe, B. A. (2013), 'What Does Προέχω Really Echo in Romans 3.9? Photius, Arethas and a "Fourth Possibility"', in D. M. Patte and V. Mihoc (eds), *Greek Patristic and Eastern Orthodox Interpretations of Romans*, 179–202, Romans through History and Cultures Series 9; Edinburgh: T&T Clark.
Malinowski, B. (1923), 'The Problem of Meaning in Primitive Languages', in C. K. Ogden and I. A. Richards (eds), *The Meaning of Meaning: A Study of the Influence of Language Upon Thought and of the Science of Symbolism*, 296–336, New York: Harcourt, Brace and World.
Martin, R. P. (1980), *Philippians*, NCB, Grand Rapids: Eerdmans.
Martin, R. P. (1988), *James*, WBC 48, Waco: Word.
Morrice, W. G. (1985), *Joy in the New Testament*, Grand Rapids: Eerdmans.
Moule, H. C. G. (1893), *The Epistle to the Philippians*, The Cambridge Bible, London: Cambridge University Press.

Mussner, F. (1975), *Der Jakobusbrief*, HTKZNT, Freiburg: Herder.
North, J. A. (2000), *Roman Religion*, New Surveys in the Classics: Greece & Rome 30, Oxford: Oxford University Press.
O'Brien, P. T. (1991), *The Epistle to the Philippians: A Commentary on the Greek Text*, NIGTC, Grand Rapids: Eerdmans.
Pao, D. W. (2010), 'Introductory Thanksgivings and Paul's Theology of Thanksgiving', in S. E. Porter and S. A. Adams (eds), *Paul and the Ancient Letter Form*, 101–28, Pauline Studies 6, Leiden: Brill.
Peterman, G. W. (1991), '"Thankless Thanks": The Epistolary Social Convention in Philippians 4:10–20', *TynBul*, 42: 261–70.
Radcliffe-Brown, A. R. (1952), *Structure and Function in Primitive Society*, Glencoe: Free Press.
Reed, J. T. (1996a), 'Are Paul's Thanksgivings "Epistolary"?', *JSNT*, 61: 87–99.
Reed, J. T. (1996b), 'Philippians 3.1 and the Epistolary Hesitation Formulas: The Literary Integrity of Philippians, Again', *JBL*, 115: 63–90.
Reed, J. T. (1997), *A Discourse Analysis of Philippians: Method and Rhetoric in the Debate over Literary Integrity*, JSNTSup 136, Sheffield: Sheffield Academic Press.
Sacks, H. (1975), 'Everyone Has to Lie', in M. Saches and B. G. Blount (eds), *Sociocultural Dimensions of Language Use*, 57–80, New York: Academic.
Sampley, J. P. (2003), 'Paul and Frankness', in J. P. Sampley (ed.), *Paul in the Greco-Roman World: A Handbook*, vol. I: 303–30, Harrisburg: Trinity.
Saville-Troike, M. (2003), *The Ethnography of Communication: An Introduction*, 3rd edn, Language in Society 3, Malden: Blackwell.
Schegloff, E. A. (1986), 'The Routine as Achievement', *Human Studies*, 9: 111–51.
Scheid, J. (2003), *An Introduction to Roman Religion*, Bloomington: Indiana University Press.
Schumacher, T. (2009), 'Der Begriff Πίστις Im Paulinischen Sprachgebrauch: Beobachtungen Zum Verhältnis von Christlicher Und Profangriechischer Semantik', in U. Schnell (ed.), *The Letter to the Romans*, 487–501, BETL 226, Leuven: Peeters.
Schweitzer, A. (2005), *The Quest of the Historical Jesus*, Mineola: Dover.
Stowers, S. K. (1991), 'Friends, Enemies and the Politics of Heaven: Reading Theology in Philippians', in Jouette M. Bassler, David M. Hay and E. Elizabeth Johnson (eds), *Pauline Theology*, vol. I: 105–21, SBLSymS 4, Minneapolis: Fortress.
Swift, R. S. (2009), 'Robert Edward Armstrong (1911–1988)', in D. Langmore (ed.), *Australian Dictionary of Biography, 1981–1990*, Melbourne: Melbourne University.
Thurston, B. B., and J. M. Ryan (2009), *Philippians and Philemon*, Sacra Pagina 10, Collegeville: Liturgical.
Tolkien, J. R. R. (2012), *The Hobbit*, New York: Houghton Mifflin Harcourt.
Trapp, M. B., ed. (2003), *Greek and Latin Letters: An Anthology, with Translation*, Cambridge Greek and Latin Classics, Cambridge: Cambridge University Press.
Van Voorst, R. E. (2010), 'Why Is There No Thanksgiving Period in Galatians? An Assessment of An Exegetical Commonplace', *JBL*, 129: 153–72.
Vincent, M. R. (1911), *A Critical and Exegetical Commentary on the Epistles to the Philippians and to Philemon, ICC 37*, New York: C. Scribner's Sons.
Vouga, F. (1984), *L'Epître De Saint Jacques*, CNT 13a, Genève: Labor et Fides.
Weima, J. A. D. (1994), *Neglected Endings: The Significance of the Pauline Letter Closings*, JSNTSup 101, Sheffield: Sheffield Academic.

Weiss, B. (1897), 'The Present Status of the Inquiry Concerning the Genuineness of the Pauline Epistles', *AJT*, 1: 328–403.

White, J. L. (1984), 'New Testament Epistolary Literature in the Framework of Ancient Epistolography', in W. Haase (ed.), *ANRW II.25.2*, 1730–56, Berlin: De Gruyter.

Wierzbicka, A. (1991), *Cross-Cultural Pragmatics: The Semantics of Human Interaction*, Trends in Linguistics 53, New York: de Gruyter.

Wright, N. T. (1992), *The New Testament and the People of God (Christian Origins and the Question of God)*, Minneapolis: Fortress.

Youssouf, I. A., A. D. Grimshaw and C. S. Bird (1976), 'Greetings in the Desert', *American Ethnologist*, 3: 797–824.

Chapter 3

PAUL OF TARSUS AND MARY OF MAGDALA: VIRTUAL HISTORY, POLITICS OF IDENTITY, POSTMODERN ENCOUNTERS*

Ingrid Rosa Kitzberger

Grace-ful Encounters: Preliminary Fragments

'How would you sum up Paul's gospel?' one of my students asked me. 'The word of the cross,' I answered. 'And how would you sum up Paul's theology?' another student inquired. 'Grace,' I responded promptly.

***

A few months later, on Palm Sunday in 2002, I encountered Mary Magdalene in San Francisco's Grace Cathedral – a powerful, transformative experience. One of my students, from the Paul class at the Graduate Theological Union (GTU) in Berkeley, California,[1] had invited me over to the Cathedral, where he was doing his field work. He became associate pastor soon afterwards. 'Grace,' he called it, as he reflected on how God had been active in his life, calling him late, just like Paul. The student's name was John, like the Evangelist in whose gospel Mary Magdalene features prominently.

The image of Mary Magdalene in Grace Cathedral, and the story related to it, differ from her portrait in the Gospel of John. And yet, they can be seen as potential and reality, the possible continuation of an open-ended story. Mary Magdalene in John can be envisioned in the light of her counterpart in Grace Cathedral.

---

* A first version of this essay was presented at the International Meeting of the Society of Biblical Literature (SBL) in Groningen, the Netherlands, in the Paul and Pauline Literature section, on 27 July 2004.

1. In the fall semester of 2001, I offered the course 'Paul – the Man and His Writings' at the GTU in Berkeley, where I was Visiting Professor of New Testament at the Jesuit School of Theology (JSTB). I gratefully remember my students from different parts of the world and social locations. Our exciting border-crossing journeys with Paul have contributed significantly to my re-viewing the apostle in a global perspective.

There, she is dressed in bright red, the colour of life, with hair as black as the icon's background and a golden halo around her head. With her right index finger, she points to the white egg in her left hand. With determination and eyes wide open, she is looking at the viewer, and beyond him or her, challenging whoever encounters her face to face. Often, I was standing at the foot of this impressive icon of Mary Magdalene, with the Chapel of Grace to my right and the Spanish Crucifix from Catalonia behind me. Lighting a candle, I was silently communicating with her in the magical twilight of flames piercing the darkness.

While it was still dark, Mary Magdalene came to the tomb on Easter morning. She left the garden with a burning heart, transformed by her encounter with the Risen Christ, his garments shining white as no fuller on earth could bleach them. Turning around she finally embarked on her first missionary journey.

> According to the Eastern tradition, after Jesus' ascension Mary Magdalene journeyed to Rome where she was admitted to the court of Tiberius Caesar because of her high social standing. After describing how poorly Pilate had administered justice at Jesus' trial, she told Caesar that Jesus had risen from the dead. To help explain his resurrection she picked up an egg from the dinner table. Caesar responded that a human being could no more rise from the dead than the egg in her hand turn red. The egg turned red immediately, which is why red eggs have been exchanged at Easter for centuries in the Byzantine East.[2]

***

'Have I not seen the Lord?' Paul asked his troublesome yet beloved community in Corinth, pleading for their loyalty. 'Am I not an apostle? Are you not my work in the Lord?' Regardless of the conflicts that had caused him to write again, he trusted in the deep bonds between them: 'If I am not an apostle to others, at least I am to you; for you are the seal of my apostleship in the Lord.'[3]

***

> Paul, a servant of Jesus Christ, called to be an apostle, set apart for the Gospel of God, which he promised beforehand through his prophets in the holy scriptures, the gospel concerning his Son, who was descended from David according to the flesh and was declared to be Son of God with power according to the spirit of holiness by resurrection from the dead, Jesus Christ our Lord, through whom we have received grace and apostleship to bring about the obedience of faith

---

2. Text by Bridge Building Images, Inc., Burlington, Vermont, describing the icon of Mary Magdalene in Grace Cathedral.

3. All biblical quotations are, unless otherwise stated, from the New Revised Standard Version (NRSV).

among the Gentiles for the sake of his name, including yourselves who are called to belong to Jesus Christ.

Exhausted from constructing the sentence and his identity, Paul took a little breath before he continued, finally thinking of those he was writing to.

'To all God's beloved in Rome, who are called saints: Grace to you and peace from God our Father and the Lord Jesus Christ.'

For some time, he had intended to visit them, but he had always been prevented for one reason or another. Now, at least, he attempted to write a letter. It turned out to be the longest he had ever written. 'Who knows,' he thought, 'it might be my last one.' And yet, he was full of plans. In fact, Rome would be just a stopover. His heart was set on Spain, to proclaim the gospel where Christ had not yet been named. He was a pioneer by vocation; building on another's foundation was not for him. Sailing to new shores was his destiny.

***

When he came into Rome, Paul was allowed to live by himself, with the soldier who was guarding him. They came to his lodging in great numbers. From morning until evening, he explained the matter to them.

'What, if I had not appealed to Caesar?' he sometimes wondered. 'Would I ever have come here?'

And he lived there two whole years and welcomed all who came to him, proclaiming the kingdom of God and teaching about the Lord Jesus Christ with all boldness and without hindrance.

***

'I have seen the Lord,' Mary Magdalene, filled with great joy, exclaimed as she ran away from the garden tomb. And thus, commissioned by the Risen Christ, she told the other disciples, hidden behind closed doors. Listening into the silence, she anxiously waited for their response.

***

The icon in Grace Cathedral was commissioned to commemorate the consecration of Barbara Clementine Harris, the first woman bishop in the Anglican Communion, on 11 February 1989, and to honour her on her visit to the Cathedral on 22 July 1990, the feast day of Saint Mary Magdalene.[4]

---

4. Barbara Clementine Harris was Suffragan Bishop of the Episcopal Diocese of Massachusetts from 1989 to 2003. The artist, Robert Lentz, was the grandson of Russian immigrants and learned icon painting in a Greek Orthodox monastery in New York. I am grateful to Michael Lampen, archivist at Grace Cathedral, for providing these pieces of information back in 2004, when I wrote the first draft of this essay. Now, in 2020, I have obtained additional information: the most striking is that Bishop Harris died shortly before her ninetieth birthday earlier this year, on 13 March, right at the time I returned to this

On 24 May 2002, I met Barbara Harris after the graduation ceremony at Church Divinity School of the Pacific (CDSP) in Berkeley.[5] A brief yet impressive encounter, full of grace, in the garden next to the fountain. Listening to her powerful speech at the ceremony, I had been reminded of Mary Magdalene with the egg in her hand, facing Caesar and the (male) powers that be, with determination, passion and humour. Bishop Harris's robe was not red, though, but purple, the colour of transformation.

> Barbara Clementine Harris is an extraordinary woman of joyful passion, hopeful vision, and inspired speech. ... She is a woman of courage, who faces both challenges and threats with strength forged in a steadfast trust that 'God will make a way' ... No matter where ministry has led her or the circumstances, challenges and conditions she faces, she says, 'Hallelujah anyhow!' ... As a woman of inspired speech, a gifted storyteller, and a compassionate servant of God, Barbara stands in the long line of prophetic voices as a woman of singular courage. She is at once a pioneer and advocate for all those who have been excluded from the table.[6]

From Salzburg to San Francisco and Berkeley: My Missionary Journeys with Paul and Mary Magdalene

When I encountered Mary Magdalene in San Francisco – and her modern counterpart on Holy Hill in Berkeley – I had already journeyed with her for more than a decade, through the biblical texts, their inter-texts and contexts, ancient and modern, in oral and written traditions, and in the arts, a never-ending source for studying the 'reversing of the hermeneutical flow' (Kreitzer 1993, 1994). Crossing many borders, I had journeyed with her through countries and paradigms, with many surprise encounters. I had turned around several times, transformed in the

---

essay. This is synchronicity. And so is the fact that she served at Saint Paul's Cathedral in Boston. Lentz is a Franciscan friar. He lived in New Mexico in 2004 and is now stationed in Silver Spring, Maryland, in the Holy Name Province.

5. John, my student mentioned above, was among the graduates, and so was another John from my Paul class who was ordained deacon at Grace Cathedral on 1 June 2002. At the same ordination ceremony, three women were ordained priestesses (in fact the only priests this time), and three women (one my student) were ordained deacons. This was indeed a powerful heritage of the first woman who passed on the good news on Easter morning, and a very special experience for me as a woman in the Roman Catholic Church, where all offices are for men only.

6. From the *laudatio* on the occasion of conferring upon Barbara Clementine Harris the degree of Doctor of Divinity, *honoris causa*, at the CDSP graduation ceremony on 24 May 2002.

encounters. An open-ended story, just like hers. Pioneers by vocation, sailing to new shores.

When I crossed the Atlantic for the first time in July 1993, I was accompanied by Mary of Magdala and her namesake, Mary of Bethany. Significantly, the paper I presented at the General Meeting of the Society for New Testament Studies (SNTS) in Chicago (Kitzberger 1995) marked the beginning of a new chapter in my professional career. A few years earlier, also on a journey, I had decided to focus my research on Jesus's most prominent female disciple.[7] Since then, I have encountered her many times, and she has encountered me, when I was re-reading the biblical texts, in particular the Gospel of John, and in many places I visited on my extensive travels.[8]

When I encountered Mary Magdalene in San Francisco, I had already journeyed for several decades with Paul the Apostle. My vocation as a biblical scholar is intimately linked to him, from my first years as a student at the University of Salzburg (Austria) in the 1970s to my graduation as Doctor of Theology in 1986.

My enthusiasm for biblical studies was sparked off in a two-semester seminar on conflicts and conflict solutions in the New Testament during the academic year 1974–5. I chose to work on the conflict between the 'weak' and the 'strong' in Corinth (1 Corinthians 8–10) for my final paper. Thus, I encountered Paul, the man and his writings, his powerful letters. I learned about his own struggles and those of a first-century community founded by him on one of his missionary journeys. I was fascinated by a man of great zeal and passion, facing challenges, threats and persecution extensively, an apostle who never ceased to proclaim the power of the crucified and resurrected Jesus Christ, who had made him what he was. 'Grace', he called it.

After the seminar paper, I wrote my diploma thesis, in which I addressed also the parallel conflict in the community of Rome (Romans 14–15) (Kitzberger 1977b). When the thesis was completed, I still could not let go of Paul. Therefore, I started to work on a doctoral dissertation, in which I focused on Paul's concept of community building (Kitzberger 1986). I had got stuck with Paul and through him with the New Testament and also the Hebrew Bible, in which he was deeply rooted. Eventually, I became a biblical scholar by vocation.

---

7. In loving memory of the late Professor Eugen Ruckstuhl, University of Lucerne (Switzerland), strongest advocate of Mary Magdalene and myself. On our train journey back home from the SNTS meeting in Göttingen in July 1987, he encouraged me to work on Mary Magdalene for my *Habilitationschrift*.

8. I encountered Mary Magdalene in familiar but also very unusual places, when I was actively searching for her and when I met her just by chance (or providence): in churches and art galleries, in paintings and sculptures, and in gardens with and without tombs. A place of special significance to me is the Cistercian Abbey of Lilienfeld, in my home country Austria, where Mary Magdalene is prominent, in particular as the patron saint of the abbey parish. I first encountered her in this place shortly after my close friend, Richard, had died in an accident on Saint Mary Magdalene's feast day, 22 July 1995.

When I crossed the border from Austria to Germany in 1981 and started my first academic position at the University of Freiburg, Paul was still the main focus of my work. At that time, I was the only female assistant and teacher at the Catholic-Theological Faculty, one of the largest in the country. The professorial ranks, however, were still exclusively male and mostly clerical. Soon after my arrival, I made my first appearance to the wider public as the leader of a workshop on 'Paul and Women' which I offered in the context of a *dies academicus* on 'Church and Theology Facing the Woman Question'.[9]

A woman teaching theology was a novel and extraordinary experience for all students. However, it turned out to be particularly relevant for my female students who had a kind of female 'role model' for the first time. On the other hand, there were also those voices who claimed that women should be silent in church and therefore also in academic theology, according to the words of 'Saint Paul' (cf. 1 Cor. 14.33b-36).

I went through profound changes and paradigm shifts with regard to Paul over the years. His halo and glorious image of 'the Apostle' collapsed when I became a feminist and began to ask challenging questions, and I eventually accused him of misogyny. More often than not, I became a resisting reader of his letters.

Finally, when I shifted my attention to the gospels, due to teaching requirements but also driven by a personal longing to learn more about the 'original' beginnings, I encountered the women in the Jesus movement, especially Mary Magdalene, and their powerful presence, even amidst the textual silences. As I journeyed with them from Galilee to Jerusalem and beyond, I re-viewed my own journey through a male-dominated academic world and church, in which women's voices had been muted and their memory forgotten. The 'tip of the iceberg' became a powerful, liberating *and* challenging image to me, offered by my fore-sister Elisabeth Schüssler Fiorenza (1983), a pioneer by vocation, who, by necessity, had sailed to new shores.[10] I imagined Mary Magdalene sitting on top of the 'tip of the iceberg', freezing but still alive, waiting to be fully resurrected.

***

I had come a long way, both in a geographical and metaphorical sense, when I offered the course 'Paul – the Man and His Writings' at the GTU in Berkeley. From Salzburg and my first encounter with Paul in 1974–5, to Freiburg and the

---

9. A very telling title, characteristic of those early days when 'women' or 'the woman question' were defined as a problem that had to be faced by theology and the church, an object to be dealt with, willingly or unwillingly. Professor Catharina Halkes from the University of Nijmegen, the Netherlands, was the keynote speaker, a powerful woman of the courageous first generation of feminist theologians in Europe.

10. Coincidentally, I was introduced to the icon of Mary Magdalene in Grace Cathedral by Schüssler Fiorenza, who had sent me a picture of it several years prior to my face-to-face encounter. I must confess, though, that I did not like this image of the (so I thought) fiercely looking woman very much at the time, but now I just love it!

workshop in 1981, to Berkeley and San Francisco in 2001–2, I had journeyed with him, the border crosser,[11] through many struggles and conflicts, becoming aware of the light *and* the shadow, a picture of different shades of colour, not simply black and white, reading his letters *with* the grain and *against* the grain.

Coincidentally,[12] I offered the course 'Paul – the Man and His Writings' alongside the course 'Jesus and Women: Transformative Encounters'[13] in which Mary Magdalene featured prominently. Vacillating between Paul and Mary during this semester added new dimensions to a process of mine which had already begun much earlier, the process of viewing both together, not separately.

As far as I can trace my handwritten notes, it was back in 1988 that I first asked the questions 'What if Paul and Mary Magdalene had met?' and 'What if Paul and Mary Magdalene met?' Since then, I have been pondering these two possibilities in my heart and have found myself standing at the crossroads of their encounters, in the first century and in the twentieth (or twenty-first) century. As I re-constructed their identities and her-/his-stories in dialogue with each other, I, too, was affected and transformed. By asking new questions and imagining alternatives, a new vision started to take shape that was born *from* struggle, not by avoiding it, as a result of 'speaking with'.[14]

Virtual History and the Politics of Identity

Generally, Paul of Tarsus and Mary of Magdala have been regarded as belonging to different worlds and, therefore, have been viewed independent of each other. Pauline studies do not deal with Mary Magdalene, and gospel studies focusing on women in the Jesus movement generally, and Mary Magdalene in particular, do not deal with Paul. In case they are mentioned together, it is usually within a paradigm of conflict.

---

11. To my Paul class, I introduced the Apostle as the 'border crosser' as his prominent identity marker. My students, coming from all over the globe, whom I regarded as border crossers like myself, embraced this image wholeheartedly, and it became a kind of *leitmotif* for us throughout the semester. Eventually, it was reflected in many of their final research papers.

12. I had handed in the topics for four courses at JSTB for the academic year, but the distribution per semester was decided by the dean. It worked out very well.

13. The course was based on Kitzberger (2000). I gratefully remember and thank the women and two men, from different parts of the world, churches and faith traditions, whose powerful presence and encouraging contributions added many new and meaningful dimensions to the women in the New Testament and Early Christian traditions. I especially thank Orna Teitelbaum, who, learning of Mary Magdalene for the first time, has kept my vision of Mary Magdalene alive to this day.

14. For this important concept and the ethics behind it, I am gratefully indebted to Patte (1995) and West and Dube (1996).

The Crucial Text 1 Corinthians 15.3-5

The essential text with regard to Paul and Jesus's female disciples is 1 Cor. 15.1-11, especially vv. 3-5. In the context of addressing the resurrection of the dead,[15] which has been contested in the community at Corinth, Paul mentions as their common ground traditions that have been handed down to him and which he, in turn, has passed on to them. Citing one of the earliest creed formulas, he reminds them of Christ's death, burial and resurrection (vv. 3-4). This is followed by a list of those to whom the Risen Christ appeared. The list contains two pairs: Cephas and the twelve (v. 5), and James and all the apostles (v. 7). Both pairs are commonly regarded as traditional material, while the mention of the appearance to more than five hundred 'brothers' at one time, some of whom have died while others are still alive (v. 6), was possibly added by Paul, even though it may have been based also on (another) tradition. Finally, Paul mentions Christ's appearance to himself as to one 'untimely born', 'the least of the apostles, unfit to be called an apostle' because he persecuted the church of God (v. 9). 'But by the grace of God I am what I am,' he explains, 'and his grace toward me has not been in vain' (v. 10).

It is indeed striking that Paul mentions only men in this list of appearances, although 'sisters' might be, and I think should be, included among the five hundred, if 'brothers' is understood as androcentric-inclusive language.[16] The absence of women, especially of Mary Magdalene and her first encounter with the Risen Christ according to the traditions in the Gospel of John (20.1-18) and the Gospel of Matthew (28.8-10, together with 'the other Mary'), has been noted especially in feminist interpretations. The supposed omission of the Easter traditions featuring women has been regarded as underscoring Paul's misogyny. This was also my opinion for some time, after I had become a feminist and sided with Mary Magdalene against Paul.

But things are not as simple as that. The main problem is that we do not really know for sure which traditions Paul knew and which he did not. For this reason, any conclusions as to what he omitted or not must remain hypothetical and will always be biased, one way or another.

However, it seems more likely that Paul did not know the empty tomb stories featuring women. For this reason, he was also ignorant of the appearance of the

---

15. The bodily resurrection of the dead was the topic of the Paul class session on the morning of 11 September 2001. Amidst the shock and chaos, working on 1 Corinthians 15 became one of the most impressive and transformative experiences for both the students and myself. Since then, whenever I encounter 1 Corinthians 15, I recall the morning of 9/11 and my faithful students of the Paul class. All had come that morning, except one student who, as she was on the road already, had been warned not to cross the Bay Bridge from San Francisco to Berkeley, since it was expected to be closed, so that she would not have been able to return home.

16. The NRSV, for example, adds 'sisters' in the text, with a footnote to the Greek original, 'brothers'. It is indeed very unlikely that such a large group of men only would have gathered in Galilee, the most plausible location of this appearance.

Risen Christ to them. Therefore, 1 Cor. 15.3-5 cannot be understood as a sexist omission of women.

Another argument that has been voiced with regard to the women's absence is their omission not because of Paul's sexism but because women could not serve his purpose of listing witnesses in the legal sense, since their testimony did not count. This argument, too, is based on the assumption of Paul's knowledge of the empty tomb traditions in the first place and thus collapses once the presupposition no longer holds.

The debate about 1 Cor. 15.3-5 is so essential because the listing of Easter witnesses is closely linked to respective claims of authority in the emerging Christian communities, claims based on 'having seen the Lord'.[17] The mention of Cephas and James refers to the leaders of the Jerusalem church, and the mention of the twelve and the apostles refers to related groups of authorities, limited in number. In addition, Paul presents himself as an apostle in his own right, based on his call/conversion experience which he regarded as an encounter with the Risen Christ.

The absence of women as Easter witnesses has far-reaching consequences especially with regard to the authority of women in general and of Mary Magdalene in particular.[18]

While it is most likely that Paul did not know the Easter morning traditions of the open tomb, it seems quite certain that he did not personally know Mary Magdalene or any other woman of Jesus's entourage who had come up with him from Galilee to Jerusalem and become members of the post-Easter church, whom Paul persecuted so vehemently before the turning point in his life.

Virtual History and Counterfactuals

Based on the assumption that Paul and Mary Magdalene never met, the question 'What if?' opens up a new horizon in terms of virtual history, which, according to J. Cheryl Exum, refers to 'serious scholarly inquiry into alternative historical

---

17. There has been a debate, especially in the German context, about the nature and relevance of Christ's appearances. To be sure, they are part of the creed formula and proof of the resurrection. The claim to 'have seen the Lord' was probably not a 'Legitimationsformel' (formula of legitimation) in the first place, but it became such in further development. For an early passionate discussion of the problem, see Vögtle and Pesch (1975).

18. Schüssler Fiorenza draws attention to the striking fact 'that the narrative presentations of Jesus' suffering, death, and resurrection ascribe to women a leading role in these events', whereas the 'confessional formula' in 1 Cor. 15.3-6 'does not mention women at all but gives the place of eminence to Peter and the twelve'. The 'various appearances of the Resurrected One', which seem to be later accretions to the basic kerygmatic formula, 'legitimate a male chain of authority' (1994: 122). Accordingly, she advocates to differentiate between a 'male and female' or 'Peter and Mary Magdalene' tradition, in contrast to the mainstream divide between a Jerusalem and Galilee tradition (1994: 124).

possibilities, not simply fiction or fantasy'; it asks the question of 'what could have been' and thus considers 'counterfactuals'. Furthermore, it is also 'about how biblical historians work to synthesize and evaluate evidence, posit theories, and test historical reconstructions' (2000: 2–3). 'Counterfactuals are helpful as a heuristic device; investigating alternative historical scenarios can sharpen our framing of the important questions' (2000: 7).

'What if Paul had not appealed to Caesar?' According to Acts 26.32, he might indeed have been set free.[19] With the help of others, he could have managed to escape the Sanhedrin's predictable condemnation on religious charges, just as he once escaped from Damascus (cf. 2 Cor. 11.32-33; Acts 9.23-25). Eventually, he would have been able to journey to Rome, not as a prisoner but in pursuit of his original missionary plans, sailing on to Spain (cf. Rom. 15.23-24). Perhaps he would not even have died a martyr.

'What If Paul Had Travelled East Rather Than West?' Thus Richard Bauckham (2000) asks in his intriguing chapter. Western Christianity would still exist, but it would be naturally quite different without Paul's shaping it. However, flourishing Mesopotamian churches would have come into existence in what used to be the Eastern Jewish diaspora, to which, according to Bauckham, Paul's original missionary strategy was aimed, had he not been threatened by the Nabatean ethnarch and forced to flee from Damascus (cf. 2 Cor. 11.32-33). For this reason, he had to change his plans, and he went to the Western Jewish diaspora in the Mediterranean.

Paul's First Visit to Jerusalem

'What if Paul and Mary Magdalene had met?' In terms of virtual history, this question implies the possibility of an encounter in the first place. Where and when could this encounter have happened? The most likely place and time would have been Paul's first visit to Jerusalem.

This visit is rendered differently in Paul's own voice in Galatians 1 and in Luke's voice in Acts 9. It followed after Paul's conversion[20] and flight from Damascus, according to the latter source (Acts 9.25-26). According to Paul's own record, he went to Jerusalem the first time only three years after his call/conversion (Gal. 1.18).[21] It seems to have been a spontaneous and rather informal, not a planned

---

19. For the legal aspects of Paul's imprisonment and trial, see the excellent study by Marie-Eloise Rosenblatt. 'The supreme irony is that in appealing to the Roman juridical bench, Paul has short-circuited the effectiveness of his defense' (1995: 84). 'Yet Paul hinders his own vindication' and 'he had enmeshed himself in a political process ... Paul's self-protective maneuver to change the venue of his trial to Rome backfired' (1995: 85).

20. According to Acts, Paul's Damascus experience was a conversion; according to his own understanding, it was also a call experience, God's calling him to the Gentile mission (cf. Gal. 1.15-16).

21. For the problem of the 'three years', Betz (1979: 76) refers to the different counting in ancient times, the first year being counted as a full year; hence he arrives at 'two or three

and official, visit. According to Paul's voice, he 'visited Cephas'[22] and stayed with him for fifteen days, but he did not see any of the other apostles except James, the Lord's brother (Gal. 1.18-19). Paul's intention to emphasize his independence from the Jerusalem church and any authorities is obvious. It is indeed striking that he did not go up to Jerusalem, to those who were already apostles before him after his call/conversion, but started his own mission in Arabia right away (Gal. 1.17).[23] After his first visit, he was not to return to Jerusalem for another fourteen years, when he met with the three 'pillars' James, Cephas (Peter, vv. 7-8) and John, and his mission to the Gentiles was confirmed (Gal. 2.1-10).

According to Acts 9.26-27, however, Paul attempted to join the disciples when he came to Jerusalem the first time, but they were afraid of him because of his past as a persecutor. It was Barnabas who took him and brought him to the apostles, to whom he reported about his conversion and preaching in Damascus. In sharp contrast to the private stay with Cephas according to Galatians 1, Luke has Paul 'go in and out among them (the disciples) in Jerusalem and speaking boldly in the name of Jesus' (v. 28). According to Acts 9, Paul's stay was suddenly terminated because of the threat from the Hellenists to kill him (v. 29). Therefore, he was brought to Caesarea and sent off to Tarsus (v. 30).

According to the alternative account in Acts 22.17-21, within Paul's speech, he departed because of a vision of Jesus in the Temple, who sent him to the Gentiles because the Jerusalem inhabitants would not accept Paul's testimony.

Paul himself, in his letter to the Galatians, does not mention any reason for leaving Jerusalem and Cephas after fifteen days. It seems rather natural that he moved on after the purpose of his visit was accomplished.

Paul's own account is usually given preference over Luke's, although the latter need not be considered altogether non-historical. Perhaps there was indeed some kind of threat that caused Paul to depart, but he chose not to mention it. After all, Paul's letter to the Galatians is written in defence against his opponents; it is not a full-fledged autobiographical record. For this reason, Paul's visit was more private than official and meant to be kept secret, at least not to attract much attention.[24]

---

years'. In addition, it is not clear whether the counting starts from his conversion or from his return to Damascus. For the purpose of this study, however, it does not make much difference.

22. The verb *historein* occurs only here in the New Testament. According to Betz (1979: 76), it is a 'non-committal phrase and refers to an "informal visit"'; it 'had no official character or purpose'.

23. Betz (1979: 74): 'Although Paul does not say why he went to Arabia, we can assume that he did so for the purpose of mission ... Gal 1:17 is the oldest reference to Christian activity in Arabia.'

24. Hengel and Schwemer (1997: 136) refer to the 'tense and always threatening situation of the Jerusalem community between the martyrdom of Stephen and the ensuing expulsion of the Jewish-Christian Hellenists and the persecution under Agrippa I'.

In any case, because of 'Peter's presumably spontaneous hospitality', and the mutual interest of the two men in each other, there 'was ample occasion for exchanges', and both 'not only got to know each other properly, but also learned from each other' (Hengel and Schwemer 1997: 145). 'These two weeks were thus a good occasion for demolishing prejudices on both sides and building up a relative basis of trust.' And further:

> One thing is for certain, that this was not just a 'courtesy visit', for which even in the Orient half a day would have sufficed, but a real encounter which was important for the further development of earliest Christianity. ... For without these fourteen[25] days together, the encounter at the 'Apostolic Council' roughly thirteen years later would have hardly been so positive. (1997: 146)

In addition to the intensity and importance of their encounter, the question arises as to what they shared and talked about. For Martin Hengel and Anna Maria Schwemer, it is quite certain that Jesus Christ stood at the centre of their conversation: Jesus's words and actions passed on by Peter, and Paul's report of his call/conversion by the Risen Christ and his own missionary preaching. While Paul learned from Peter, Paul would also have affected Peter and made 'an impression on the leading disciples in Jerusalem', and was thus 'not unimportant for the further fortunes of the young movement' (1997: 147–9).

Mary Magdalene in Jerusalem and Her Open-Ended Story

'What if Paul and Mary Magdalene had met?' This virtual-historical question implies the possibility of a personal encounter between Mary Magdalene and Paul in the first place. If Mary Magdalene was still present in Jerusalem after Jesus's resurrection and ascension, she would have been among the 'disciples' mentioned in Luke's account of Paul's visit in Acts 9. However, if Luke's account is secondary to Paul's own voice, he did not 'go in and out among them' but stayed in Peter's house.[26] However, it seems unlikely that Paul did not see any other disciples, male or female members of the Jerusalem church, during such a long stay.

According to Acts 1.14, 'women' – that is, the women who had come up with Jesus to Jerusalem, witnessed his death and burial and went to the tomb on Easter morning (Lk. 23.49, 55-56; 24.1-12) – were present, together with Mary, Jesus's

---

25. There is no explanation for the 'fourteen days'; on p. 145, 'fifteen days' is mentioned.

26. The accounts in Galatians 1 and Acts 9 cannot be harmonized. Although Paul's own voice is usually considered to be more authentic than voices about him, one needs to bear in mind that both writings have their 'tendencies' and agenda. In Galatians, Paul has to defend himself and argue for the sake of 'his gospel' against the Judaizing agitations of his opponents. Therefore, his reference to Cephas, and then also James, is essential for the thrust of his argument. Luke, on the other hand, has a special interest to let Paul get into contact with the Jerusalem church, not Peter alone, as soon as possible after his conversion.

mother, the apostles and Jesus's brothers, waiting for the coming of the Holy Spirit. It is quite telling that in the remainder of Acts all these women are silenced, never to be mentioned again. This applies also to Mary Magdalene, who even in the Gospel of Luke was always mentioned first among the women who followed Jesus (e.g. Lk. 8.1-3).

According to the Gospel of Matthew and especially the Gospel of John, Mary Magdalene encounters the Risen Christ and is entrusted with the Easter message (Mt. 28.8-10; Jn 20.11-18). However, in these narratives, too, she disappears from the scene right afterwards. Even in the Gospel of John, where she features prominently, she is not portrayed as actually passing on the message to the other disciples. It is only the narrator's comment which states the fact, without telling (Jn 20.18). Her story is open-ended.

These women, including Jesus's own mother, share in the fate of all women in patriarchal societies and writings. For this reason, their stories need to be reconstructed from textual silences. To be sure, this is always a challenging, hypothetical enterprise. Nevertheless, it is an essential and indispensable task. Therefore, the question of what became of Mary Magdalene is legitimate and necessary with regard to the reconstruction of women's stories and early Christian history.

If Paul paid his first visit to Jerusalem three years after his call/conversion, the most likely date would have been 36 CE, six years after Jesus's death. Where was Mary Magdalene at that time? According to later legends, both Western and Eastern, Mary Magdalene went on a missionary journey after Jesus's ascension.[27] However delightful these traditions are, and in accordance with Mary Magdalene's prominence in the Jesus movement, it indeed seems more plausible that she stayed on in Jerusalem and became a member, perhaps even a foundational member, of this earliest community.[28] Belonging to the fraction of the 'Hebrews', she would still have been there after the expulsion of the 'Hellenists'. Perhaps she stayed in the house of another Mary, the mother of John Mark (Acts 12.12).[29]

---

27. According to the Eastern tradition, portrayed in the icon at Grace Cathedral, Mary Magdalene went to Rome. According to the Western tradition of the thirteenth-century *Legenda Aurea* by Jacobus de Voragine, Mary Magdalene sailed as far as southern France and preached the gospel there. However, her identification with Mary of Bethany and the 'sinner woman' of Lk. 7.36-50 makes it clear that this is not an authentic tradition.

28. According to Moloney (1998: 164), commenting on Jn 20.11-18, she was a 'foundational character from the early Christian community'.

29. The church in Jerusalem soon became the centre and focus. Little is known, by contrast, about the church in Galilee. It is only mentioned, together with the church in Judea and Samaria, in Acts 9.31, without further information, apart from the summary statement that the church 'had peace and was built up', and 'living in the fear of the Lord and in the comfort of the Holy Spirit, it increased in numbers'. See also note 34 for further suggestions with regard to the origin of the Galilean church.

The virtual-historical question 'What if?' draws attention to causation and contingency. With regard to Paul and Mary Magdalene, this implies the following: What if Paul did not have to keep his first visit to Jerusalem a secret, meeting only Cephas and James? What if he, as Acts indicates, could indeed have 'walked in and out' and met with at least some other members of the Jerusalem church, eventually encountering Mary Magdalene? I assume that something similar to what Hengel and Schwemer reconstructed for Paul's visit with Cephas/Peter and its significance would apply, with a lasting effect on the development of the post-Easter Christian movement or at least Pauline Christianity.

Having Seen the Lord and Apostolic Authority

To be sure, Paul and Mary Magdalene would have talked about and shared the most important event in their lives: the encounter with the Risen Christ, at the garden tomb in Jerusalem and on the road to Damascus. 'I have seen the Lord!' they would have claimed, enjoying their common ground and foundation of their apostolic authority (cf. Jn 20.18; 1 Cor. 9.1-2). Furthermore, Mary would have shared with Paul her experience of walking with Jesus, from their first encounter, most likely in Magdala,[30] through Galilee and up to Jerusalem, finally witnessing Jesus's death and burial, together with the other women, after the male disciples had fled at Jesus's arrest (Mk 14.50 par Mt. 26.56). Therefore, what Mary shared with Paul would have been more, and something more intimate, than what Cephas/Peter was able to share.[31] If theirs was a real encounter, both Mary and Paul would have been transformed in the process. As a result, Paul would have mentioned her in his list of appearances of the Risen Christ when he wrote his first letter to the Corinthians many years later.[32] How could he *not*

---

30. Since I had the unique opportunity to give a sermon on the shore of the Sea of Galilee, at Tabgha, in June 1990, with Magdala to my left, I have imagined Mary meeting Jesus over there, in her hometown, after he had come down from Nazareth to Magdala when he started his mission. And she was the first one to be called and to follow him. I have drawn inspiration to imagine their encounter in such a manner from Bargil Pixner, whom I had met a few days before my sermon and from whom I learned about the Wadi Hammam ('Doves Valley') through which Jesus most likely came; it starts near Nazareth and ends at Magdala (Pixner 1991: 64).

31. Paul and Peter might also have shared their experiences of the Risen Christ, although we do not know much about Peter's experience. It is not narrated in the gospels but only referred to by the Eleven and their companions in Lk. 24.34: 'The Lord has risen indeed, and he has appeared to Simon.' Besides that, it is only in the traditional formula taken up by Paul in 1 Cor. 15.5 that an appearance of the Risen Christ to Cephas is mentioned.

32. With regard to the Easter witnesses and the origin of the account in 1 Cor. 15.2-8, Hengel and Schwemer comment that, 'Why not should its content (its formulation may have been later) at least in part have been discussed at this memorable visit, on which the only three individual witnesses listed there by name, Cephas, James, and Paul, met for the first time?' (1997: 147).

have acknowledged Mary Magdalene's unique vocation and role? After all, he only knew too well, even at this time and increasingly in the years to come, what it means to struggle for being acknowledged by others for one's unique vocation and apostolate.

Their respective unique experiences of the Risen Christ would have bonded Paul and Mary Magdalene. Paul's attitude towards women and his theology in general might have developed differently, besides a more equal 'distribution' of authority between men and women in the emerging Christian communities. Paul and Mary might even have become a missionary pair on equal terms, like Prisca/Priscilla and Aquila (Rom. 16.3-5; Acts 18.1), or Andronicus and Junia (Rom. 16.7). Paul might have claimed, rather than renounced, his right to take a 'sister' with him on his missionary journeys, like the other apostles and the brothers of the Lord and Cephas (cf. 1 Cor. 9.5). Many passages in his letters would most likely convey a different message and speak a different language.

Alternatively, Mary Magdalene could have been inspired to set out on her own missionary journeys and leave the stability of the Jerusalem church – if she had not done so before. For it is also possible that she had not stayed on in Jerusalem all the time since Jesus's final departure but had begun to preach in other places, passing on the good news of the resurrection that Christ had entrusted to her.[33] Perhaps she was also influential in the origin and growth of the church in Galilee, of which we know so little.[34] Even in this case, it is likely that she commuted between Galilee and Jerusalem and, therefore, could also have been present in the city when Paul came to visit. Unfortunately, there is a huge gap with regard to Mary Magdalene and the other female followers of Jesus in the New Testament writings. Nor do we have any other sources, such as letters the women might have written but which were not preserved.[35]

---

33. Cf. Moloney's (1998: 169) comment on John 20: 'The conclusion of the report of Mary Magdalene's experience of the risen Jesus is sufficiently "missionary" (vv. 17–18) to suggest to the reader that the faith experience of Mary Magdalene might be communicated beyond the boundaries of the characters and the time of the present story.'

34. Galilee is most likely the location of the Risen Christ's appearance to the five hundred 'brothers' mentioned in 1 Cor. 15.6. This could have been the foundation of the Galilean church. 'Brothers' has to be understood as androcentric-inclusive language, including also 'sisters'. In addition, we might think of Simon Peter's wife (cf. Mk 1.30) and others who had remained in Galilee and who could have formed the basis of house churches, before some became missionaries themselves (see 1 Cor. 9.5). On the other hand, there is no substantial reason for the idea that the Galilean Judeo-Palestinian women who had followed Jesus (Acts 1.14) had returned from Jerusalem to Galilee, voluntarily and without persecution (Dormeyer and Galindo 2003: 154, on Acts 9.31).

35. Mary Magdalene and Joanna, for example, could indeed have been literate; in spite of the small percentage of literacy among people in antiquity, and less in women than men (Bar-Ilan 1998: 31–51).

Epilogues: Postmodern Encounters

It is 22 July 2002, Mary Magdalene's feast day, and I am back in Münster. Attending the service in Saint Paul's Cathedral, I look up to Paul the Apostle in the stained-glass window in the apse, just behind the crucifix, raised high above the altar.

> *And I, when I am lifted up from the earth will draw all to myself.*
> Even Saul, the persecutor.
> *For I decided to know nothing among you except Jesus Christ, and him crucified.*

Dressed in bright red, the colour of life and the martyrs, his face radiating, like a golden halo turned inside, against the deep blue background, blue as the sea he crossed on his missionary journeys. In his right hand he holds the sword, signifying his persecution of Christians and his own death. In his left hand he holds a book, signifying his letters.

Since my return from Berkeley three weeks prior, on the feast day of Saints Peter and Paul, I have reconnected with Paul in a special way, becoming even more aware of divine providence that led me, the Pauline scholar, to Münster and Saint Paul's Cathedral.[36] But I do miss the icon of Mary Magdalene. Sitting in the pew and looking to the left of the apse, where she was located in Grace Cathedral, I experience the void. I am searching for her but do not find her.

> *If anyone is in Christ, there is a new creation: everything old has passed away; see, everything has become new! (2 Cor 5.17)*

The first Scripture reading from 2 Corinthians[37] is still echoing in my heart when I listen to the gospel – John's account of Mary Magdalene's encounter with the Risen Christ. Suddenly, both Paul and Mary Magdalene are intensely present to me, visible and invisible. I envision Mary Magdalene's icon on the left, and looking up into the apse I see Paul in the stained-glass window. I am reconciled.

***

It is 29 June 2003, the feast day of Saints Peter and Paul, the special feast day here, celebrating Saint Paul, the patron saint of this Cathedral and the Diocese of Münster. Communicating with Paul in the stained-glass window, I recall my

---

36. Paul, with the sword and the book, is also the logo of the Catholic-Theological Faculty at the University of Münster, which I joined in January 1989, shortly before Barbara Clementine Harris became the first woman bishop in the Anglican Communion (but at that time I did not yet know this). Paul is the patron saint of the Cathedral and the Diocese of Münster, which reaches from the Lower Rhine to the North Sea.

37. This has held a special significance to me since one of my earliest, and one of my few German-language, publications focused on it (Kitzberger 1990).

departure from San Francisco exactly a year ago, bidding a last farewell to Mary Magdalene in Grace Cathedral from aboard the plane taking me home, where home was not but now is.

The bishop is celebrating a special Eucharist with the Knights of Malta on the occasion of their centenary. This order, dedicated to serving others, is named after the isle of Malta, where Paul is supposed to have been shipwrecked on his voyage to Rome. Listening to the bishop's sermon, talking about serving others with grace, I recall his sermon on Mary Magdalene only a few days ago, on the occasion of another centenary jubilee, that of a Catholic women's organization. The bishop, a strong advocate of women past and present, had referred to her as a prophetess and the first witness to Christ's resurrection.

Mary Magdalene – her name voiced so powerfully, filled the air in the Cathedral, like the ocean's waves resonating, finally reaching Paul in the multicoloured stained-glass window and breaking into a thousand images of loveliness.[38] Shipwrecked they both were, many times, and resurrected. So am I.

No matter where ministry has led us, or the circumstances, challenges and conditions we face, we say, 'Hallelujah anyhow!'

***

It is 22 July 2004, Mary Magdalene's feast day again, and I am back to Saint Paul's Cathedral for the morning service, with this paper in my bag. Waiting in the silence before the service, I imagine Mary Magdalene's coming to the garden tomb, early in the morning, while it was still dark. The morning sun is shining brightly through the stained-glass window, illuminating Paul from behind. I am thinking of Mary Magdalene's icon in Grace Cathedral.

Two priests enter – a member of the Cathedral Chapter, accompanied by a visiting priest who is dark-skinned, just like Mary Magdalene in the icon and like Bishop Barbara Harris. *There is no longer male and female; for you are all one in Christ Jesus.*

The main celebrant introduces Mary Magdalene as the one to whom the Risen Christ appeared first. I am delighted, having heard the myth of the 'repentant sinner' in the same place on a previous occasion. And I learn some fascinating new details.

On 22 July 1225, the foundation stone for this present Cathedral was laid by Bishop Dietrich, who was elected bishop of Münster on Saint Mary Magdalene's day and therefore introduced it as a special feast day in the diocese. According to later records, he was also supposed to have been born and to have died on that day.

38. This image is inspired by Percy Bysshe Shelley's Fragment to Epipsychidion, 19–26:

> Like ocean, which the general north wind breaks / Into ten thousand waves, and each one makes / A mirror of the moon – like some great glass, / Which did distort whatever form might pass, / Dashed into fragments by a playful child, / Which then reflects its eyes and forehead mild; / Giving for one, which it could ne'er express, / A thousand images of loveliness. (Kitzberger 1977a)

The large statue of Mary Magdalene, with the ointment jar in her hands, located in the Cathedral's entrance hall called 'Paradise', opposite the statue of Bishop Dietrich, is a vivid reminder of these impressive biographical links.[39] Between these two statues, one on the right and the other on the left, a mighty statue of Saint Paul stands between the two doors, welcoming all visitors who enter the sanctuary.

I bid farewell to Saint Paul and Saint Mary Magdalene, and, with this paper in my bag, I head for Groningen.[40]

***

After the International Meeting of the Society of Biblical Literature and the presentation of my paper, I decided to visit Dokkum, a town near the North Sea and not far from Groningen. It was there that Saint Boniface, the great 'Apostle of the Germans', died a martyr's death in 754, exactly 1250 years earlier, a jubilee year as it were in 2004. In his self-understanding, Saint Boniface was strongly influenced by the Apostle Paul and considered himself to be his successor. Saint Boniface was named after Boniface of Tarsus (who had died a martyr's death around 300 CE), and the Pope appointed him to become a missionary to the pagans. Thus, Saint Boniface was closely linked to Saint Paul through the apostle's birthplace, Tarsus, and his special vocation, the gentile mission. However, I had not yet known all this when I had decided to offer the paper to the Paul and Pauline Literature section at the International Meeting in Groningen, but it turned out to be most appropriate and providential.[41] Furthermore, Saint Ludgerus, the great missionary who became the first bishop of Münster in 805, built the first church at Dokkum in the place where Saint Boniface died. And he chose Saints Paul and Boniface as the church's patron saints. Later, Saint Ludgerus proceeded on his missionary journey to Münster and dedicated the Cathedral and Diocese to Saint Paul.

***

---

39. For these exciting pieces of information I am gratefully indebted to Dieter Geerlings, the priest who celebrated the Eucharist that morning. He was the first to ever mention the link between Saint Paul's Cathedral and Mary Magdalene! And he drew my attention to further illuminating material on the subject. A member of the Cathedral Chapter, he became auxiliary bishop six years later, on 29 August 2010. Bishop Barbara Harris was also auxiliary bishop at a Cathedral dedicated to Saint Paul. That's another synchronicity!

40. The paper in my bag was the first draft of this essay which I presented at the SBL meeting. I took it to Saint Paul's Cathedral shortly before my journey to Groningen in order to ask Saint Paul for his blessing. I left with Saint Mary Magdalene's blessing, too.

41. While I knew some basic facts prior to my journey to Dokkum, I learned further interesting details later when I read the excellent biography of Saint Boniface (von Padberg 2003: esp. 29–32).

> *Er blieb zwei volle Jahre in seiner Mietwohnung und empfing alle, die zu ihm kamen.*
> *(He lived two whole years in his rented apartment and welcomed all who came to him.)*

How often have I heard these words before? They are familiar to me. But now they resonate so differently in my heart, they are startling. It is the Saturday before Pentecost, 30 May 2020. And it is the Corona pandemic. Only earlier this month, services in Saint Paul's Cathedral were resumed, though with strict regulations and far from 'back to normal'. For the past two months, life has been shaped by a general lockdown in all areas of life. Depending on one's location and personal situation, staying at home, or in quarantine elsewhere, was strongly advised or even required by law. Being confined for two weeks or even two months can be hard enough and very testing – but two years?! I look up to Paul the Apostle in the stained-glass window, radiating in his bright red robe, and wonder. 'How did you manage?' I ask him. 'How, for God's sake, could you endure two years inside a place, which was not even your home?' To be sure, a rented apartment[42] was much better than a prison cell, like the one in Caesarea, and receiving visitors alleviated the situation. Nevertheless, what a challenge in particular to someone who had been on the move for three decades, eager to preach and disseminate the gospel in the entire Mediterranean. Now he was stuck, finally deprived of any prospect to ever fulfil his missionary dream of sailing on to Spain. Instead, he was awaiting his sentence. Furthermore, by the time he was shipwrecked, he had certainly lost all personal belongings he might have been able to take with him on his voyage to Rome. And yet, he continued his mission, preaching the gospel.

How could he make a living? I wonder. It is unlikely that he was able to set up a tentmaker's workshop in the apartment.[43] Who, then, paid the rent and provided for him?[44] And whom did he receive during these two years? Apart from the 'local leaders of the Jews' (Acts 28.17), there is no further information. Certainly, members of the Roman church also came to visit him, appreciative of the unique occasion to discuss what he had written in his letter to 'all God's beloved in Rome'.

---

42. The Greek *en idiō misthōmati* in Acts 28.30 is best translated 'in his own rented apartment', as in the German translation of the *Neue Einheitsübersetzung* (2016) quoted above. Both NRSV and RSV read 'at his own expense'. Although this translation is possible, it does not really fit in the present context. See also v. 16 (*kath' heauton*) and v. 23 (*ēlthon pros auton eis xenian*). For this argument, see Balz (1992). Also Lichtenberger (1996): 'his rented quarters' (2152); whether v. 16 refers to the same place as v. 30 'cannot be determined' (2151); for a detailed discussion of Paul in Rome, see Lichtenberger (1996: 2149–54).

43. This is another reason why the translation 'at his own expense' does not make much sense here.

44. Pesch (1986: 303) suggests that the Roman 'brothers' (i.e. fellow-Christians) who had come to meet him in Forum Appii and Tres Tabernae (v. 15) provided the apartment.

Since this Pentecost Saturday, contemplating Paul's fate in Rome, I have been intrigued by an idea that suddenly sparked off in my mind. What if Mary Magdalene had visited Paul in his apartment? According to the legend behind the icon in Grace Cathedral, she travelled to Rome and was admitted to the court of Tiberius Caesar, describing how poorly Pilate had administered justice at Jesus's trial and telling Caesar about Jesus's resurrection. What if she travelled to Rome (again) later and had been admitted to the court of Nero Caesar, describing how poorly Paul had been treated on his return to Jerusalem and how he had enmeshed himself by appealing to him, Caesar? And she got permission to visit Paul in his apartment and talk with him face to face, for as long as they wished.

To be sure, this is not virtual history but imagination. According to Paul Ricoeur (1976), imagination can create alternative realities and visions for the future.[45] To imagine Paul of Tarsus and Mary of Magdala sitting in his rented apartment in Rome, both far from home and reconnecting after their first encounter in Jerusalem some thirty years ago,[46] has an irresistible charm.

'We have seen the Lord!' they confirm, recalling also their own deaths and resurrections. No matter where ministry has led them or the circumstances, challenges and conditions they faced, they kept saying, 'Hallelujah anyhow!' And Mary, picking up an egg from Paul's kitchen table, tells him the story of her encounter with Tiberius Caesar during her first visit to Rome. 'That's a good one,' Paul says smiling, amused and immediately the egg in Mary's hand turns red.

References

Balz, Horst (1992), 'Misthōma', in Horst Balz and Gerhard Schneider (eds), *Exegetisches Wörterbuch zum Neuen Testament*, 2nd edn, vol. II: 1065–6, Stuttgart: Kohlhammer.

Bar-Ilan, Meir (1998), *Some Jewish Women in Antiquity*, Brown Judaic Studies 317, Atlanta: Scholars Press.

Bauckham, Richard (2000), 'What If Paul Had Travelled East Rather Than West?', in J. Cheryl Exum (ed.), *Virtual History and the Bible*, BibInt 8 (1–2): 171–84, Leiden: Brill.

Betz, Hans Dieter (1979), *Galatians: A Commentary on Paul's Letter to the Churches in Galatia*, Hermeneia, Philadelphia: Fortress.

Dormeyer, Detlev, and Florencio Galindo (2003), *Die Apostelgeschichte. Ein Kommentar für die Praxis*, Stuttgart: Katholisches Bibelwerk.

Exum, J. Cheryl (2000), 'Why Virtual History? Alternatives, Counterfactuals, and the Bible', in J. Cheryl Exum (ed.), *Virtual History and the Bible*, BibInt 8 (1–2): 1–7, Leiden: Brill.

---

45. Imagination belongs to a postmodern approach. According to Edgar V. McKnight, 'Postmodernism challenges an intellectual certitude that is the antithesis of freedom, faith, and imagination' (1990: 13).

46. An alert reader will notice that this applies only if Paul and Mary had not become a missionary pair, as suggested earlier. However intriguing this idea may be, for two such strong individual characters, it is more likely that they went separate, independent ways.

Hengel, Martin, and Anna Maria Schwemer (1997), *Paul between Damascus and Antioch: The Unknown Years*, trans. John Bowden, London: SCM.
Kitzberger, Ingrid R. (1977a), ''A Thousand Images of Loveliness' in Percy Bysshe Shelley's Love Poetry*, Salzburg Studies in English Literature; Romantic Reassessment 69, Salzburg: Institut für Englische Sprache und Literatur.
Kitzberger, Ingrid R. (1977b), '*Die "Starken" und "Schwachen" in Rom und Korinth. Eine Darstellung des Konfliktes und des paulinischen Lösungsversuches*', Mag. theol. diss. Katholisch-Theologische Fakultät, Paris-Lodron-Universität, Salzburg.
Kitzberger, Ingrid (1986), *Bau der Gemeinde. Das paulinische Wortfeld oikodomē/(ep) oikodomein*, FzB 53, Würzburg: Echter.
Kitzberger, Ingrid R. (1990), '"Wenn also jemand in Christus ist, ist er/sie eine neue Schöpfung" (2 Kor 5, 17). Paulinische Perspektiven zu Friede – Gerechtigkeit – Schöpfung', *BK* 44: 163–70.
Kitzberger, Ingrid Rosa (1995), 'Mary of Bethany and Mary of Magdala – Two Female Characters in the Johannine Passion Narrative: A Feminist, Narrative-Critical Reader Response', *NTS* 41: 564–86.
Kitzberger, Ingrid Rosa, ed. (2000), *Transformative Encounters. Jesus and Women Re-viewed*, BibInt 43, Leiden: Brill.
Kreitzer, Larry J. (1993), *The New Testament in Fiction and Film: On Reversing the Hermeneutical Flow*, The Biblical Seminar 17, Sheffield: JSOT.
Kreitzer, Larry J. (1994), *The Old Testament in Fiction and Film: On Reversing the Hermeneutical Flow*, The Biblical Seminar 24, Sheffield: JSOT.
Lichtenberger, Hermann (1996), 'Jews and Christians in Rome in the Time of Nero: Josephus and Paul in Rome', in Wolfgang Haase and Hildegard Temporini (eds), *ANRW*, Part II, vol. 26/3, 2142–76, Berlin: W. de Gruyter.
McKnight, Edgar V. (1990), *Postmodern Use of the Bible: The Emergence of Reader-Oriented Criticism*, Nashville: Abingdon.
Moloney, Francis J. (1998), *Glory not Dishonor: Reading John 13–21*, Minneapolis: Fortress.
Padberg, Lutz E. von (2003), *Bonifatius. Missionar und Reformer*, Munich: Beck.
Patte, Daniel (1995), *Ethics of Biblical Interpretation: A Re-evaluation*, Louisville: Westminster John Knox.
Pesch, Rudolf (1986), *Die Apostelgeschichte (Apg 13–28)*, EKKNT V/2, Zürich: Benziger; Neukirchen-Vluyn: Neukirchener.
Pixner, Bargil (1991), *Wege des Messias und Stätten der Urkirche*, ed. Rainer Riesner, Gießen: Brunnen.
Ricoeur, Paul (1976), *Interpretation Theory: Discourse and the Surplus of Meaning*, Fort Worth: Texas Christian University Press.
Rosenblatt, Marie-Eloise (1995), *Paul the Accused: His Portrait in the Acts of the Apostles*, Collegeville: Liturgical Press.
Schüssler Fiorenza, Elisabeth (1983), *In Memory of Her: A Feminist Theological Reconstruction of Christian Origins*, New York: Crossroad.
Schüssler Fiorenza, Elisabeth (1994), *Jesus: Miriam's Child, Sophia's Prophet*, Critical Issues in Feminist Christology, London: SCM.
Vögtle, Anton, and Rudolf Pesch (1975), *Wie kam es zum Osterglauben?*, Düsseldorf: Patmos.
West, Gerald, and Musa W. Dube, eds (1996), *'Reading With': An Exploration of the Interface between Critical and Ordinary Readings of the Bible*, African Overtures, Semeia 73, Atlanta: Scholars Press.

Part II

HERMENEUTICAL LENS

Chapter 4

PAUL AND THE 'MOMMY WARS': READING PAUL'S MATERNAL METAPHORS IN CONTEMPORARY AMERICAN CONTEXT

Jennifer Houston McNeel

It is rather remarkable that the apostle Paul, as a first-century man, employs maternal imagery six times in his seven undisputed epistles. In three of these six occurrences, Paul describes himself as a mother to one of his church communities, and in the other three Paul uses maternal imagery more broadly. What did Paul mean to convey by using these maternal metaphors? What was Paul's idea of motherhood, and how might someone in a different context read them, particularly if that reader is herself a mother?

In 2011, I completed a dissertation focused on the maternal metaphor found in 1 Thess. 2.7. During my research and writing, I also became a mother. While my writing during that period retained a historical and literary focus, outside of my writing I did a lot of reflecting on my experience of becoming a mother and how that experience related to Paul's understanding of motherhood and my reading of his maternal metaphors. In this essay, I will explore some of the implications of those reflections. I will begin by briefly introducing Paul's maternal metaphors. Then, after considering Paul's context and my own context separately, I will put these contexts in conversation with one another through an exploration of five themes related to motherhood. Finally, I will draw some conclusions and propose a way forward by taking one of Paul's maternal metaphors to heart.

Paul's Maternal Metaphors

Paul employs maternal metaphors in four out of the seven undisputed epistles. This includes two metaphors found in 1 Thessalonians. In 1 Thessalonians 2, Paul is defending himself and his past conduct to the Thessalonian community as a way of strengthening his relationship with them and their relationship with the gospel that he preached. As part of this defence, Paul emphasizes that while he was with the community, he did not use flattery to influence them, did not have a greedy motive and did not seek honour from human beings. On the contrary, he was as innocent as an infant.[1] Paul goes on to say that he cared for the community like a nursing mother. Like a wet nurse who is finally able to care for her own children rather than the children of another, Paul and his co-workers shared with them not only the gospel but also their very selves. In addition to this rich metaphor, Paul also employs a maternal image in 1 Thess. 5.3. This metaphor is more conventional, tapping into Old Testament birth pangs imagery and its association with the 'day of the Lord'. Just when people are saying 'peace and security', then sudden destruction will come upon them, Paul writes, like labour pains coming upon a pregnant woman.

There are also two maternal metaphors in 1 Corinthians. In 1 Cor. 3.2, Paul again takes the role of nursing mother, as he did in 1 Thess. 2.7. But this time it is not to express his deep affection for the congregation, but rather to reprimand those who still need milk when they should be ready for solid food. As the mother, Paul has the authority both to decide when his children are ready for solid food and to reprove them for their lack of maturity. Later in the letter (1 Cor. 15.8), when Paul is listing those to whom the risen Christ appeared, he refers to himself as an *ektrōma* (a miscarriage, abortion or premature birth), because he was last in the list of those to whom Christ appeared. Here, Paul is the child, not the mother, but the image relates to birth nonetheless.

Another maternal metaphor is found in Gal. 4.19. Here Paul portrays himself as a woman in labour, giving birth again to the Galatian community. Frustrated with the Galatians for listening to those urging them to be circumcised and worried that they are abandoning the gospel as he preached it to them, Paul portrays himself as a mother who reprimands her children for their lack of faithfulness. Faced with the prospect of losing them to his theological opponents, he feels as though he is experiencing the pain of labour all over again, attempting once more to birth them in the gospel so that Christ will be formed in them.

Finally, maternal imagery is also employed in Rom. 8.22. Here Paul takes maternal imagery to the cosmic scale, writing that all creation has been groaning together and having labour pains together until the present time, as it waits with longing for the children of God to be revealed. Like 1 Thess. 5.3, this image is also tied to Old Testament language associating birth pangs with the coming day of the Lord, but in Romans, the image is less conventional and more creative. Here, Paul paints a grand picture of all creation, our place in it and the experience of living with suffering while awaiting a glorious future. There is suffering, but it is experienced together, and it is all part of the work of giving birth to new creation.

---

1. For my arguments regarding the punctuation of this passage and the text critical issue of 'infants' versus 'gentle', see chapter 2 of McNeel (2014).

Motherhood in the Roman Empire

Paul created maternal metaphors within his own context, as a first-century, educated male living in the Roman Empire. What can we know about what his ideas of motherhood would have been in that context? Metaphors are not created and cannot be understood in a vacuum, and so to understand something of Paul's metaphors, we must ask what ideas, experiences and beliefs Paul would have associated with motherhood, since it is these ideas, experiences and beliefs that he applies to himself and his communities through the metaphors. Therefore, we must include in our analysis of these metaphors historical questions about motherhood in the Roman Empire.

Motherhood has its inception in pregnancy and fully begins with childbirth. Childbirth in the ancient world was far more dangerous than in modern America, with high maternal mortality rates and even higher infant mortality rates.[2] Birth in the ancient world was witnessed almost exclusively by women, presided over by a midwife and assisted by female family members (Osiek, MacDonald and Tulloch 2006: 53-4; Soranus, *Gynecology* 1.67-69). Once an infant was born alive, a determination was made by the father (or the master in the case of a slave mother) about whether or not to accept the child into the family. If the child was not accepted, both infanticide and exposure were practiced in the ancient Mediterranean (Corbier 2001: 57-8). If the child was accepted, practices varied by culture, but typically there was a naming day ceremony eight to nine days after the birth, which celebrated the child's entrance into the family (Rawson 2003: 110-11).

While maternal mortality rates were high in the ancient world, infant and child mortality rates were even higher. Historians estimate that 50 per cent of infants born alive were dead by their tenth birthday (Osiek, MacDonald and Tulloch 2006: 78; Rawson 2003: 104). Scholars debate about the effect that this reality would have had on the development of the bond between parents and children. Some have argued that the prevalence of wet nurses and other caregivers employed by those who could afford them indicate that parents resisted close involvement with their children until the children were older, which may have been a defence mechanism against the grief of losing children so often (Bradley 1986: 216). Nevertheless, there is also evidence from inscriptions and letters that there were parents in the ancient world who were very attached to their children and deeply grieved their deaths (Dixon 1988: 114).

---

2. According to the World Health Organization, the maternal mortality rate for developed countries in 2015 was 12 per 100,000 live births (see http://www.who.int/mediacentre/factsheets/fs348/en/ (accessed 27 February 2018)). By contrast, historians estimate that the maternal mortality rate in ancient Rome was about 2,500 per 100,000 live births, making childbirth about 200 times more dangerous in the ancient world as compared to developed countries today (see French 1988: 1357).

Society had certain expectations for the relationship between mothers and their children. Along with the father, the mother was expected to love her children and provide for their physical needs, as well as guide their moral development and see to their education (Rawson 2003: 236). But in some ways the mother's role was viewed as distinctive from the father's, though in exactly what way was not uniform across ancient Mediterranean cultures. For example, ancient Roman culture (before Greek influence) viewed mothers as the primary disciplinarians for young children, while ancient Greek culture (before Roman influence) associates mothers with indulgence and fathers with discipline (Dixon 1988: 131). In the Graeco-Roman culture of Paul's day, the Greek view seems to have been more prevalent. Several ancient authors wrote that mothers and fathers both love their children but show that love in different ways. Seneca, for example, expressed that fathers show their love by urging their children to be disciplined and engaged in active pursuits while mothers show their love by physical affection and wishes for their comfort and happiness (Seneca 1928: *De Providentia* 2.5).

Before leaving the ancient context, we also need to consider breastfeeding in the ancient world, since Paul portrays himself as a wet nurse or nursing mother in two of his maternal metaphors. Whereas the modern question when a baby is born is 'bottle or breast?', the ancient question was 'mother or wet nurse?' Wet-nursing appears to have been a common practice in ancient Roman society (Bradley 1986: 203). There were many reasons why infants in the ancient world were often breastfed by someone other than their mothers. Wet nurses were needed when mothers died in childbirth or when they chose not to breastfeed for a variety of reasons.[3] Wet nurses were usually slaves but could also be poor free women (Bradley 1986: 203). In Graeco-Roman literature, nurses are generally portrayed positively in terms of their care of and affection for their charges. Epitaphs and letters attest to the fact that the nurse–nursling relationship could be a strong, affectionate and lasting one (Bradley 1986: 221; Dixon 1988: 145; Rawson 2003: 126). Doubtless the relationship was not positive in every case, but overall, the literature gives a sense of the ideal nurse as one who loves, plays with, cares for, comforts, guides and tells stories to the children in her care.

---

3. For upper-class women, these reasons included a desire to conceive again sooner, a desire to maintain normal engagements and activities, and possibly a sense that the work of nursing was beneath them (Bradley 1986: 215-16). For lower-class women, these reasons included a need to return to work sooner or even, in extreme situations, to turn the care of their children over to foster parents (Dixon 1988: 146; Rawson 2003: 124). It should be noted that slave mothers would not have had a choice in the matter. It was up to the master of the house to decide who nursed the infants in his household. Some large households had a slave woman designated as the household wet nurse, in order to allow new slave mothers to return to their regular duties more quickly (Bradley 1986: 211-12).

Motherhood in Modern America

Like Paul, I also reflect on motherhood from within my own context. In my case, I do this as a twenty-first-century, educated, white, middle-class, married American woman. Motherhood in my own context can, of course, be defined in many ways, but in recent decades, it has often been portrayed in popular media through the lens of the 'mommy wars'. The term 'mommy wars' defined narrowly refers to the supposed conflict between working mothers and stay-at-home mothers. However, the term is also used more broadly to refer to all the parenting decisions and values mothers might disagree about as well as conflict over the basic idea of what a mother is and how she ought to think and behave. This section will not so much be about what mothers actually *do* in America but more about how mothers *feel* about what they do, and popularly expressed notions of what mothers ought to be like.

Leslie Morgan Steiner makes the following summary: 'Motherhood in America is fraught with defensiveness, infighting, ignorance, and judgment about what's best for kids, family, and women' (2006: 6). This negative picture, while far from encompassing the full experience of motherhood in America, nevertheless taps into a common experience of mothers, who often feel judged for the choices they make, and sometimes judge others for making different choices. According to Miriam Peskowitz, the reason for this kind of conflict is that there is no consensus in American society about the proper way to raise children. Without consensus, no matter what choice a mother makes, someone will disagree with it (Peskowitz 2005: 13). So mothers make choices and take sides: working or staying at home, breastfeeding or bottle-feeding, crib sleeping or co-sleeping, cloth or disposable diapers, baby-wearing or stroller-pushing and so forth. And the debates over these issues become so intense that sometimes it seems like the future stability of society surely depends on whether infants eat jarred baby food, have mothers who make their own from organic ingredients or go right from breast to table food.

Despite the fact that there are so many differences of opinion about these individual parenting decisions, there is also an overarching and powerful image in American society of what a 'good mother' is. Namely, a good mother is someone who puts her children first in her life and makes sacrifices for them. According to Ayelet Waldman, from society's viewpoint, a mother's life is supposed to be completely centred around her children: 'The single defining characteristic of iconic Good Motherhood is self-abnegation' (2009: 10). The good mother in modern times is the mother who invests all her emotional resources in her children and gives them as much time as she possibly can. And she does so gladly. This is sometimes called 'intensive mothering' (Vandenberg-Daves 2014: 258–9). In the past, people used to worry about the detrimental effects of mothers being over-involved with their children; now it hardly seems possible that a mother could be over-involved.

For her book, Waldman asked people to describe what a good mother is like. This is one of the responses she received:

She remembers to serve fruit at breakfast, is always cheerful and never yells, manages not to project her own neuroses and inadequacies onto her children, is an active and beloved community volunteer; she remembers to make playdates, her children's clothes fit, and she does art projects with them and enjoys all their games. And she is never too tired for sex. (2009: 9–10)

The standard for good motherhood is so high that mothers are certain to fall short of it and, consequently, to feel guilt. Jodi Vandenberg-Daves, writing about working mothers in the 1990s, describes it this way: 'Guilt was a common, but also prescribed, emotion among working mothers. If these women did not feel guilty on their own, the mass media was there to help them along' (Vandenberg-Daves 2014: 257). Modern mothers often feel guilty for not giving more to their children, for needing to work or even for wishing for some time to themselves.

It is important to examine our ideas about what makes a good mother, not only to give relief and support to mothers burdened by an unreachable ideal, but also because our ideas about motherhood say something bigger about us as a society: 'Motherhood has provided a critical reference point for social, political, and religious agendas of all sorts and a field on which Americans have wrestled with their ambivalence about female power, social justice, the needs of families, and even the social order' (Vandenberg-Daves 2014: 4). What does it say about our view of these issues that we believe the 'good mother' spends almost all of her time with her children, while in reality 70 per cent of women with children under eighteen are in the workforce (Vandenberg-Daves 2014: 249)? Are 70 per cent of mothers failing? Or are we failing to create the kind of society in which motherhood in a variety of forms is both valued and supported?

Paul's Metaphors in Ancient and Modern Contexts

What meanings arise from Paul's maternal metaphors when they are put in conversation with the realities of motherhood in both the ancient and the modern American contexts? This section will explore the metaphors through the lens of five themes related to motherhood: (1) status inconsistency; (2) conflict; (3) choice (or lack thereof); (4) self-denial and suffering; and (5) the authority–nurture balance. In each case, both the ancient context and the modern context will be referenced in a reading of the metaphors.

Status Inconsistency

Status inconsistency refers to the social state of a person who has both high and low markers of social status simultaneously. Mothers in the ancient world could be placed in this category because of the way they both had authority and were under authority. Mothers were authority figures and role models for their children, yet almost always lived under the authority of a husband or father. This aspect of ancient motherhood may be one reason Paul chose to employ maternal images: because he had a spiritual authority but not a legal authority in the communities he founded (Aymer 2009: 195). When Paul wanted the Galatians to accept his views on circumcision, or when he wanted the Corinthians to live out the implications of the gospel, he had to use the persuasive power of a mother rather than the legal authority of a father.

While most modern mothers do not live under authority structures similar to ancient times, many can, nevertheless, relate to the concept of status inconsistency. Mothers are often told that there is no higher calling than raising their children, yet many stay-at-home mothers feel judged for being 'just' mothers, and working mothers may feel their parental role not at all accommodated in the workplace. American society sends mothers mixed messages about their value and status. Mothers experiencing this kind of status inconsistency can relate to the image of Paul as nursing mother in 1 Thess. 2.7. As a nursing mother, she has a deep bond with her children, and they love her as she nurtures them. Yet by profession she is a nurse, a role most commonly held by slaves and poor women. Somewhat like modern American mothers, within her own small circle, this nurse has status and respect, but she is not viewed highly by the larger society.

Paul also expresses a kind of status inconsistency when he portrays himself as an *ektrōma* in 1 Cor. 15.8. Paul repeatedly claims the title 'apostle' in his letters, a title that defines his role and also gives him authority in the communities. Yet here he portrays himself as 'least' among the apostles (but still an apostle!) through the image of an untimely birth. Paul's apostleship is like a pregnancy gone wrong, ended before its appointed time by miscarriage, abortion or preterm labour. An appropriate metaphor for one who viewed himself as, without question, having the right to claim the term 'apostle', but whose apostleship was proven by weakness, imprisonments, floggings, danger, toil, hunger and anxiety (2 Cor. 11.23-30). Status inconsistency, indeed.

Conflict

As discussed above, motherhood in modern America is fraught with conflict over the right way for children to be raised. This conflict often results in mothers feeling like they are being judged for their choices. If they work, they are neglecting their children, but if they stay home, they are lazy or not setting a good example for their daughters. If they bottle-feed, they are harming their children's physical and emotional well-being, but if they breastfeed too long, they are likewise damaging their children's proper development. If they co-sleep with their infants, they are needlessly endangering them for selfish reasons, but if they put them in a crib, they are abandoning them to a cold and lonely night that will traumatize them. Mothers take to blogs and social media to defend their own choices and argue against the choices of others.

We cannot know if similar conflicts and arguments about raising children happened around wells and at other gathering places in the ancient world, but it is certain that people did project societal issues onto the choices mothers made and blamed mothers for society's perceived decline. This can be seen clearly in the issue of whether a mother ought to nurse her own children or employ a wet nurse to care for them. Elite male authors had strong opinions on this subject. Plutarch, Favorinus, Quintilian and Tacitus all advocated for maternal breastfeeding. These men felt that wet-nursing interfered with mother–child bonding, and they worried about the influence of low-born and especially foreign-born nurses on the children (Gellius, *Attic Nights* 12.1.8-23; Plutarch, *Moralia* 3C; Quintilian, *Institutio Oratoria* 1.1.4-5; Tacitus, *Dialogus* 29.1). Consequently, they worried that the choices these mothers were making were causing a degeneration of society, degraded from the 'good old days' when mothers had virtuously cared for their own children and considered it an honour to maintain the home (Tacitus, *Dialogus* 28). Favorinus accused mothers who had abortions or employed wet nurses of vanity and laziness (Gellius, *Attic Nights* 12.1.8-9).

Into this context comes Paul, who in 1 Thess. 2.7 imagines himself as a wet nurse caring for her own children and in 1 Cor. 3.2 presents himself as the mother who decides when her children are ready to be weaned. Placing himself in the maternal role, Paul might to some extent agree with those elite male authors, that a mother ought to care for her own children. Viewing his communities as his own children, Paul portrays himself as giving birth to them, providing for their nourishment and guiding their weaning. He is an attentive mother. Nevertheless, Paul does not denigrate the low-born wet nurse, often a slave, as other writers of his time did. Rather, he presents her in a tender light, giving her the chance in his metaphor to care for her own children, though she usually cares for the children of others.

A look at the conflict surrounding motherhood in both the ancient and modern contexts also serves to highlight Paul's conflict with other apostles and Christian preachers during his ministry. This connection between motherhood, conflict and Paul's metaphors is especially clear in Gal. 4.19. When Paul is contending for the Galatians, trying to convince them to stay true to the gospel as he had preached it to them, and not listen to those proclaiming another version, one of the things he does is portray himself as their mother. Not only did he give birth to them, but he also feels he is currently giving birth to them all over again. Paul asserts his rights as their mother to determine how they are to be raised and does not take kindly to others who intervene advocating another way.

Choice

So far in this essay I have referred repeatedly to the choices mothers make, as though all mothers are free to make any decision they choose about all the issues related to raising their children. This, of course, is not really the case. Need, rather than choice, often prevails. This is especially true when it comes to the question of whether or not mothers work outside the home. Some would choose to stay home but cannot afford to because they are single mothers or mothers with partners who do not have a high enough income to support the family. Some would choose to work but cannot find a job or cannot find one that covers childcare costs. Some are free to choose, others are not.

Ancient mothers would have had even more restrictions on their choices than American women today. For one thing, with less reliable forms of birth control, they would have had less choice about if and when to become mothers. Even after giving birth, a woman's choice related to caring for the infant was restricted, since the legal right to decide if an infant was accepted into the family lay with the father, not the mother. To be sure, some women could make some choices, such as elite women deciding whether or not to breastfeed their children or hire wet nurses. But overall, women's choices surrounding motherhood were fairly restricted in the ancient world by social convention, economic necessity and the authority of husband or father.

How might we view choice when it comes to Paul's maternal metaphors? There is a level at which Paul feels he is compelled to proclaim the gospel, rather than it being his own choice.[4] Certainly, the *ektrōma* has no choice about if or when to be born, and similarly Paul views his apostleship as a calling and the gospel as a revelation, not a choice. However, in his other maternal metaphors, even if Paul did not choose this role, he does not project any resentment about fulfilling it. He expresses deep care about his communities and tries to stay intimately involved with what is happening in them. One could even say he has an 'intensive mothering' style. With the Corinthians, he is the one who gets to choose when they are weaned from the breast and ready for solid food. With the Galatians, he is willing to go through labour all over again to maintain his relationship with them. And he tells the Thessalonians that he was 'pleased' to care for them as a mother and nurse. Whether or not the choice was his in the beginning, Paul now wants to care for these children, and he is willing to invest himself wholeheartedly in their development.

Self-Denial and Suffering

As we have already seen, one of the central ideas of what a 'good mother' is in American society is that a good mother centres her life around her children and makes sacrifices for them. We have also already seen that some elite male authors in the ancient world felt that good mothers were those who were happy with their prescribed role of keeping the home and were willing to sacrifice their lifestyles and comfort in order to care for their children themselves. Those who had abortions or employed wet nurses were deemed vain and lazy. Paul seems to have shared this idea of good motherhood to some extent. When he describes himself as a wet nurse with her own children in 1 Thess. 2.7-8, he writes that he and his co-workers were pleased to share with them 'not only the gospel of God but also our very selves, because you had become beloved to us'. Paul as mother shares not only information but also his very self with them. And with the Galatians, he does not shy away from the notion

---

4. See, for example, 1 Cor 9.16: 'If I proclaim the gospel, this gives me no ground for boasting, for an obligation is laid on me, and woe to me if I do not proclaim the gospel!' (NRSV).

of maternal sacrifice but is willing to suffer the ordeal of obstinate, disobedient children, even to the point of going through labour with them all over again.

The death of children can produce suffering for mothers of any era, but this reality was ever-present for those in the ancient world, in which 50 per cent of children died by the age of ten. Therefore, a link between motherhood and suffering would have been more apparent in the ancient world than in twenty-first-century America. When we keep this in mind, it adds poignancy to Paul's maternal worry about his churches. He worries not only that his 'children' may choose the wrong path, but also that they will go so wrong that he will lose them. We can also sense in his metaphors the distress of a mother separated from her children. Throughout 1 Thessalonians, Paul expresses his distress at being separated from the community and his strong desire to see them again. His distress and desire are emphasized when he pictures them as infants too young for weaning and yet separated from him, their mother. As Trevor Burke notes, the metaphor of Paul as nursing mother highlights both 'the apostle's anxieties *and* the Thessalonians' vulnerability' (2003: 153).

The Authority–Nurture Balance

In modern America, most people would acknowledge that motherhood combines elements of nurture and authority. There, are however, differences of opinion about where exactly on that continuum 'good motherhood' falls. The 'attachment parenting' movement, for example, places a much greater emphasis on nurture than on authority. Others are more traditional in promoting discipline. As discussed above under 'status inconsistency', mothers in the ancient world also had a complex relationship with authority, though not in the same way as modern mothers. For them, the complexity lay in being at the same time an authority figure for their children but usually under the authority of a husband or father. This inconsistency plays out in the question of whether mothers should be more nurturing or more authoritative in relation to their children. Of course, both can be, and usually are, present at the same time, but some see one as more important than the other. Consider, for example, this quote from Seneca:

> Do you not see how fathers show their love in one way, and mothers in another? The father orders his children to be aroused from sleep in order that they may start early on their pursuits, even on holidays he does not permit them to be idle, and he draws from them sweat and sometimes tears. But the mother fondles them in her lap, wishes to keep them out of the sun, wishes them never to be unhappy, never to cry, never to toil. (1928: *De Providentia* 2.5)

Seneca here expresses the Greek cultural view that fathers are the disciplinarians and mothers are the nurturers. Nevertheless, Graeco-Roman culture also acknowledged the important responsibility mothers had as role models for their children. Mothers shared with fathers the parental duty of teaching their children to live moral lives through instruction, example and discipline.

Not surprisingly, Paul's maternal metaphors contain elements both of nurture and of authority. In fact, the metaphors are so effective precisely because they express an interplay between intimacy and authority. Through them, Paul can express deep love for the churches and his willingness to care for them and sacrifice for them, while at the same time these metaphors also enhance his authority in the communities. The nursing mother metaphor in 1 Thess. 2.7 might seem at first to only contain intimacy and nurture, since Paul uses it to express his deep love for them and his willingness to give himself to them. But when you look deeper, you realize that if Paul is the nursing mother, then the Thessalonians are his infants. This places them in a dependent role with him as the giver and nurturer, and them as the receivers. Additionally, the metaphor makes Paul and the congregation kin to one another, so if the Thessalonians buy into it, they will owe Paul trust and loyalty. And, in fact, this is exactly what Paul is aiming for in the first few chapters of the letter, in which he defends his conduct when he had been with them and seeks to inspire their continuing commitment and loyalty to the gospel message as he had preached it to them.

Conversely, the metaphor in Gal. 4.19 might seem at first to contain only the element of authority, as Paul castigates them for their disloyalty to his message and instructs them on the only proper course for them to take. But this metaphor, too, contains more than one might see at first glance. For Paul, as a mother in the metaphor, does not abandon his children when they are disloyal to him, but fights for them and is willing to go through pain for them, in order to maintain the relationship and set them back on the right path. He is perplexed about them, desires to be present with them and wishes he could change his tone, presumably to something more affectionate. Paul is fighting to maintain the intimacy of their relationship, so that more nurturing aspects can reappear. In a similar way, the metaphor in 1 Cor. 3.2 is more authoritative in feel, with Paul reprimanding the community for not being ready for solid food. But here also, the metaphor communicates not just reprimand but also Paul's willingness to stick with the community and work with them despite the fact that their maturation is not happening as quickly as he might have hoped or expected. Paul's maternal metaphors illustrate the way in which he simultaneously asserts authority and seeks to create or strengthen an intimate bond of affection.

Changing the Conversation

For this essay, I have chosen the 'mommy wars' as the lens through which to see motherhood in modern America. But this conflict surrounding issues related to motherhood, work and child-rearing choices by no means encompasses the full experience of what it means to be a mother in America. In fact, it not only is a partial representation of motherhood but also can be a harmful one, since focusing only on the conflict can 'obscure the issues facing us' (Peskowitz 2005: 6). With the media's focus on the 'mommy wars', we can fail to notice how little progress we are making in supporting mothers and creating a society in which parents feel empowered both to provide for and to nurture their families.

For mothers in America today, there is often a disconnect between the words we hear about motherhood and the lack of practical support given to back up those words. As Vandenberg-Daves points out, there is often a lack of connection between recommendations and social policy. For example, while the American Academy of Pediatrics recommends that mothers breastfeed rather than bottle-feed their children, little is done to work towards an expansion of the Family and Medical Leave Act or a provision for better options for workplace childcare, both of which would make it much easier for working mothers to breastfeed (Vandenberg-Daves 2014: 279). Similarly, mothers in America often hear that nothing in their lives is more important than their role in raising children, and yet America lags behind most of the developed world on maternity leave, funding for quality childcare and flexibility in workplace hours that would allow working mothers to feel supported in their parental role.

With these issues facing mothers in America, it is hardly fruitful for mothers and others in traditional and social media to continue to focus the conversation on conflict between mothers who make different choices or who are in different situations. It is time for a change in conversation. I propose that one of Paul's maternal metaphors can help us facilitate such a change in conversation.

The Cosmic Mother of Romans 8

In the first seven chapters of Romans, Paul casts a wide theological net over all of humanity. God is the God of all people, but all have sinned and turned away from God (1.18–3.20). Likewise, there is now hope for all humanity because of Jesus Christ, the 'New Adam' whose faithfulness is stronger than Adam's sin (5.12-21). In ch. 8, however, our perspective is broadened even more, as Paul invites us to view what God has done in Christ in light of its effect, not just on humanity, but also on the entire cosmos. After imploring his readers to have the point of view of the Spirit and to recognize that they have been made heirs of God through receiving a spirit of adoption, Paul addresses the suffering of the Christian community by placing it in the context of what the entire cosmos is experiencing:

> I consider that the sufferings of this present time are not worth comparing with the glory about to be revealed to us. For the creation waits with eager longing for the revealing of the children of God; for the creation was subjected to futility, not of its own will but by the will of the one who subjected it, in hope that the creation itself will be set free from its bondage to decay and will obtain the freedom of the glory of the children of God. We know that the whole creation has been groaning in labor pains until now; and not only the creation, but we ourselves, who have the first fruits of the Spirit, groan inwardly while we wait for adoption, the redemption of our bodies. (Rom. 8.18-23, NRSV)

Paul makes sense of Christian suffering by placing it in the context of the suffering of all creation – a creation that has been subjected to futility and waits with eager longing for God's redemption. Christians who suffer, especially those who are suffering for the sake of the gospel, can understand their suffering as a participation in the labour pains of all creation. Through these labour pains, creation is in the process of giving birth to new creation (Polaski 2005: 85). And those who groan in pain along with creation also eagerly long for God's promised future.

The words Paul uses to describe the labour pains of creation (*systenazei* and *synōdinei*) are quite interesting. Forming compound verbs, Paul has taken *stenazō* ('groan') and *ōdinō* ('suffer labour pains') and added the Greek preposition *syn* to them, resulting in verbs that mean 'groan together' and 'suffer labour pains together'. A more literal translation of the text than the NRSV provides would read as follows: 'We know that all creation groans together and suffers labour pains together until now.' All things that are part of creation are groaning together, experiencing together the birth pains that lead to new creation. In this way, Christians at Rome are assured that even if they are suffering due to persecution or other causes, they are not suffering alone but rather suffering along with all creation. Not only that, but their suffering is not pointless; it is part of the labour of all creation that is in the process of bringing forth the new age. In this way, the metaphor is a call to participate in this hard work of groaning in labour and actively anticipating the redemption of God.

This kind of groaning together in labour pains suggests a solidarity between all creatures and all created things. It suggests that all things share a common bond and strain forward together in hope towards the future. What if we could view motherhood in modern America through this metaphor rather than through the lens of the 'mommy wars'? Perhaps mothers could honour their common bond of motherhood and humanity rather than tearing each other down for their choices. Perhaps working mothers and stay-at-home mothers could view each other according to Steiner's vision: 'Working moms might conceivably be grateful to moms who stay home and run our schools, our communities, a good chunk of our kids' worlds. And stay-at-homes might arguably appreciate the working moms' who work hard not only to support their families but to increase women's participation and representation in economic and political life (Steiner 2006: xxii). They might see that they are interdependent as different parts of one society. Through Paul's birth pain metaphor, perhaps those who are not mothers could see themselves as also groaning in the same labour with mothers to raise our children, and all could work together to create a society that supports parents and children in all their different stages and different situations. After all, the metaphor of all creation groaning in labour pains does not imply a passive suffering, but hard labour in which all work together, straining towards the promise of a better future.

Conclusion

As a white, middle-class American, the experience of considering what motherhood might have meant to Paul and how it is different from my experience also serves to remind me that not all contemporary mothers experience motherhood the way

I do, because their lives, experiences and world views are different. We do not all experience motherhood the same way for a variety of reasons, and we would all do well to recognize and remember this. On the other hand, we are all human beings longing for liberation and peace, and in that respect, we are all in it together. Paul's metaphor of all creation groaning together and suffering labour pains together can serve to inspire solidarity between mothers and with all people.

While not entirely unique, Paul's maternal metaphors are unusual for male writers of his era. He must have been purposeful in choosing this type of imagery on occasion, rather than sticking with more conventional masculine imagery, especially when it comes to the metaphors in which he portrays himself as a woman. This essay, while far from a thorough exploration of these metaphors, has served to illuminate some of the reasons why Paul might have chosen to employ this imagery. Specifically, exploration of the five maternal themes in ancient and modern contexts served to illustrate some of the meanings that motherhood may have had for Paul, and therefore the particular rhetorical impact he expected these metaphors to have. For Paul, these metaphors expressed his status inconsistency within the communities and the Empire, the conflict he had with other leaders about how new Christians should be 'raised', his compulsion to spread the gospel but willingness to parent the churches, his readiness to give of himself and suffer for their sake, and the interplay between intimacy and authority in his dealings with his congregations. And this ministry of the gospel, with all of its rewards and challenges, he saw as his own participation in a cosmic, apocalyptic labour that was in the process of giving birth to God's new age.

References

Aymer, Margaret (2009), '"Mother Knows Best": The Story of Mother Paul Revisited', in Cheryl A. Kirk-Duggan and Tina Pippin (eds), *Mother Goose, Mother Jones, Mommie Dearest: Biblical Mothers and Their Children*, 187–98, Atlanta: Society of Biblical Literature.
Bradley, Keith R. (1986), 'Wet-Nursing at Rome: A Study in Social Relations', in Beryl Rawson (ed.), *The Family in Ancient Rome: New Perspectives*, 201–29, London: Croom Helm.
Burke, Trevor J. (2003), *Family Matters: A Socio-Historical Study of Kinship Metaphors in 1 Thessalonians*, London: T&T Clark.
Corbier, Mireille (2001), 'Child Exposure and Abandonment', in Suzanne Dixon (ed.), *Childhood, Class, and Kin in the Roman World*, 52–73, London: Routledge.
Dixon, Suzanne (1988), *The Roman Mother*, Norman: University of Oklahoma Press.
French, Valerie (1988), 'Birth Control, Childbirth, and Early Childhood', in Michael Grant and Rachel Kitzinger (eds), *Civilization of the Ancient Mediterranean: Greece and Rome*, vol. 3, 1355–62, New York: Scribner's.
McNeel, Jennifer Houston (2014), *Paul as Infant and Nursing Mother: Metaphor, Rhetoric, and Identity in 1 Thessalonians 2:5–8*, Atlanta: SBL Press.
Osiek, Carolyn, Margaret Y. MacDonald and Janet H. Tulloch (2006), *A Woman's Place: House Churches in Earliest Christianity*, Minneapolis: Fortress.

Peskowitz, Miriam (2005), *The Truth behind the Mommy Wars: Who Decides What Makes a Good Mother?*, Emeryville: Seal Press.
Polaski, Sandra Hack (2005), *A Feminist Introduction to Paul*, St. Louis: Chalice.
Rawson, Beryl (2003), *Children and Childhood in Roman Italy*, Oxford: Oxford University Press.
Seneca (1928), *Moral Essays*, trans. John W. Basore, Loeb Classical Library, New York: G. P. Putnam's Sons.
Steiner, Leslie Morgan (2006), *Mommy Wars: Stay-at-Home and Career Moms Face Off on Their Choices, Their Lives, Their Families*, New York: Random House.
Vandenberg-Daves, Jodi (2014), *Modern Motherhood: An American History*, New Brunswick: Rutgers University Press.
Waldman, Ayelet (2009), *Bad Mother: A Chronicle of Maternal Crimes, Minor Calamities, and Occasional Moments of Grace*, New York: Doubleday.

Chapter 5

'GOD'S WORK. OUR HANDS.': A LUTHERAN READING OF ROMANS 7.15–8.13

Amy Lindeman Allen

Living the Liturgy

In the culture of church advertising that permeates most American churches, it is not uncommon to see a place of worship tout itself as either a 'bible' church or a 'liturgical' church. Such labels may imply that these categories are mutually exclusive or that a particular church possesses or can possess a monopoly on the 'Bible' or on the 'Liturgy'. But this, quite simply, is not the case. The term 'liturgy' itself is a biblical concept, weaving the two claims intricately together. 'Liturgy' comes from the Greek word *leitourgia*, which means 'public service'. Within traditionally defined liturgical churches, this most often refers to the role either of God or of the assembly *in worship*; however, liturgy is and can be understood far more expansively as well.

When Paul stakes his imperative to write to the Romans on his calling to be a *leitourgon* of the gospel (Rom. 15.16), he has this expansive sense of liturgy in mind. Here, Paul classifies the whole work of his mission to the Gentiles as *herourgounta*, defined as acting 'in some cultic or sacred capacity' (Bauer 2000: 591). In other words, all that Paul does for the sake of the gospel is, for him, liturgy. For Paul, the liturgical gathering of the assembly, centred around the proclamation of the gospel and the reception of the sacraments, propels Christians into the world to live and serve the gospel of the incarnate Christ where they are. Thus, any exercise in biblical interpretation rightly begins with an identification of context – where, as interpreters of the gospel, we begin this encounter with the incarnate Christ.

Within the frames named above, I identify as a liturgical Christian. Specifically, I am a *liturgist* – ordained to the public service of proclaiming the gospel through the act of preaching and enacting the gospel by presiding at the sacraments. I carry out this ministry as a pastor of the Lutheran Church (Evangelical Lutheran Church in America (ELCA)), in which capacity I served, from 2016–18 in the specific context of a downtown church of approximately three hundred members in the western part of the United States. Although there is some diversity within this congregation and, more broadly, the ELCA as a whole, in terms of race, class, gender, ability and sexual orientation, I myself am a white, middle-class, cisgender heterosexual woman of German immigrant descent, and our communal liturgy most typically reflects similar realities among such majority groups, albeit typically multiple generations removed from either German or Scandinavian immigrants who brought the Lutheran Church to the Americas. The largest service of worship therefore most typically follows the orders for worship set out in the *Evangelical Lutheran Worship* book (Evangelical Lutheran Church in America 2006) that are arranged for organ and reflect these European traditions.

This liturgical grounding to my context of interpretation is significant because, as testified by Paul, liturgy has been at the heart of the way in which God's people both receive and live out the gospel in their lives since the very beginnings of the Christian Church. In this way, liturgy as ritual enactment serves both as a reflection of the interpretive principles of a worshipping body and as a lens through which to read the Scripture that such a body holds sacred. As a Christian called into service of the gospel through the proclamation and enactment of the gospel in the liturgy, I read that same gospel in light of my liturgical context. The Word of God proclaimed and enacted in the liturgy thus shapes my understanding of and lived response to that very Word, even as the Word itself shapes the movement of the liturgy.

Within the scope of this essay, I will therefore: (1) contextualize the Lutheran liturgy as embodied by this context as a lens for reading Paul's letter to the Romans, (2) examine Rom. 7.15–8.13 through the lens of the 'Brief Order for Confession and Forgiveness' found in the *Evangelical Lutheran Worship* book and (3) imagine creatively how such a reading might impact a uniquely Lutheran enactment of liturgy in its broadest sense as sacred service to the world.

Liturgy in the Evangelical Lutheran Church in America: 'God's Work. Our Hands.'

Liturgy as Public Service

Acknowledging its ancient roots in the biblical *leiturgia*, or sacred service, the ELCA defines liturgy as 'the rite or body of rites prescribed for public worship'.[1] Liturgy is thus rooted in one's participation in a service of corporate worship. It is in such worship that God promises to make God's self present to humanity through the proclamation of the Word and the administration of the sacraments as means of God's grace. Martin Luther writes, 'Neither you nor I could ever know anything about Christ, or believe in him and receive him as Lord, unless these were first offered to us and bestowed on our hearts through the preaching of the gospel by the Holy Spirit' ([1529] 2000: 436). God in the person of the Holy Spirit is the primary actor in a Lutheran conception of the liturgy – serving those present

---

1. http://www.elca.org/What-We-Believe/The-Basics/Glossary-of-Terms.aspx (accessed 21 March 2011).

by offering up God's self. The liturgy is God's service to those gathered, God's work for the sake of the world.

God's work occurs in the context of community, through the interaction of the gospel enacted by preacher, presider and all those gathered together in holy encounter. Of the church as a communion, or community, of saints, Luther continues,

> I was brought into [this community] by the Holy Spirit and incorporated into it through the fact that I have heard and still hear God's Word … Through [the Holy Spirit] [God] gathers us, using it to teach and preach the Word. By it he [*sic*.] creates and increases holiness, causing it daily to grow and become strong in the faith and in its fruits, which the Spirit produces. ([1529] 2000: 438)

The holiness that God brings about in the Christian community is the means through which those assembled engage in God's work for the world. Those who participate in the liturgy thus enact God's work through their hands. For the past decade, the ELCA has been fostering community service activities with the slogan: 'God's Work. Our Hands'.[2] This captures the relational interdependence between God and the gathered community through the liturgy. From an ELCA Lutheran context, liturgy, both as participation in a service of corporate worship and the subsequent enactment of public service for the sake of the world, thus stands at the core of what it means to live a Christian life.

Moreover, as I have argued elsewhere, 'to this end, we stand in good company. In his letter to the Romans, the apostle Paul describes his whole mission to the Gentiles – preaching and social action – as a "priestly service" (Rom. 15.16). This is liturgy – and the Christian life – at its finest' (Allen 2014: 102). As God reaches out to us through the liturgy, so we, in enacting the liturgy in our lives and in our world, reach out to one another, as well as to our local and global neighbours. Within this context, however, there remains a present tension between those in the worshipping community who prioritize the divine service of the liturgy in itself and those who prioritize the social service towards which the liturgy impels its participants beyond the church walls.

This dual character of liturgy as both a source of spiritual nourishment and an impetus for mission is expressed in the primary worship resource of the ELCA, *Evangelical Lutheran Worship*. In the introduction to this book, the editors state their purpose on the grounds that 'because the worship that constitutes the church is also the fundamental expression of the mission of God in the world, worship is regularly renewed in order to be both responsible and responsive to the world that the church is called to serve' (Evangelical Lutheran Church in America 2006: 6–7). Denominational definitions of what it means to be a public church thus hold these two aspects of service in tension with one another. The public service of worship serves the public service of action, and the public service of action serves the public service of worship.

---

2. https://www.elca.org/dayofservice/ (accessed 10 October 2023).

Liturgy as Gospel-Centred

While the axes of worship and work coexist within an understanding of liturgy as public service, the direction towards which the pendulum of church identity seems to sway can become a point of tension and even conflict for those within worshipping communities. In studying the ELCA's most recent social statement on faith, sexism and justice, I received feedback that the national church 'needs to do *more* to publicly achieve greater justice and equality for women and girls' alongside critiques that 'in church we ought to be talking about the "gospel" not "justice" in a social sense'.[3] I firmly believe that a public church living out our calling to do liturgy is responsible to *both* the gospel of God's gracious will for humanity *and* the enactment of God's justice for all people. As a Christian, I experience both of these embodied in the person of Jesus Christ and his life, death and resurrection as it is described in Scripture. To this end, I feel strongly that the gospel must remain at the centre of all service.

As a liturgist, my task is thus to present that gospel in such a way that it is faithful to this understanding of public service most broadly conceived. Crafting the proclamation of the gospel through both the liturgical order and the sermon event, my task is to proclaim the gift of God's love for humanity in such a way that it inspires the movement of the Holy Spirit among the worshipers (all liturgists in their own right!) to proclaim the same gospel through words and deeds throughout God's world. A sermon is thus distinct from an inspirational talk or a rally speech in that it is not *about* human action; rather, it is *about* God's actions for us. Nevertheless, the proclamation of God's action for the world ought to, by the very nature of God's act, *inspire* human action for the world in which God acts. 'God's Work. Our Hands'.

God's concomitant embrace of the Christian in grace and call to the Christian for service is perhaps nowhere more deeply experienced in the liturgy than in the sacrament of baptism. Baptism itself envelops the Christian in the very embodied experience of Christ's death and resurrection through descent and ascent in the life-giving waters. To this end, *Evangelical Lutheran Worship* talks about baptism as a 'lifelong gift' nurtured within the context of Christian community (Evangelical Lutheran Church in America 2006: 225). Within the liturgies of worship that this book provides, it thus offers additional orders including 'Welcome to Baptism, Affirmation of Baptism, and Confession and Forgiveness' to 'provide several ways by which God's people in worship may participate in the lifelong gift of baptism' (Evangelical Lutheran Church in America 2006: 225).

Generally speaking, ELCA Lutherans teach that because we are reborn into God's gracious love through the waters of baptism, we are called to live out our baptismal vocations by sharing that love with our neighbours and, indeed, the entire world. As a result, the responsibilities entrusted to the baptized and/or their sponsors are quite extensive and include the charge to 'proclaim Christ through

---

3. Paraphrased from anonymous participants in a four-session study session that I facilitated at an ELCA Lutheran congregation in the spring of 2017.

word and deed, care for others and the world God made, and work for justice and peace' (Evangelical Lutheran Church in America 2006: 228).

The liturgical rite of confession and forgiveness reflects this dual relationship between the free gift of God's grace through baptism and the continued call for the baptized to live into God's grace in our still broken and sinful world. Luther expresses this as *simul iustus et pecator* ('simultaneously justified and a sinner') (Luther, *LW* 25:260).[4] The baptized remain in relationship with the broken sinful world, thus, *pecator*; and yet, on account of God's gift in baptism, are no longer ruled by it, thus, *iustus*. It is, therefore, appropriate, in light of a Lutheran understanding of baptism, to both *give thanks* for the gift of justification God has freely and completely given in baptism and to *confess* the continued need of the baptized to receive God's daily forgiveness. Reflecting this now-and-not-yet experience of justification through baptism, *Evangelical Lutheran Worship* frames both the rites of thanksgiving for baptism and confession and forgiveness within the gift of God's gracious action for and through the baptized in the sacrament of baptism.[5]

An Analysis of Romans 7.14–8.13 in light of a Lutheran Liturgy of Confession and Forgiveness

Captivity to Sin

In the brief order for confession and forgiveness in *Evangelical Lutheran Worship*, the worshipping body confesses before God and one another 'that we are captive to sin and cannot free ourselves' (Evangelical Lutheran Church in America 2006: 167).[6] It is with this liturgy as public service – God's work through our hands – in mind that I approach Paul's struggles with sin and justification in Rom. 7.14–8.13.

This liturgical utterance places its emphasis on the action of God with and for the community and the individuals that make it up. Here, human action is passive – there is nothing directly that the community has done to incur captivity; it is simply a power and reality in their life. In the words of the epistle to the Ephesians, which was penned by a leader within the Pauline school of thought, 'our struggle is not against enemies of blood and flesh, but against rulers, against the authorities, *against the cosmic powers* of this present darkness, against the

---

4. Martin Luther, *Lectures on Romans* (1516), translated and edited by Wilhelm Pauck, in *LW* 25:260 (Jaroslav Pelikan, Helmut T. Lehmann and Christopher Boyd Brown (eds), *Luther's Works*, 75 vols (Philadelphia: Fortress, 1955–86)).

5. For a brief analysis of the biblical and theological implications of each of these rites, see Allen (2014: 103–8). Given the contextual setting mentioned in the introduction, I focus the remainder of my analysis specifically on the brief order for confession and forgiveness.

6. Note that this is a minor variation from the rite as written in the ELCA's preceding worship resource, *Lutheran Book of Worship*, that reads, 'in bondage': see *Lutheran Book of Worship* (1978: 56).

spiritual forces of evil in the heavenly places' (Eph. 6.12, emphasis added). In more contemporary terms, the baptized remain captive to the structures of sin that infuse our systems of government, commerce and interpersonal interaction in this broken world.

The liturgical language of captivity mirrors Paul's description of fleshly humanity as 'sold under sin' (Rom. 7.14). This phrase, in light of the context and sociocultural reality of Paul's time, is almost universally translated with an implied reference to 'slavery', 'bondage' or 'captivity'.[7] As Emerson Powery explains, 'slavery was fundamental for how Paul thought about relationships of all kinds' (Powery 2022: 83). As such, the NRSV renders this phrase in Rom. 7.14 as 'sold into slavery under sin'. Such translations highlight the connection to the sin-as-slave-master metaphor used extensively in Paul's letter to the Romans from 6.16 onwards. Practically, for those attuned to the experience of enslavement whether in the ancient world or today, this metaphorical frame conjures 'the legacy of violence, abuse, dishonor, lack of volition, [and] loss of a communal self that was associated with human bondage' (Powery 2022: 85). Theologically, the most basic implication seems to centre around the loss of volition, specifically the ability to choose between good and evil central to the fall narrative of Genesis 2. In this reading of Paul, human agency is thus displaced by the dominion of sin.

Paul's troubling treatment of humans as commodities is furthered with a shift to militaristic language in 7.23 with phrases such as 'this "other law" is "at war" (*antistrateuomenon*) with the "law of my mind" (*ta noma tou noos mou*) and is "holding me captive" (*aichmalotizonta*)'. These images of the human relationship to sin continue to leave human beings subject to another agenda outside of themselves, driven by the acquisition of power and wealth typical of war. Brendan Byrne compares these metaphors with a similar usage in Rom. 6.12-13 and notes that this use of terms becomes 'all the more significant where one realizes that the usual fate of prisoners of war in ancient times was to be sold into slavery (cf. v. 14)' (2007: 228). According to this reading, human beings in the condition of sin are thus forcibly untethered from their sense of self and community and made to submit themselves to sin as a force outside of themselves with an agenda all of its own.

---

7. Cf. NRS, NAS, NIV, NJB. A notable exception to this is NKJ, which translates this phrase more rigidly as 'sold under sin'; however, even in the NKJV where the specific language of captivity is avoided, the reference to the buying and selling of human beings still clearly draws upon a social and political context of slavery. For more on the embedded nature of enslavement within Pauline thought and communities, see Emerson B. Powery, 'Reading with the Enslaved: Placing Human Bondage at the Center of the Early Christian Story', in *Bitter the Chastening Rod: Africana Biblical Interpretation after Stony the Road We Trod in the Age of BLM, SayHerName, and MeToo*, edited by Mitzi J. Smith, Angela N. Parker and Ericka S. Dunbar Hill (Lanham, MD: Lexington/Fortress, 2022): 71–90.

In light of this context of captivity, J. Christiaan Beker describes Paul's relationship with sin expressed in Romans 7 as an experience in which 'sin controls my innermost being by paralyzing my will and by deceiving me through the law' (1990: 57). In this way, sin is seen as 'a part of the human condition' and as 'the source of all idolatries' (Patte 1983: 266-7). Through its embedded and deleterious powers, sin not only prevents the good that Paul wills to do, but also entangles him in the very harm that he wishes to avoid (Rom. 7.19-20). In a concrete sense, I have found myself shopping at discount retailers in an effort to do good by saving funds for my family and the ministries that I support, only to find myself complicit in the structures and organizations that oppress through failing to pay a living wage and contracting with manufacturers who hold both human beings and the environment captive through their unethical practices targeted at yielding the highest profit. I do not do the good I want, but the evil that I do not want is what I do. This is the insidious power of sin.

However, by itself sin is dormant – a dangerous force infesting but not yet at war with the human will. With reference to baptism, Luther maintains that the power of sin is taken away completely, while in this world the structures remain, thus rendering sin a passive agent (*LW* 32:209). The freedom that we have in Christ is a freedom of perspective. It is the ability to will and act differently because Christ so willed and acted for us. So, Paul exclaims, 'Thanks be to God through Christ Jesus our Lord!' (Rom. 7.25a). This is not solely a prayer transmitted to God through Christ but, rather, an expression of thanks *on account of* Christ, through whom the baptized are liberated from the hold of sin on our lives.

And yet, the catch: nearly two thousand years after Christ's death and resurrection, our world is still broken. Powers and principalities, structures of sin and evil, continue to dominate, oppress and wreak havoc on human life, animal life and all of creation. While we may be liberated from the hold of sin, the structures remain all around us. Paul makes this distinction in terms of mind and flesh. 'So then, with my mind I am a slave to the law of God, but with my flesh I am a slave to the law of sin' (Rom. 7.25b). Paul, however, never advocates a complete abdication of the flesh. Indeed, the mind (*nous*) was understood in both Greek and Hebrew thought of his time as a part of the whole human body – the flesh (*sarki*). So, Jesus explains the greatest commandment: 'You shall love the Lord your God with all your heart, and with all your soul, and with all your mind' (Mt. 22.37) – with your whole self.

The distinction between mind and flesh, rather, is in the gap that occurs between Paul's willing and his doing as described above. While the structures of sin already and always infest humanity in our broken world in advance of the *parousia*, the force of that sin is only activated when a person's desire to *will* the good translates into concrete action. Apart from a will to act, the power of sin remains dormant. However, when the baptized act on a desire to do good, noble though their desire may be, their action activates the dormant power of sin and leaves them vulnerable to the structures and systems of sin that they are entangled in.

Challenged by such righteous intentions, as, for example, a desire to live into the charge to do justice given at one's very baptism, sin gains power over people by absolutizing desires. Thus, what we rightly perceive as good becomes for us an idol, placed above the gospel and the actual doing of good that we willed. For example, when the baptized place their priority on the doing of justice rather than on the gospel of God's gracious love that rightly pushes them towards the pursuit of justice, then justice becomes for them an idol. This has the tendency not only to set aside other needs, such as the pursuit of environmental justice over humanitarian justice or vice versa, but also, more dangerously, to place these ends above the very gospel that motivated them to begin with. In such instances, the baptized then end up bending to sin in the supposed service of this idol, or false good (Rom. 7.5). So, Paul laments, 'The very commandment that promised life proved to be death to me' (Rom. 7.10). Throughout his letter, Paul most clearly defines this corruptible good as *the law* (esp. Rom. 7.5-12). In my contemporary liturgical context, this sin could just as readily be equated with any of the righteous charges presented to candidates and their sponsors at the time of their baptism.

Freed and Forgiven

Just as the liturgy uplifts the baptismal charges as in themselves good and worthy pursuits (although they can be absolutized to our detriment) Paul insists that while the law too can activate the destructive force of sin, the law itself remains 'holy' (Rom. 7.12) and 'good' (Rom. 7.16).[8] It is only when it is lifted up as *the good* itself rather than as God's revelation pointing to the ultimate good that the law is corrupted (Rom. 7.12). Transforming what is good into an idol in this way is the evil that sin accomplishes. Byrne calls this 'the distinction between what the law of God is in itself ("holy", etc.) and the effect it has in the prevailing situation in human affairs' (2007: 229). The law is in itself good, but when it comes into contact with the power of sin that dominates human life, this good agent is corrupted and works evil instead.

To illustrate this relationship, Paul personifies sin 'as a slave master (cf. 6.15-23)' and an 'infestation' (Byrne 2007: 227).[9] This view is captured well by an Eastern Orthodox conception of sin, which, apart from our Western predilection towards the individual, offers a 'less individual-centered anthropology, [and] sees sin more in terms of error (being deceived by the devil) and illness that need correction and healing' (Shuster 2010: 1159). Paul's use of sin in Romans 7 depicts this corruption of the whole person similar to the way in which a disease can infect the whole body. Carefully avoiding assigning any active agency to the power of sin at each point in

---

8. It is significant that Paul reserves the term *kalon* (translated as 'good') to indicate a superlative form of moral perfection (7.16, 18, 21), which he assigns to the law; whereas, in its more practical applications in relationship to the specific commands of the law (7.12) and actualized human action/desire (7.13, 18, 19), he uses the more common term *agathon*.

9. Cf. Jewett 2007: 461-4. Thus, 'sin functions in Paul's expression as the alien power that enslaves its helpless victims' (462). This 'involved an unacknowledged hostility against God' (464).

his rhetoric where sin might take an active role, Paul describes it instead as acting 'through the law' (Rom. 7.8, 11, 13). In this way, Paul resists understanding sin as error or deception equivalent to an evil being or force (e.g. devil) acting in the world. Instead, he identifies sin as a destructive power that is activated by outside agents and structures that take advantage of sin's hold on humanity. Contemporary definitions of sin that 'stress constraints on individuals' and 'structural or systemic sin' best align themselves with Paul's imagery here (Shuster 2010: 1159). Captivity to sin in this context is the direct result neither of individual or communal actions in a Christian community nor of an active and malevolent evil force. Captivity to sin is the compilation of factors and corruptions that have grown and will continue to grow over time such that human nature is constrained (captive) and paralysed (infested) by this powerful force.

This force is still active in the world. Like an epidemic, sin has infested human communities to the point that no one is immune. Thus, 'Without [God's intervention] any human being is irremediably caught under the power of sin and condemned to death as his or her life – a living death – already manifest' (Patte 1983: 277). Yet, in the light of the infestation or bondage of the human flesh by this power, Paul proclaims, 'God has done what the law, weakened by the flesh, could not do' (Rom. 8.3). God has provided a cure. Byrne explains, 'This powerful depiction of the plight of the "I" left to its own merely human resources *(autos ego)* [in 7.21-24] prepares the way for the contrasting proclamation of liberation at God's hand that is to follow (8.1–4)' (2007: 230). The *Brief Order for Confession and Forgiveness* that begins with communal acknowledgement of our own captivity ends with a word of mercy in the form of the absolution: 'In the mercy of almighty God, Jesus Christ was given to die for us, and for his sake God forgives us all our sins' (Evangelical Lutheran Church in America 2006: 167). Christ joins with sin-infested humanity as an inoculation against the death-dealing power of sin. Paul boldly proclaims, 'For the law of the Spirit of life in Christ Jesus has *set you free* from the law of sin and of death' (Rom. 8.2, emphasis added).

Similarly, Luther speaks of baptism as a liberation, or inoculation, from sin in terms of a patient and a doctor. Luther writes,

> Justification is similar to the case of a sick man who believes the doctor who promises him a sure recovery and in the meantime obeys the doctor's order in the hope of the promised recovery and abstains from those things which have been forbidden him, so that he may in no way hinder the promised return to health or increase his sickness until the doctor can fulfil his promise to him. (Luther, *LW* 25:63)

This metaphor of illness provides an alternative entry point for understanding Paul's first-century language of slavery, especially in predominantly White, liberal contexts such as my own. From both a social and biblical perspective, it remains imperative that preachers and Bible scholars continue to name and critique biblical complicity with enslavement, including Paul's own too easy acceptance of enslavement both practically and rhetorically. Moreover, slavery is not an entirely past phenomenon. While universally condemned, untold numbers of people, especially girls and young women from the most vulnerable populations, continue to be victimized by sex slavery in an underground market in the United States, while bonded labour in various forms also continues in pocketed areas across the globe. Moreover, inter-generational impacts of slavery, especially as it was imposed upon the African American community, persist on social, economic, psychological and physical levels today. Naming and addressing these truths is necessary work for the church of the twenty-first century.

At the same time, in my context, addressing these truths effectively requires first recognizing that much of twenty-first-century White America prefers to forget about, or at least avoid talking about, the continued practice and legacies of human enslavement. In general, White Americans are more comfortable naming and discussing experiences of victimization at the hands of disease, especially in the wake of Covid-19.[10] The point here is not to cave to White fragility, which prefers to condemn universally experienced, natural sources of suffering, rather than repent of and make reparations for our own complicity. While not downgrading the important distinctions between slavery, both initiated and sustained by human sin, and illness, with its roots in the natural world, some important parallels can create an entry point for the conversation. In this way, my hope is that by highlighting the oppressive and dehumanizing effects of some experiences of serious and prolonged illness that White Christians might better grapple with the overwhelming power of sin-as-slavery described by Paul.

Moreover, as emphasis on living well with some diseases such as HIV, cancer and Alzheimer's continues to grow, the distinction between *freedom from* and *cure of* a disease has gained traction. Similarly, there is no immediate cure for the intergenerational traumas of enslavement; the impacts of slavery cannot simply be wished away or tucked under a proverbial rug and forgotten about. There is, rather, the work of reaching across racial and ethnic boundaries to end racial inequity – in other words, the pursuit of freedom.

Through the gift of justification made manifest in baptism, the baptized are *freed from* the power of sin even as the structures of sin continue to infect them. This is so even as the full effects of this freedom continue to work themselves out in the life of the baptized, much as medicine works on an illness over time. Living well in the face of the powers and principalities of this world thus requires the patients both to trust God's intent and ability to make them well and to live into the fullness of life in Christ *as it is presently*. So, Paul concludes, 'To set the mind on the flesh is death, but to set the mind of the Spirit is life and peace' (Rom. 8.6). Here, the question is not one of detachment from or engagement in worldly existence but, rather, the

---

10. The higher infection and mortality rates among African American communities effected by Covid-19 highlight the impacts of American chattel slavery that continue to spill over even into the realm of illness and disease. See Maritza Vasquez Reyes, 'The Disproportional Impact of COVID-19 on African Americans', *Health Human Rights* 22.2 (December 2020): 299–307.

mindset with which one engages in this world. When sin is thus viewed as a disease, atonement is seen as 'the "salvific effect of the Incarnation" that heals humans from this disease and extends to the entire cosmos' (Byrne 2007: 230). The baptized are thus called to engaged with the whole world as *ones who are freed* from the powers of sin and death. Just as the liturgy presents an alternate reality, 'a foretaste of the feast to come',[11] so the baptized are called as liturgists to enact an alternate reality – one in which sin and death and, indeed, slavery, no longer have the final word.

In light of the healing that occurs through Christ, such a redemption model of atonement typically interprets Romans 7 as a description of Paul's life before Christ (Byrne 2007: 226). However, because the law is read as only one among many possible revelations/goods that sin corrupts by making it to seem absolute, this passage cannot be merely autobiographical. Beker argues, 'Paul develops an anthropology that in an autobiographical manner depicts the internal conflict of the old Adam under the law' (1990: 57). Under this anthropology, the 'I' of Rom. 7.14-23 represents not just Paul but rather the pre-Damascus Paul as a literary *type* for the common experience of one who is bound by the law. Daniel Patte adds that this experience of being bound by the law 'is also the situation of all sinners whatever their origin and the time in which they live' (1983: 264). Byrne further nuances this by observing that while

> the issue is usually couched in terms of 'before' and 'after' / 'pre-Christian' and 'Christian' ... purely temporal categories in fact hardly reflect what Paul is about, which is to depict the situation of anyone who finds himself or herself confronted by the demands of external law without the aid of the grace of Christ. (2007: 226)

Paul's reflection on the power of sin in such a reading no longer centres around the temporal relationship between his discussion of sin and his own call and baptism. Rather, the spiritual power of justification conveyed by the sacrament is read in relationship to Paul (and every person!) and their experience of the carcinogenic powers and structures of sin that constrain them.

The question is thus not so much one of captivity to the Law of Moses, caricaturized in some interpretations as a uniquely Jewish problem,[12] but, rather, one of captivity to the power of sin as experienced by Jews, Christians and any person impacted by the corruption and brokenness of this world (Rom. 7.14, 23). This is made most clear in Rom. 7.25 when Paul contrasts service to the law of God with service to the law of sin. Byrne explains,

---

11. *Evangelical Lutheran Worship*, 'Let the Vineyards be Fruitful Lord (Offering Song)', Hymns 181–4.

12. Paul himself, as a Jew, is unlikely to have seen the Law of Moses as a problem at all. In contrast, first-century Jewish teaching, especially in the Pharisaic tradition with which Paul identifies, understands God's covenant, including the Law, as a freeing gift. See Pamela Eisenbaum, *Paul Was Not a Christian: The Original Message of a Misunderstood Apostle* (New York: Harper Collins, 2009), 208–39.

> By 'law of sin' Paul ... means the controlling force of 'sin', metaphorically described in terms of *nomos*, which compels the law of God – in itself always 'holy' and 'spiritual' – to have disastrous effects when it comes into contact with human nature 'sold into slavery under sin' (v. 14). (2007: 229)

Paul believes that this power is broken by the atoning act of Christ in the world. In the words of the liturgical absolution, 'by [Christ's] authority' (Evangelical Lutheran Church in America 2006: 167). Through baptism as an experience of dying and rising with Christ in his atoning sacrifice, the baptized are thus buoyed by this grace of Christ. Through baptism and trust in the justification that God offers, the baptized come to understand themselves as immune to the power of sin and freed from its captivity, analogous to Paul's Jewish understanding of covenant.

Within this framework, the law, while grounded in the Law of Moses, 'becomes increasingly more general as it proceeds [in Paul's description] and so is capable of more universal applications' (Byrne 2007: 226). The law as it is represented in Romans 7 for Paul is analogous to the creation that Paul describes in Romans 1. Both convey the will and promise of God and both are good; however, neither is intended to be *the* good (instead, each is intended to point to the good i.e. God) (cf. Patte 1983: 276). Sin is the power or force that overtakes a right perception of God and makes a false god (idol) out of it. The law of sin 'refers to any system or factor seeking to control behavior' in this way (Byrne 2007: 228). Paul is speaking in this broad sense when in 7.25 he

> powerfully depicts the bankruptcy of any attempt to correct moral failing simply through the imposition of an external code where the inner root problem of human life (what Paul calls 'flesh' infested with sin is not addressed). (Byrne 2007: 230)

The concern is not the inadequacy of the law to convey the promises of God but rather the corruption that has occurred as a result of sin absolutizing the law. The only answer to such corruption is in the person of Jesus Christ.

Corporate Confession and Forgiveness

According to Byrne, 'only a more powerful "law" – the Spirit – can break the grip of the "law of sin", as Paul will proclaim in 8.1-4' (2007: 229). This is why Byrne and others place Paul's first-person reflection in Romans 7 as an echo from his pre-Damascus past and attribute the present tense use of first-person in 7.14-23 to rhetorical effect. The logic is that since the Spirit shatters the power of sin through Christ, those who are 'in Christ' are no longer bound to sin as their master. The experience of captivity that Paul describes in 7.14 and 7.23 in such a reading cannot describe his present experience in Christ.

Commenting on the remaining oppositions between good and evil described in Rom. 8.5, however, Byrne concedes that '"outside" of Christ, sin and death still very much prevail and even those "in Christ", as they journey to full salvation, continue to feel the buffet of those powers' (2007: 235). When contemporary believers succumb to such powers, Byrne suggests that this is an indication not of 'the "normal" situation for the Christian' but a case of such believers 'trying to "go it alone" (*autos ego* [v.25b]) apart from God in a way more redolent of life "before" Christ' (2007: 230). Hence, if Christians become incapacitated by sin, it is a result not of sin's continued dominion in the new life in Christ but rather of their intentional or unintentional abandonment of the ends of this new life to pursue selfish ends of their own.

While this may fit neatly into Byrne's theological framework, the communal nature of the brief order for confession and forgiveness in the Lutheran liturgy draws out its fallacy. In the real world, prior to the *parousia* (what Byrne calls 'full salvation'), Paul's words are typical of 'normal' Christians. All people are captive to sin. Without knowing the precise conditions of my neighbour in the pew, I can confess these words confident that they reflect a shared reality. The structures and systems of sin in this world not only hold individual believers in captivity but indeed hold the whole world and all its inhabitants in its grip. The fact that Byrne feels the need to address this cognitive dissonance at such length and on multiple occasions is an indication of such truth. The presupposition that those who feel the power of the infesting and enslaving forces of sin pressing down upon them are in fact living 'before Christ' effectively excludes most, if not all, baptized Christians from the experience of the graces 'in Christ'. Or at least such an interpretation excludes every Lutheran who takes seriously the words of this confession.

Recognizing this lived experience of bondage in the Christian life, Luther prefers a simpler reading of the text. When Paul is speaking in the present tense in this address to the Romans, Luther interprets Paul to, in fact, convey his (and others') present experiences (Luther, *LW* 25:332). Therefore, for Luther, who himself identifies as such, the baptized Christian is *simul iustus et pecator* – at once both saint and sinner. Sin is an unyielding infestation and force that holds the human life in captivity. Only another powerful force is capable of breaking this bondage. For the Christian, this comes in the form of Christ.[13] This is affirmed in the celebratory tone and thanksgiving of Romans 8. In opposition to the experience of sin he has just described, Byrne insists, 'The "condemnation" (*katakrima*), which in the apocalyptic scenario presupposed by Paul hung over human beings because of sin (v. 1), falls not upon them – or at least not upon those "in Christ" – but upon sin itself' (2007: 237). Sin, in Christ, is condemned; yet sin continues to infest humanity with personal and intergenerational impacts. Just as inoculations do not instantly end the debilitating effects of plagues, so the cure in Christ has not instantly ended all of the effects of individual constraints and structural sin. 'For this reason, Christians continually return to the font, remembering the freeing power of their baptisms and confessing their captivity, confident that the power of Christ can and does break these bonds' (Allen 2014: 105). Byrne calls this 'the new

---

13. In this interpretation, it remains plausible that God can, has and will manifest God's self, in a parallel way, through forces other than Christ that can break the power of sin.

era of freedom and ethical "possibility" brought by the Spirit' as described in 8.1-13 (2007: 234-5). The legacy of American chattel slavery makes evident that such possibility can only come to fruition when a whole society and the individuals within it acknowledge the deleterious impacts of such bondage and do the work of liberation.

Reading Rom. 7.14-8.13 in light of the brief order for confession and forgiveness in the Lutheran liturgy described above, I concur with Byrne, Beker and Patte about the pervasive and paralysing role that sin can play in human life. Nevertheless, I experience this reality not solely or even predominantly in the past (pre-baptismal) existence, but rather as a past, present and future experience of captive consciousness characteristic of individuals unwilling or unable to look beyond their own gain. I read Paul to maintain that freedom from this captivity is only possible through divine intervention. Lutheran Christians experience such intervention through the continual acknowledgement of the need for Christ's atoning action in their present lives, as acknowledged in the communal confession. However, confession alone, if it is not outward oriented and accompanied by the works to which it points, cannot itself effect this liberating change.

Doing God's Work across Contexts

Under this understanding of sin as a slave master and infestation, for Christians, sin holds the power to corrupt the good revelations of God (such as nature, law and even Christ) into idols. In this way, sin can also warp the good intentions of humanity (such as service to God, the good, etc.) into idol worship. This is the dilemma of captivity described by Paul in Rom. 7.13-25. Those who believe that the ELCA is correct in pursuing the good of social action and love of neighbour above all else view Scripture primarily as a revelation of gospel. Those who believe that the ELCA is moving away from Scripture in favour of socially oriented agendas view Scripture primarily a revelation of law. The problem is that both of these views absolutize only one aspect of God's revelation in Scripture. In seeking to do good, the baptized thus become captive to the absolutizing power of sin instead.

This limited vision, while well-intentioned, is the result of giving primacy of place to the means of revelation rather than to God to whom it points, and this is the fault of the corrupting power of sin. Rom. 7.13-8.13 'powerfully depicts the bankruptcy of any attempt to correct moral failing simply through the imposition of an external code where the inner root problem of human life (what Paul calls "flesh" infested with sin) is not addressed' (Byrne 2007: 230). What is needed is a new vision that broadens believers' understanding of God's intended good. Reading Scripture through the metaphor of a corrective lens that reorients one's vision thus helps to resolve the conflicting interpretations of moral (and scripturally oriented) action within the ELCA. By broadening the vision of what is good beyond any individual commandment to the pursuit of *leitourgia* – the full work of God in one's life – divine revelation resumes its proper place in opposition to the absolutizing constructions of sin. This is what I believe is meant by the powerful phrase, 'God's Work. Our Hands'.

In order to enact this teaching in the life of the liturgical community, it is necessary to make clear the manifestation of God in the common work of God's people experienced in the liturgy. This experience of God's power combats the infestation of absolutizing idolatries by giving a central place to the crucified and resurrected Christ. In the particular worshipping community described above, immediately following the sacrament of baptism, the newly baptized is anointed with oil. This anointing occurs as the baptized is commended to

> Receive the sign of the cross, a sign of God's endless love and mercy for you.
> That you may hear the gospel of Christ, the word of life,
> Receive the cross on your ears.
> That you may see the light of Christ illumining your way,
> Receive the cross on your eyes.
> That you may sing the praise of Christ, the joy of the church,
> Receive the cross on your lips.
> That you God may dwell within you by faith,
> Receive the cross on your heart.
> That you may bear the gentle yoke of Christ
> Receive the cross on your shoulders.
> That God's mercy may be known in your work,
> Receive the cross on your hands.
> That you may follow in the way of Christ,
> Receive the cross on your feet.[14]

Through this ritual, the gift of God's freeing power in baptism is received physically through the sign of the cross. At the same time, that sign is accompanied with a charge to action in relation to each part of the body on which it is marked. The justifying power of Christ's life, death and resurrection is thus embodied in the baptized. They become a *part* of the liturgy – of the public service of the church.

With the community's vision reoriented on the pursuit of Christ as the ultimate good, the baptized are empowered to do the good that, through Christ, they desire to do and in so doing to manifest Christ for others. Revealing that by one's own power one can neither pursue the good nor turn from sin, a Christ-centred vision renders irrelevant the conflict about whose reading of God's revelation in Scripture is correct. Instead, this vision focuses believers on living into God's revelation, acknowledging that apart from Christ everyone is captive to sin and in Christ everyone is set free.

Within the liturgical context of an ELCA worshipping community founded upon the sacrament of baptism and rooted in liturgical rites that accompany baptism, in particular, the brief order for confession and forgiveness, this interpretation has

---

14. *Evangelical Lutheran Worship*, 'Welcome to Baptism', 234.

the power to open up and expand believers' understandings of sin. Reading Rom. 7.15-8.13 in conversation with the rite of confession and forgiveness in this context can have the spiritual effect of emphasizing the dependency of all the baptized upon the grace and forgiveness of God while striving to live a moral life. Such an interpretation fits with the grace-centred tradition of the Lutheran church, while not letting believers off the hook for their own wrongdoing – a tension lived out in the liturgical act of confession and forgiveness.

However, an apocalyptic approach to Romans 7–8 is hardly individual-centred either. The neighbour is not and cannot be forgotten in any communal act of liturgy. Thus, in the corporate acts of confession and forgiveness prescribed in *Evangelical Lutheran Worship*, the individual comes to an awareness of both their sinfulness and God's grace in light of their role in the worshipping community. They confess not 'I', but '*we* are captive to sin'. Rather than a desire to solely love or correct the neighbour, as when one acknowledges their neighbour's sinfulness and not their own, this experience of communal complicity creates an empathy for neighbours who are also caught in the effects of sin. This is particularly important in predominantly White middle- and upper-class worshipping communities such as my own, as we come to terms with our own complicity in the structures of sin that oppress and stigmatize groups who have been historically marginalized on account of race, gender, sexual orientation, age, ethnicity and ability, both in the United States and abroad. Such sin, in the case of each individual and, indeed, the community as a whole, is often structural and systematic sin that is not solely the individual's doing and, yet, sin that the whole community participates in.

The experience of communal confession, acknowledging the captivity and powerlessness on the part of all brings about an awareness of the constraints brought upon everyone by the forces of sin. This, in turn, fosters a humility among neighbours that allows them to acknowledge each other's equal complicity without judgement, self-righteousness or condemnation. Ethically, this has the potential to encourage further social concern and action that does not judge others in the community, who are recognized as equally in need of God's grace as anyone else, but rather seeks to condemn 'the power of sin' itself. When the ELCA, or any church, is able to focus on this deep need of the world instead of on individual controversies and disagreements, the work of God – the liturgy – is best done. Preaching thus focuses on the gospel as a *gospel of justice*, with the liberating effect of Christ's love inextricably attached to the baptismal vocation of service.

As such, the church must be cautious that this emphasis on divine rather than human agency is not misunderstood in a fatalistic way. Believers, aware that they cannot escape the power of sin by themselves, may resolve not even to try. In order to avoid such a reading, it is necessary to understand Paul's argument in Romans 7–8 within its larger context. By reading the theological argument of these chapters within the context of Paul's admonition to the Romans in ch. 6 to stop living in sin and to 'present your members to God as instruments of righteousness', it is clear that human participation in the work of God is both needed and desired (6.12-13). Paul's own active participation in this liturgical work is emphasized in his self-description of Rom. 15.16. The way in which God's grace is lived out and experienced today is through the work of God's people – the liturgy – which is empowered and enabled through the atoning sacrifice of Christ. Therefore, a church united around Scripture and liturgy in the ELCA today ought to take seriously the ways in which both the captivating powers of sin and the freeing power of Christ unites it so that, empowered by Christ, it might seek to be a sign of God's freeing grace in an otherwise sin-bound world.

References

Allen, Amy Lindeman (2014), 'Captivity, Turning, and Renewal: Three Liturgical Readings of Romans 7:15–8:13', *Currents in Theology and Mission*, 41 (2): 102–9.

Bauer, Walter, ed. (2000), *A Greek-English Lexicon of the New Testament and Other Early Christian Literature*, 3rd edn, revised and edited by Frederick William Danker, Chicago: University of Chicago Press.

Byrne, Brendan (2007), *Romans*, Sacra Pagina, Collegeville: Liturgical.

Beker, J. Christiaan (1999), *The Triumph of God: The Essence of Paul's Thought*, trans. Loren T. Stuckenbruck, Minneapolis: Fortress.

Eisenbaum, Pamela (2009), *Paul Was Not a Christian: The Original Message of a Misunderstood Apostle*, New York: HarperCollins.

Evangelical Lutheran Church in America (2006), *Evangelical Lutheran Worship: Leader's Desk Edition*, Minneapolis: Augsburg.

Jewett, Robert (2007), *Romans: A Commentary*, Hermeneia, Minneapolis: Fortress.

Luther, Martin (2000), 'Large Catechism', in Robert Kolb and Timothy J. Wengert (eds), *The Book of Concord*, Minneapolis: Fortress.

Lutheran Book of Worship (1978), Philadelphia: Board of Publication, Lutheran Church in America.

Patte, Daniel (1983), *Paul's Faith and the Power of the Gospel: A Structural Introduction to the Pauline Letters*, Philadelphia: Fortress.

Pelikan, Jaroslav, Helmut T. Lehmann and Christopher Boyd Brown, eds (1955–86), *Luther's Works*, 75 vols, Philadelphia: Fortress.

Powery, Emerson B. (2022), 'Reading with the Enslaved: Placing Human Bondage at the Center of the Early Christian Story', in Mitzi J. Smith, Angela N. Parker and Ericka S. Dunbar Hill (eds), *Bitter the Chastening Rod: Africana Biblical Interpretation after Stony the Road We Trod in the Age of BLM, SayHerName, and MeToo*, 71–90, Lanham, MD: Lexington/Fortress.

Reyes, Martiza Vasquez, 'The Disproportional Impact of COVID-19 on African Americans', *Health Human Rights* 22 (2) (December 2020): 299–307.

Shuster, Marguerite (2010), 'Sin', in Daniel Patte (ed.), *The Cambridge Dictionary of Christianity*, 1159–60, Cambridge: Cambridge University Press.

Vasquez Reyes, Maritza, 'The Disproportional Impact of COVID-19 on African Americans', *Health Human Rights* 22 (2) (December 2020): 299–307.

Part III

ETHICS OF INTERPRETATION

Chapter 6

WHEN ALLEGORIES ATTACK: HAGAR AND SARAH IN GALATIANS 4.21-31

Sid D. Sudiacal

When it comes to theological studies, it is difficult to find any position where there is consensual agreement among its adherents. One thing is certain. Everyone, in some way, shape or form, will disagree on how to properly interpret the Bible. Biblical theologians will approach the Bible from a certain hermeneutical lens that systematic theologians will not. Interpreting the Bible can lead to much disagreement, since each theologian comes to the text with their own set of biases, presuppositions and ulterior motives. The question of who has the proper interpretation can often lead to the question of who has the power to make their particular school of thought the dominant way of exegeting the text.

Biblical exegesis has been profoundly influenced by the Reformation and modernist thinking. Especially within the North American evangelical context, any discussion of proper or improper way of exegesis will somehow end up revolving (or devolving?) around the Reformed school of thought. With the rise of postmodern readings of the Bible, its power has slightly waned. Yet, as we look back to the early days of Christianity, we are quick to realize that the way they interacted with the sacred Scripture is somehow different and, to be honest, strange to how we think exegesis should be done. The use of allegory, in particular, is so foreign to our modern sensibilities that we eschew such exegetical methods because it does not align with the prevailing views on biblical interpretation. Yet, this exegetical method was used prolifically by the early church fathers. From Origen to Augustine, allegory was used by the church's early theologians to help give us a better understanding of the Christian sacred texts.

The first section of this essay will provide a brief background on Augustine and the Donatist Controversy. The second section will provide a brief exploration into the world of allegory and how it has been understood within patristic hermeneutics and Henri de Lubac from the *Nouvelle Théologie* movement. The final section will revisit the Hagar–Sarah allegory through the feminist lens of Letty Russell. The purpose of this essay is to examine how we can learn and benefit from the use of allegory as a legitimate exegetical tool in interpreting the Bible while also exploring the limitations and boundaries of allegorical readings as it pertains to biblical exegesis.

Context

This essay was born out of a question I encountered while studying the Donatist Controversy. I am a first-generation Filipino immigrant to Canada. I grew up in Canada and, for the most part, have been thoroughly assimilated into the Canadian culture. However, Canadian culture is something that is very difficult to define. In jest, we say that although we may not be able to properly define what it means to be 'Canadian', we are not Americans! Our identity can only be understood by what we are not. I also served as a missionary to a restricted-access nation in North Africa with a para-church organization for two years. Living overseas, I had to, yet again, come to terms with the question of identity within a culture that is foreign to me. Once, while riding in a taxi, the driver asked me where I came from. I told him that I was Canadian and he expressed his surprise. 'I don't believe you,' he said. My white teammate who was sitting at the back of the taxi responded by telling him that, indeed, I was Canadian. After hearing his approval of my Canadian-ness, the taxi driver readily agreed. This driver took the word of my white friend concerning my identity as Canadian with no hesitation, but questioned it when I myself told him about it. While this was a negative experience for me and made me think about the pervasive nature of systemic racism from a global perspective, it has also fascinated me, especially as I think of issues concerning identity. Who are the authoritative voices that we believe in with no qualms or hesitation? Why do we believe them? In many ways, the predominant reason why we believe any one's word is because in some way, shape or form, this individual is the embodiment of that particular topic or issue. The taxi driver believed my white friend because of the strong belief that a Canadian must be white. Since he was white, he was the authority on what it means to be Canadian. If the white Canadian can vouch for the Canadian-ness of someone who looks like a Filipino, then he must be Canadian. Even though I told the taxi driver about Canada's multicultural society, it still took a white person to validate what I said. Even though we both spoke the truth, the taxi driver saw my friend's white skin as the authority on what it means to be Canadian.

This anecdotal example hopefully highlights how our experiences affect the way in which we view the world. The North American society has this strong, pervasive belief that my truth is just as true as your truth. The belief that truth is personal and needs no other referent than the self which proclaims it to be truth is rampant. However, in cultures that are less individualistic, truth is understood as being communal in nature. If I am the only person that believes something, the chances of it being accepted as a truth by others is almost non-existent. It is the fact that there are also others who similarly believe in what I believe in that increases the chances that what I am saying is also true. It is easy to believe that one person may believe a lie; it is another to believe that a whole community, or even a whole society, believes a lie. The question of 'who can we believe?' is linked to the question of 'who is a truth teller?' A person in authority is one that we believe in because we believe that person to be a champion of truth.

Having grown up in the evangelical tradition, the idea that the Scripture is the highest form of authority is paramount. Tradition is a bad word, and since it is human-made, it is almost always seen in a suspicious light. Scripture, however, is God-breathed and infallible. Scripture is authoritative in a way that tradition is not. However, what happens when two individuals handle the same biblical passage and fail to come to a similar conclusion concerning its interpretation? Who should we believe? Who holds the truth? Who is the authority to whom we must submit? Faced with such a dilemma, being able to properly identify who the authority is on the subject becomes increasingly important.

This is the question that triggered my fascination concerning the Donatist Controversy. In particular, I am intrigued by Augustine's allegorical interpretation of Hagar and Sarah in Galatians 4.21-31. Initially, Augustine did not advocate for the use of force against the Donatists. Yet, later on in his ministry, he changed his mind. He uses the story of Hagar and Sarah as the proof-text for his change of heart. This event aroused my curiosity about the question of allegory and how our particular hermeneutical approach affects the way we understand and interpret the Bible. It also goes back to the question of who, or perhaps what, is the approach that should be seen as the authority in how we should interpret this passage? Why should Augustine be the sole authority in interpreting this Scripture when there are other methods and figures who provide a different reading of this biblical passage? Also, why should an allegorical reading of this passage be seen as less authoritative because it employs an allegorical reading versus a more literal reading grounded in the historico-grammatical approach that evangelicals are more prone to use? These are but some of the questions I would like to reflect on in this essay.

The Donatist Controversy: A Brief Overview

During the Great Persecution instituted by Diocletian in 303 CE, Christians were faced with the option of recanting or being tortured or killed by the state. Confiscation of sacred Scriptures played an integral role in the state's attempt to eliminate Christianity. There were some Christians who recanted and handed over sacred Scriptures to evade the state-sanctioned persecution. There were also others who only pretended to give up sacred Scriptures; in reality, they gave Greek treatises that looked like it was sacred Scriptures. The Edict of Milan, enacted in 313 CE, put an end to the state's oppressive acts against Christians.

While the state's role in persecuting Christians officially ended in 313 CE, the church's role in persecuting other Christians was about to begin. As a result of the Edict of Milan, the church was confronted with the problem of figuring out how to deal with the *traditores* (traitors) and the *lapsis* (lapsed). One faction argued that it is possible to readmit them back to the church, provided they underwent penance, the conditions of which are determined on a case-by-case basis. Another faction disagreed with this idea. Those who abandoned the faith when it was inconvenient for them to maintain it should not be readmitted back into the fold now that it is convenient for them to do so. Over time, this faction would be called the Donatist Movement.

The beginning of the Donatist Controversy is usually attributed to the appointment of Caecilianus as bishop of Carthage. According to the rules, three bishops must be present for the appointment of a new bishop. The bishop of Numidia was customarily invited and a key part of the appointment ritual. However, in an attempt to fast-track Caecilianus's appointment, the bishop of Numidia was not invited. Instead, only two bishops were present. To further complicate things, Felix, one of the bishops who appointed Caecilianus, was accused of being a traitor. Caecilianus, having been appointed by a traitor, could not be properly acknowledged as a bishop because Felix, who was able to proclaim him as bishop, forfeited his ability to act within that capacity, being a traitor himself. Since Felix's role as bishop was compromised, the process by which Caecilianus was appointed bishop was also suspect and illegitimate. Caecilianus's rival, Majorinus, was elected as the 'true' bishop of Carthage. After Majorinus died, Donatus came into power, and it is through him that we derive the term 'Donatists'.

The Donatists claimed that they were the true and pure church. This is the claim that animated and defined their thoughts and their actions. The Roman Catholic Church, with its refusal to agree with the Donatists' theological convictions concerning impurity, as evidenced by the appointment of Caecilianus and acceptance of *traditores* and *lapsis*, forfeited the Donatist claim of being faithful Christians, and of being the true church, by their actions. Furthermore, the Donatists were the true African church. They traced their lineage back to Cyprian, an African, and not to a foreign power like Rome. Their desire for purity informed the way they spoke and acted out against those who opposed them.

Augustine and the Donatist Controversy: Hagar and Sarah according to Augustine

By the time that Augustine dealt with the Donatist Controversy, Donatism had been around for eighty years. Charles Scalise comments that 'during the early years of his controversy with the Donatists (392–404) Augustine clearly advocates a position opposing religious coercion' (1996: 499–500). Yet, by 408 CE, Augustine's sentiments would completely change. By this time, he held the position, once foreign to him, that violence can be used to promote religious unity. Any change in thinking for Augustine necessitated a shift in his theological thinking. If it is appropriate to use violence in certain situations, he needed to ensure that he had a biblical basis for his change of heart. By looking at Sarah and Hagar's relationship in the Old Testament, Augustine had the exegetical proof text he needed to bolster his new position (Scalise 1996: 499–500). His exegesis of this passage would provide him the necessary theological foundation he needed to advocate the use of violence against those who opposed the ways of the Roman Catholic Church. In his letter to the Donatist bishop, Petilian, Augustine argued, 'See then that we act not with the sword, but with the word' (Schaff 1956: 567). Later, he would change his stance and say,

I have, then, yielded to the facts suggested to me by my colleagues, although my first feeling about it was that no one was to be forced into the unity of Christ, but that we should act by speaking, fight by debating, and prevail by our reasoning, for fear of making pretended Catholics out of those whom we know as open heretics. But this opinion of mine has been set aside, not because of opposing arguments, but by reason of proved facts. (Augustine 2008: 72–3)

When exegeting the Galatians passage concerning Hagar and Sarah, Augustine said,

Did not Sara readily punish her rebellious handmaid when the authority was given her? Yet she obviously did not hate her cruelly, since she had previously done her the kindness of allowing her the opportunity of becoming a mother, but she restrained the pride of her maid for her own good. You know that these two women, Sara and Agar, and their two sons Isaac and Ishmael, are figures of the carnal and spiritual, and although we read that the handmaid and her son suffered harsh treatment from Sara, the Apostle Paul says that Isaac suffered persecution from Ismael: "But as then he that was born according to the flesh persecuted him that was after the spirit, so also it is now" [Gal. 4:29]. Let those who are able understand that it is rather the Catholic Church which suffers persecution through the pride and wickedness of the carnal-minded, and that it attempts to correct these through temporal penalties and fears. (Augustine 2008: 61–2)

Scalise opines, 'Through a clever exegetical reversal, which follows the pattern of Paul's interpretation of the Sara-Hagar story, Augustine manages to convert the Catholic Church's sufferings from the Donatist schism into a *warrant* for persecuting the Donatists' (1996: 499). To further bolster his claim, Augustine compares what happened to the Donatists as to what happened with Daniel. In *Epistle 185*, Augustine notes,

The same thing happened to the Donatists as happened to the accusers of holy Daniel. Just as the lions were turned against the latter, so the laws by which they tried to oppress the innocent were turned against the former, except that, by the mercy of Christ, those laws which seemed to be against them were rather favorable to them, since many through them have been and are daily being converted. (Augustine 1981: 147)

Through these works, we see how Augustine's interpretation of Hagar and Sarah served as his scriptural reasons for advocating the use of force against the Donatists.

Allegory: A Brief Exploration

Since Augustine was willing to use an allegorical method to further understand the passage in question, the purpose of this section is to try and better understand what the definition of an allegory is and how it has been employed to better understand the story of Hagar and Sarah. Allegory is a Greek term meaning 'other-speaking' and is defined as 'the search for secondary and hidden meaning underlying the primary and obvious meanings of a narrative' (Lampe and Woollcombe 1957: 40). Hans Dieter Betz comments that 'the term *allēgoroumena* ("interpret allegorically") is a *hapax legomenon* in primitive Christian literature' (1979: 243). Furthermore, he states that

> the method rests upon the assumption that the material to be interpreted contains a 'deeper meaning' not visible on the surface. The allegorical method was believed to be able to bring this deeper meaning to light. The fact is, however, that for the most part the deeper meaning is secondary to the material which it claims to explain, and that the deeper meaning has its origin in the interpreter and his ideas and frame of reference. (1979: 243)

Philip Rollinson claims that 'the Galatian church to which Paul wrote was beset by a Judaizing, legalizing group which was perverting the gospel of liberty in Christ by demanding ritual and legal observances from the Old Law as prerequisites to salvation. Paul's letter argues against this legalizing perversion' (1981: 30). To counteract the Judaizers, Paul gives a non-historical interpretation of the story of Hagar and Sarah in the Genesis account. Since 'allegory may also exist as a concept in the mind of the interpreter before and during the allegorical interpretation of a piece of literature', it has the potential to influence the explication of the text in question (Rollinson 1981: ix).

For Paul, the story of Hagar and Sarah is the story of the present Jerusalem and the Jerusalem above; it is the story of two covenants.[1] Hagar, the slave woman, represents the present Jerusalem, the law and the old covenant. Sarah, the free woman, represents the Jerusalem above, the promise and the new covenant. As Christians, our mother is not the slave woman, bound by the law's chains; as Christians, our mother is the free woman, she whose son was born through the

---

1. 'Paul is not interested in the two women as historical persons, but in the two worlds they represent. The two covenants amount to two diametrically opposed systems: an "old covenant" and a "new covenant"' (Betz 1979: 243). However, James D. G. Dunn disagrees with Betz's understanding of the two covenants:

> It is tempting to understand the two covenants as old and new covenant. But in fact only one covenant is at issue here – the covenant with Abraham and his seed promising blessing to the nations; strictly speaking there was no covenant with Ishmael. It is the single issue of relationship to and descent from Abraham which is refracted into two contrasting sequences. What Paul describes as two covenants for the purposes of his exegesis are in effect two ways of understanding the one covenant purpose of God through Abraham and for his seed. What Paul is about to argue is that the Abraham covenant seen in terms of freedom and promise is a fuller expression of God's electing grace and a fuller embodiment of the ongoing divine will than the Abraham covenant seen in terms of law and flesh. (1993: 249)

promise. Our lineage is not earthly in nature; instead, our lineage is heavenly. The offspring of these two mothers testify to that reality.

Ronald Y. K. Fung remarks that 'in Paul's treatment of the Hagar-Sarah story, the main point remains the contrast between the two branches of the Abrahamic family, and it is to this that Paul returns in his final summation of the argument' (1988: 215). Although Ishmael was the first born, he does not represent the line of Abraham. It is Isaac, the son born through the promise and not of the flesh, who is Abraham's true heir. In this passage, Paul turns the table against the Judaizers. Richard N. Longenecker argues that 'the Judaizers had evidently contemporized the Hagar-Sarah story in their argument to prove that since the promises were made to Abraham and his seed ... Gentile Christians had no share in the promise unless they submitted to the Mosaic law given to Isaac's posterity and were circumcised' (1990: 207–8). In a sense, they were partly correct in their understanding that Abraham's line is through Isaac. However, they had a wrong understanding of what it meant to be in the line of Isaac. Paul, in a clever manoeuvre, paints the Judaizers as those who came from the line of Ishmael, and it is the Gentile Christians who belong to the line of Isaac. Moreover, Paul definitely puts himself within that stream as well. The new covenant meant a new way of understanding and embodying God's covenant. As Dunn remarks, 'the crucial theological point of Paul is ... that the understanding of God's purpose in terms of promise brings us closer to the heart and character of that purpose than an understanding in terms of the Torah' (1993: 248). Paul's allegorical reasoning created the theological space for the church of Galatia to conceptualize what it meant to be a true Christian.

Allegory versus Typology: The Debate Concerning Galatians 4.21-31

There is much debate concerning this passage on whether or not this should be seen as an example of an allegory or typology. While this section will primarily deal with authors who favour reading this biblical passage in a typological manner, it will not necessarily seek to give a definite response on whether or not it should be read in either an allegorical or a typological manner. The purpose of this section is to further problematize a seemingly 'easy' literal reading of this passage as an allegory.

Richard Hays (1989: 116), in his book *Echoes of Scripture in the Letters of Paul*, argues against the idea of allegory being used in the passage. Instead, we should view Paul's 'allegory' as typology. A. Berkeley Mickelsen states that

> in typology the interpreter finds a correspondence in one or more respects between a person, event, or thing in the Old Testament and a person, event, or thing closer to or contemporaneous with a New Testament writer. It is this *correspondence* that determines the meaning in the Old Testament narrative that is stressed by a later speaker or writer. (1963: 237)

A key point in understanding the concept of typology is its rootedness in history. 'The correspondence is present because God controls history, and this control of God over history is axiomatic with the New Testament writers' (Mickelsen 1963: 237). Since 'Paul is dealing with the correspondence between figures past and present rather than timeless spiritual truths' (Gignilliat 2008: 137), this passage should not be seen as an allegory but as a typology.

It must be noted that when I invoke the concept of history or historicity of the texts, I do not mean it in the modern sense by which we understand these concepts. Neal MacDonald notes that 'in the pre-critical perspective, the biblical world and the real historical world are one and the same ... Accordingly, there is no conceivable "epistemic space" in this world, no "geographical point" as it were, that does not take place within the realm of the biblical world' (2001: 316). As a modernist, the basic hermeneutic is one of suspicion. The opposite is at work in the pre-critical world. The historicity of the texts was a presupposition that was not only present but also viewed as integral in performing basic exegesis. To make any point that matters, the text is assumed to be both real and sacred.

According to Jean Daniélou, a key figure in the *nouvelle théologie* movement, 'the object of typology is the research of the correspondences between the events, the institutions, and the persons of the Old Testament and those of the New Testament, which is inaugurated by the coming of Christ and will be consummated with his parousia' (1951: 199). There are certain aspects in the Old Testament that can be linked to the New Testament through the figure of Christ (Martens 2008: 286). Although typological exegesis within the Old Testament was evident, there was a new typological emphasis in the New Testament. In the Old Testament, we have the figure of Adam; in the New Testament, Jesus is seen as the second Adam. In the Old Testament, we have the figure of Noah; in the New Testament, Jesus is seen as the second Noah. In the Old Testament, we have the figure of Moses; in the New Testament, Jesus is seen as the second Moses (Martens 2008: 286). For Daniélou, there are two types of typology in the New Testament. The Matthean typology was grounded in the idea that the events in the Old Testament corresponded with the events in Jesus's life. For example, Rachel weeping for her children prefigured the massacre of infants by Herod (Martens 2008: 286). The typology in the Johannine literature saw events in the Old Testament not necessarily as figures of circumstances in Jesus's life but rather the mysteries in that life. For example, the 'serpent in the wilderness was a figure of the mystery of salvation' (Daniélou 1951: 200–2). No matter which type of typology one finds in the Old Testament, Daniélou notices the widespread use of typology within the church, whether East or West, in Antioch or in Alexandria, and rightly argues that it should still be normative for Christian biblical scholarship today (Martens 2008: 286).

Wolfgang A. Bienert made a notable distinction between allegory and typology. Allegory 'is the vertical manner of interpretation, since it establishes unhistorical-timeless relationships between images (allegories) and their spiritual archetypes', while typology 'is the horizontal matter of interpretation, since it transports the historical events of the past into the present and future' (1972: 42). Daniélou's distinction between typology and allegory was based on whether the referent was Christological (typology) or non-Christological (allegory); Bienert's distinction was dependent on whether the referent was historical (typology) or unhistorical (allegory)' (Martens 2008: 290).

Frances Young's understanding of typology follows the same line of thought as that of Daniélou and Bienert. According to Young, typology 'requires a mirroring of the supposed deeper meaning in the text taken as a coherent whole, whereas allegory involves using words as symbols or tokens, arbitrarily referring to other realities by application of a code, and so destroying the narrative, or surface, coherence of the text' (2002: 162). In her description of allegory and typology, there are two things worth noting. First, she insists that both allegory and typology are concerned with the texts. Second, she argues that typology is more sensitive to the narrative coherence while allegory does violence to the text (Martens 2008: 291). This type of thinking lends itself to the belief that typology is a legitimate reading of the text since it preserves and safeguards history, while allegory destroys and negates history (Gignilliat 2008: 138).

Allegory: Its Place in Patristic Hermeneutics

The modern North American evangelical theologian is well aware that the Bible – written in a foreign language, amidst a foreign culture, during a foreign time – can only be properly understood when situated within its own particular social and cultural context. The process of exegeting the text is concerned with not only what the text says but also its original, intended meaning. Through the use of various textual criticisms, the theologian attempts to better understand the text. However, the process of understanding the text also involves understanding the particular cultural and social milieu in which the text was written in, along with its intended audience during the time of its writing.

The patristic commentators may not have the same concerns that we do concerning history and culture, but they are well aware that 'the literal content of the Bible needed explanation for later generations' (Kannengiesser 2004: 170). While we might turn to the historical-grammatical method to exegete the Scripture, the patristic commentators turned to their rhetorical training to help them understand the grammatical and stylistic features of the Bible. 'For ancient critics the biblical text was mediatory of God's message through the intricacies of a specific language that called for the skills of a translator' (Kannengiesser 2004: 170). They were well aware of the need to carefully scrutinize the sacred text they were handling. While sometimes our desire to correctly interpret the Scripture lay a great deal in our chosen methodology, the exegetes of the early church held the firm belief that the very act of attempting to correctly interpret the text was 'in itself a spiritual exercise' (Kannengiesser 2004: 168). For them, the decidedly human text they were interpreting was also filled with divine mysteries. The act of exegesis was one steeped in the deep understanding of the deep mysteries of the divine.

How, then, should allegory be understood within patristic hermeneutics? To answer this question, I turn to Gerald L. Bruns who talks about allegory as radical interpretation. For him, radical interpretation means 'the redescription, in one's own language, of sentences from an alien system of concepts and beliefs' (1992: 83).

It does not necessarily mean the recovering or preserving of the original message; it is more concerned with integrating a text and its meanings 'into a radically new cultural environment' (Bruns 1992: 83). In radical interpretation, there is a shift of emphasis from meaning to truth. The question changes from 'What does this sentence mean?' to 'How would this sentence have to be construed so as to be held true in our language?' (Bruns 1992: 83) This type of thinking runs contrary to the modern theologian's conceptualization of biblical exegesis.

Thomas Böhm's hypothesis is that 'the allegorical interpretation seems to presuppose a much stronger philosophical thrust than the so-called historical' (2004: 217). Among the early church fathers, it is Origen who best exemplifies and embodies the allegorical method. Origen 'believed that there were three levels of meaning in Scripture analogous to the body, soul and spirit … These three senses were literal, moral, and spiritual. Simple believers might remain at the level of the letter, but the elite should progress to the higher levels' (Young 2003: 335). Yet, Origen sometimes did not apply these three levels. It has been observed that in Origen's commentaries and homilies, there is only a twofold interpretation (Young 2003: 336). M. F. Wiles notes that

> he admits that the measurements given for the ark appear at first sight totally inadequate to house fourteen specimens of every clean and four of every unclean animal in the world, but claims on the authority of a learned Jew that the cubits there mentioned are to be understood as geometric cubits and therefore all the measurements need in practice to be squared. (1970: 471)

For someone who is often accused of 'evacuating the literal sense if it was difficult', Origen took the time and effort to factor in the literal sense within his allegorical reading of the text (Young 2003: 336). This should alert us to the fact that we need to be cautious about making a caricature out of a certain position which we may not necessarily agree with. Oftentimes, the allegorical approach has been derided for its seemingly low view of history. Yet, even someone who embodied the allegorical approach like Origen took note and struggled with the literal sense of the text, just like their 'historical' counterparts.

Henri de Lubac and Allegory: A Nouvelle Théologie *Understanding*

Henri de Lubac's first and fundamental principle of the allegorical sense of Scripture 'is that it is not situated, properly speaking, in the text, but in the events themselves' (Wood 1998: 36). Allegory is not to be found in history as narrative, but in history as event. This type of thinking concerning allegory is markedly different from the previous generation's definition of allegory. By rooting it in history, this would normally put it in the 'typology' camp. 'Such a distinction consequently sees allegory as nonhistorical and typology as historical. For de Lubac, however, Christian allegory is grounded in historical event' (Wood 1998: 37). He firmly believes that the allegorical sense 'was the dogmatic sense par excellence rooted in history' (Wood 1998: 37). He disagrees with the notion that allegories compromise the historical foundation of the faith as 'the allegorical sense assures the essentially historical character of the faith since it does not seek its referent apart from the literal or historical meaning, but within it, much as the Father is not found behind the Son, but in the Son' (Wood 1998: 37).

De Lubac's second principle is that 'the object of allegory is properly Christ and the Church ... Christ is the principal and final cause providing the reference for the interpretation of historical events. The Church is included ... by virtue of the mystery of the union of Christ and his Church' (Wood 1998: 38). The church, as Christ's bride, is forever intertwined with her Bridegroom. It is virtually impossible to understand one without understanding the other. To understand Christ is to understand the church; to understand the church is to understand Christ.

The third principle is that 'the object of allegory in reference to the Old Testament is a reality in the future. Once again, this principle underlines the historical character of Christian allegory' (Wood 1998: 39). Allegory, then, finds its referent in a historical event rather than in a historical narrative. Even the subject of allegory – Christ and the church – are historical realities. The fourth principle is that 'the structure of allegory is fundamentally sacramental. That is, the content or signification of both the historical event and the future historical reality of Christ and the church to which the allegorical meaning refers exceed what is observable within history' (Wood 1998: 39).

De Lubac's understanding of allegory provides us with the necessary rules and parameters by which we can engage in the act of allegorizing the Scripture. In a way, he provides us with a sort of *regula allegoria* (rules of allegory). Not only does an allegorical reading provide us with a higher meaning of the text, but by using de Lubac's principles, we can also be assured that our allegorical reading will be Christological and ecclesial in nature.

Letty Russell and Allegory: Hagar and Sarah Revisited

This essay began with a look at Augustine's view of Paul's allegory concerning Hagar and Sarah. Augustine, upon reading this passage, eventually used it as a means by which he ended up condoning the use of violence against the Donatists. Thus began an exploration into the world of allegory, its definition and its place in patristic hermeneutics. With everything I have laid bare so far, I want us to return to the place where it all started. This time, however, it shall be through a new set of lenses. As we re-examine this allegory anew, we are forced to consider the ways in which this allegory has been used to attack the 'other'.

Letty Russell, in her chapter 'Twists and Turns in Paul's Allegory', examines the allegory of Hagar and Sarah. If an allegory is defined as 'a rendering of truth that asserts the truth is always somewhere else, something other than where or what appears', as Elizabeth A. Castelli (1994: 229) defines it, then it is helpful to note that its usage is linked to the author's persuasion of the reader to 'reimagine the meanings of a familiar tradition' (Russell 2006: 73). Paul reverses the Judaizers' understanding of who counts as Abraham's children. In a surprising twist, Paul announces the Gentile Christians as the ones who are born from the free woman, Sarah, and the Judaizers the ones who are born from the slave woman, Hagar. 'By appealing to a familiar story that might have been used as a proof of Abrahamic descent by his opponents, Paul seeks to establish a new truth in the story. Hagar, already the castaway, becomes the ancestor of his opponents who want Gentile Christians to follow the law' (Russell 2006: 74). The allegory allows Paul to appeal to a 'deeper, hidden truth: that the promise of God is fulfilled in the death and resurrection of Christ and is now offered to all believers without the need for them to fulfill the Jewish law' (Russell 2006: 78). This could not be done through a plain reading of the text.

However, Paul's use of allegory in Gal. 4.21-31 has devastating consequences. Paul's allegory, according to Sheila Briggs, 'uses the socially accepted understanding of slavery, with freedom as its opposite' (Russell 2006: 74). Slavery, in Paul's work, has been used as metaphors of power evasion. In Phil. 2.5-11, Christ gives up his power only to become a slave. Like a slave, he was persecuted and killed. Yet, unlike other Roman slaves, Christ is raised up as Lord! Like Christ, Christians are also raised to new life. It is Briggs who also points out that Paul's rhetoric of evasion was similar to the Graeco-Roman society who did not talk about the evils and brutality of slavery even though it was so rampant and pervasive. In the story of the return of Onesimus, a Roman slave, Paul does not 'directly condemn the social reality of slavery beyond asking that slaves not be treated harshly' (Russell 2006: 85).

In addition to this, Paul's allegory of Hagar and Sarah has been used in many circumstances as a proof-text to cast out the 'other'. Paul uses this allegory as a way to frame all who disagree with him as outsiders. Augustine is not alone in reading this Pauline allegory within this us-versus-them narrative framework. Elizabeth Clark notes that Cyprian uses Galatians 4 'to claim that the formerly barren church has birthed more children from among the Gentiles than the synagogue had formerly been able to produce' (2006: 128). She also mentions how the early church fathers used 'Hagar' and 'Sarah' as codes for 'synagogue' and 'church' (Clark 2006: 129). By doing so, they imply that the former has been abandoned, and not incorporated, into the latter (Clark 2006: 129). In short, this allegory has enabled and exacerbated Christian-Jewish tensions over the centuries.

Allegory: Strengths and Limitations

Charles Cosgrove claims that in antiquity, allegories were typically used 'to bring a revered tradition in line with accepted views (especially the "modern" world view or a particular philosophy). This means that the interpreter would make points via allegorical exegesis with which his audience was already in sympathy' (1987: 220). In many ways, Cosgrove's assertion concerning allegory is helpful for us in trying to understand why Paul used an allegory in his Galatians letter. According to Anne Davis, one of the allegorical techniques employed is providing 'a statement that either explicitly or implicitly counters conventional understanding about a text, a character, or an event' (2004: 165). Paul's use of the Hagar–Sarah allegory shocks his audience and forces them to reimagine the Old Testament in novel and *nouvelle* (new) ways. The Judaizers would never have been able to conceive the thought that they could be the ones in the wrong; they were categorically and undeniably condemned by Paul as the outsiders whose very essence is the antithesis of everything that the Christian faith stands for and believes. The use of allegory allows for radical reinterpretations of what some may say as staid, comfortable and safe texts. Allegorical interpretations can direct the minds of its readers and hearers anew to the potential that the sacred texts written thousands of years ago still have the ability to be relevant to their particular generation.

It has been said that one's greatest strength can also be one's greatest weakness. One of the strengths of the allegorical method is its ability to 'update' the text and make it accessible to its current audience. Through allegory, the literature of the past is still relevant to today's discussions on various subjects. However, the person who is allegorizing is limited by their own particular time and culture. They cannot speak of anything beyond what they already know. In this way, the timelessness of the Scripture is exchanged for a timely exposition. The allegory becomes incredibly steeped in the allegorist's cultural and social milieu.

Allegory seems to be an exegetical method that has the possibility of running amok in its interpretation. The allegorist is not bound by any rules. Distinguishing between a good allegory and a bad allegory can be a seemingly impossible task. Since allegory is already seen as rhetoric rife with subjectivity and disbelief, most people seem fearful in engaging in this ancient task. De Lubac's allegorical principles can perhaps help us move forward as it provides us with a sort of *regula allegoria* that clearly demarcates the boundaries of what is acceptable or unacceptable in the act of allegorizing.

Conclusion

If you were riding a scriptural taxi, so to speak, and these historical figures told you that if you truly wanted to understand the Scripture properly, you should listen to them because they provide the true way of interpreting the Scripture, who would you listen to? Who should you listen to? I think it is safe to say that the particular hermeneutical approach we would follow, or at least show our theological leaning to, is one that is in line with how we see the world and how to make sense of it. While the literal reading of the Scripture, as best captured by the historico-grammatical approach that most evangelicals are wont to do, may yield a particular understanding of it, we cannot or should not privilege it as the only way to understand the sacred Word of God. The allegorical reading, as employed by the early church fathers, is as valid and truthful as the literal reading. An allegorical reading can even enhance our understanding of that which we are trying to understand.

Augustine's allegorical reading of Gal. 4.21-31 enabled him to advocate the use of force against the Donatists. This should alert us to the potential downfalls of allegorizing. We can unintentionally use this exegetical method to bolster our own ideas and preferences while simultaneously maintaining that this is what the

Scripture truly means. However, to rebuke Augustine's allegorical reading of Paul presents its own problems. Even if we would like to dismiss Augustine's allegorical reading, what are we to do with Paul's own allegorizing? If we disagree with the notion that allegory is a valid, legitimate tool in biblical exegesis, how can we explain Paul's usage of allegory in Gal. 4.21-31?

According to Origen, since the Scripture sanctions the use of allegory, allegory must be understood as a divinely sanctioned mode of reading the Scripture. Not only is it sanctioned, but it is also encouraged and to be emulated (Clark 2006: 130). One of allegory's salient features

> Is that the universal is not merely expressed but encrypted in the particular … that the deeper sense is felt as the discovery not the creation of the exegete, that it seems to be part of the fabric of the work, and hence … a 'real presence' that is waiting to be deciphered, not an arbitrary function that the reader has found it useful to impose. (Edwards 2002: 125)

Allegory, properly done, is not a mere creation of the exegete but a discovery of the exegete as one attempts to better understand the text. Although the use of allegory is a valid exegetical tool for the biblical exegete to use, we must be cautious in using ambiguous language where the meaning could be misinterpreted by the audience. John Chrysostom, the Golden Tongued himself, said that Paul could have used clearer language than the one he used (Kepple 1977: 244).

The diversity of contexts and experiences that each exegete brings to the table offers with it a diversity of readings of the same text. This should not come as a surprise. Living with this reality in mind, proper balance must be sought when it comes to discerning what the biblical text means. While we may have multiple ways of reading a text, there is such a thing as a 'wrong' interpretation. However, one must exert extreme caution to ensure that hasty conclusions are not made concerning a passage simply because a particular reading of the passage is unfamiliar to one's particular interpretive tradition. As discussions and debates continue concerning the place of allegory in biblical exegesis, these discussions must take into careful account the long-established tradition of allegorical readings by Paul and the early church fathers. Allegorical readings can provide us with a reading that challenges our current status quo. This is why allegories can be a powerful subversive exegetical tool for groups who are often marginalized and disenfranchised. However, one must be careful when engaging in the act of allegorizing, lest they fall into the same traps and pitfalls they condemn others of doing. Allegory, properly understood, is the human act of exploring the depths of God's mystery while simultaneously acknowledging our human finitude and limitations.

References

Augustine *Letters*, Vol IV (165–203). (Trans and ed. Sister Wilfred Parsons) Washington: Catholic University of America Press.

Augustine *Letters*, Vol II (83–130). (Trans and ed. Sister Wilfred Parsons) Washington: Catholic University of America Press.

Betz, Hans Dieter (1979), *Galatians*, Philadelphia: Fortress.

Bienert, Wolfgang A. (1972), *Allegoria und Anagoge Bei Didymos Dem Blinden Von Alexandria*, Berlin: De Gruyter.

Böhm, Thomas (2004), 'Allegory and History', in Charles Kannengiesser (ed.), *Handbook of Patristic Exegesis: The Bible in Ancient Christianity*, 213–69, Leiden: Brill.

Bruns, Gerald L. (1992), *Hermeneutics: Ancient and Modern*, New Haven: Yale University Press.

Castelli, Elizabeth A. (1994), 'Allegories of Hagar: Reading Galatians 4.21-31 with Postmodern Feminist Eyes', in Elizabeth Struthers Malbon and Edgar V. McKnight (eds), *The New Literary Criticism and the New Testament*, 228–50, Valley Forge: Trinity Press International.

Clark, Elizabeth (2006), 'Interpretive Fate Amid the Church Fathers', in Phyllis Trible and Letty M. Russell (eds), *Hagar, Sarah, and Their Children: Jewish, Christian, and Muslim Perspectives*, 127–47, Louisville: Westminster John Knox.

Cosgrove, Charles H. (1987), 'The Law Has Given Sarah No Children (Gal 4:21-30)', *Novum Testamentum* 29 (3): 219–35.

Daniélou, Jean (1951), 'Qu'est-Ce Que La Typologie?', in Paul Auvray (ed.), *L'Ancien Testament et les Chrétiens*, 199–205, Paris: Éditions du Cerf.

Davis, Anne (2004), 'Allegorically Speaking in Galatians 4:21-5:1', *Bulletin for Biblical Research* 14 (2): 161–74.

Dunn, James D. G. (1993), *The Epistle to the Galatians*, Peabody: Hendrickson.

Edwards, M. J. (2002), *Origen against Plato*, Aldershot: Ashgate.

Fung, Ronald Y. K. (1988), *The Epistle to the Galatians*, Grand Rapids: Eerdmans.

Gignilliat, Mark (2008), 'Paul, Allegory, and the Plain Sense of Scripture: Galatians 4:21-31', *Journal of Theological Interpretation* 2 (1): 135–46.

Hays, Richard B. (1989), *Echoes of Scripture in the Letters of Paul*, New Haven: Yale University Press.

Kannengiesser, Charles (2004), *Handbook of Patristic Exegesis: The Bible in Ancient Christianity*, Leiden: Brill.

Kepple, Robert J. (1977), 'Analysis of Antiochene Exegesis of Galatians 4:24-26', *Westminster Theological Journal* 39 (2): 239–49.

Lampe, Geoffrey William Hugo, and K. J. Woollcombe (1957), *Essays on Typology*, Naperville: A. R. Allenson.

Longenecker, Richard N. (1990), *Galatians*, Dallas: Word Books.

MacDonald, Neal B. (2001), 'Illocutionary Stance in Hans Frei's *The Eclipse of Biblical Narrative*: An Exercise in Conceptual Redescription and Normative Analysis', in Craig G. Bartholomew, Colin J. D. Greene and Karl Möller (eds), *After Pentecost: Language and Biblical Interpretation*, 312–27, Carlisle: Paternoster.

Martens, Peter (2008), 'Revisiting the Allegory/Typology Distinction: The Case of Origen', *Journal of Early Christian Studies* 16 (3): 283–317.

Mickelsen, A. Berkeley (1963), *Interpreting the Bible*, Grand Rapids: Eerdmans.

Rollinson, Philip (1981), *Classical Theories of Allegory and Christian Culture*, Pittsburgh: Duquesne University Press.

Russell, Letty M. (2006), 'Twists and Turns in Paul's Allegory', in Phyllis Trible and Letty M. Russell (eds), *Hagar, Sarah, and Their Children: Jewish, Christian, and Muslim Perspectives*, 71–97, Louisville: Westminster John Knox.

Scalise, Charles J. (1996), 'Exegetical Warrants for Religious Persecution: Augustine vs the Donatists', *Review & Expositor* 93 (4): 497–506.

Schaff, Philip, ed. (1956), *A Select Library of Nicene and Post-Nicene Fathers of the Christian Church*, Grand Rapids: Eerdmans.

Wiles, M. F. (1970), 'Theodore of Mopsuestia as Representative of the Antiochene School', in P. R. Ackroyd and C. F. Evans (eds), *The Cambridge History of the Bible*, 489–510, Cambridge: Cambridge University Press.

Wood, Susan K. (1998), *Spiritual Exegesis and the Church in the Theology of Henri De Lubac*, Grand Rapids: Eerdmans.

Young, Frances M. (2002), *Biblical Exegesis and the Formation of Christian Culture*, Peabody: Hendrickson.

Young, Frances (2003), 'Alexandrian and Antiochene Exegesis', in Alan J. Hauser and Duane Frederick Watson (eds), *A History of Biblical Interpretation*, 334–54, Grand Rapids: Eerdmans.

Chapter 7

THE PERSECUTOR AND THE PERSECUTED: AN INTERPRETATION OF GALATIANS 4.30 FROM A TAIWANESE CONTEXT

Menghun Goh

This essay argues that Paul's citation of Gen. 21.10 in Gal. 4.30 does not exhort, threaten or command the Galatian churches to cast out the Judaizing troublemakers. Rather, as the casting out is tied to the matter of inheritance, which is related to God's promise (Gal. 3.18, 29; cf. 4.1, 7), it should be done by God. Indeed, by turning Sarah's command in Gen. 21.10 into the Scripture in Gal. 4.30, Paul indicates that the driving out is God's prerogative. This intervention of God characterizes Galatians. From the beginning of Galatians, Paul repeatedly stresses the intervention of Jesus Christ and God in calling and sending him to proclaim the gospel among the Gentiles (Gal. 1.15-16; cf. 1.1-2, 11-12; 2.2, 7). Consequently, Gal. 1.8 tells us that even Paul and his co-workers are cursed if they preach a gospel different from what they first proclaimed! In Gal. 4.29, Paul further implies that God will drive out the persecutors – those who absolutize their viewpoints and persecute others. However, in the case of Paul, we also see that the persecutor can be transformed (Gal. 1.13-24). Likewise, if the Judaizing troublemakers are from 'the churches of Judea that are in Christ' (NRSV),[1] then the persecuted can also become the persecutor.

This interpretation of Gal. 4.30, highlighted by the interventive or apocalyptic orientation of Galatians (Martyn 1997; cf. Beker 1980), is accentuated by the apocalyptic image of 'the pains of childbirth until Christ is formed in (*en*) you' in Gal. 4.19 (Gaventa 1990) and the Jewish eschatological character of Paul's allegory in Gal. 4.1–5.1 (Di Mattei 2006). From a semiotic analysis that shows that Paul faces six systems of convictions in Galatians (Patte 1983: 39–83), we can see why God's intervention is critical, since these convictions can cause ambivalence in communication. Paul can easily be misunderstood. In the case of Gal. 4.21-31, while a binary structure in Paul's allegory (Kahl 2014: 261) can help reduce misunderstanding, it can also reify dichotomy, pitching one position against all

---

1. Unless noted otherwise, all Bible citations are from the New Revised Standard Version (NRSV).

others (Boyarin 1994: 32; Castelli 1994: 241), discouraging any further dialogue. From the context of Taiwan's transitional justice that is mired by modern Taiwan's contested history, we see that a binary structure can exacerbate the existing tension and conflict. Hence, the reminder of Martin Luther King Jr is rather pertinent. That is, just as the fundamental tension in Montgomery, Alabama, is 'between justice and injustice, between the forces of light and the forces of darkness', and not 'between white people and Negro people' (King 2010: 91), the tension in Taiwan should also be 'between the forces of light and the forces of darkness'. Therefore, this essay sees Paul subtly exposing the parasitic ambivalence in the binary structure. Without problematizing the dichotomy, both sides cannot see the cracks in their own viewpoints. They cannot see that there may be 'forces of darkness' among themselves and 'forces of light' among their opponents. In the year-round election culture of Taiwan, Gal. 4.21-31 can shed light on how to work our way out of the social polarization that is rife with double standards, political labelling and stereotypes that seek to demonize the other, in particular if stereotype 'must always be in *excess* of what can be empirically proved or logically construed' (Bhabha 1994: 66). That is, if stereotype betrays a sense of anxiety that tries to erase ambivalence by fixing the other into one's prejudiced representation of the other, then Paul's allegory that seems to make use of stereotypes can deconstruct stereotypes. Hence, this essay finds the notion of allegory as manifesting discontinuity and resistance (Dawson 1992; Greenblatt 1981; Hillenbrand 2006; Jameson 1986) – instead of a one-to-one correspondence – more appropriate to our interpretation of Gal. 4.21-31.

Ambivalence in Transition

A glance at the issue of Taiwan's transitional justice can perhaps help us appreciate the complexity of Paul's allegory that tries to address the issue of inheritance in the context of freedom and slavery. Ruti Teitel defines transitional justice 'as the conception of justice associated with periods of political change, characterized by legal responses to confront the wrongdoings of repressive predecessor regimes' (2014: 49). This definition reveals two challenges. First, as transitional justice is 'associated with periods of political change', the change is often marked by ambivalence, since the 'legal responses' are usually defined by the ruling party. Second, in presenting a genealogical perspective of transitional justice, Teitel highlights the legal, political, ethical and even religious aspects of transitional justice, which show that transitional justice should not be implemented by the ruling party alone, lest it be deemed as biased and retaliatory. This inherent problematic in executing transitional justice is well noted by Teitel. She writes,

> The paradoxical goal in transition is to undo history. The aim is to reconceive the social meaning of past conflicts, particularly defeats, in an attempt to reconstruct their present and future effects. Transitions present a threshold choice. By definition, they are times of contestation in historical narratives. Transitions

thus present the potential for counter-histories. The question is posed anew after the passage of time, which underscores the threshold challenge of remaining in history, as well as the limits to transformation. (2014: 61)

In the sociopolitical and economic contexts of Taiwan, the 'threshold challenge' is particularly thorny in the light of 'endless paradoxes' in the imagination and construction of Taiwanese social identity, as Margaret Hillenbrand points out:

China poses a constant territorial threat, yet remains a magnet for Taiwanese talent and capital; Japan is the old colonial enemy, but its popular culture is feted to the point of obsession; the notion of Taiwan as 'orphan of Asia' strikes a poignant chord, yet in recent years the island has arguably turned imperializer itself across the poorer swathes of Southeast Asia; the nation's politics are both passionately contested and ruthlessly stage-managed; cultural nativism has long preoccupied writers, but leading intellectuals devour Western literary theory. (2006: 646)

Given these paradoxes, one can imagine the difficulty of implementing transitional justice in Taiwan. Hence, for Ian Rowen and Jamie Rowen, what Tsai Ing-wen (the chair of Democratic Progressive Party, DPP) announced on 20 May 2016 in her presidential inauguration speech to 'set up a truth and reconciliation commission (TRC) inside the presidential office' was a strategy to 'legitimate the new regime', 'reframe narratives of Taiwan's democratic transition' and 'affect its geopolitical position and participation in international institutions' (Rowen and Rowen 2017: 111). However, it becomes awkward for DPP to condemn the brutality of Kuomintang (KMT) during 1947–87 without addressing the Japanese colonization of Taiwan (1895–1945). Second, one can question whether DPP can be politically against the Mainland Chinese government but economically benefiting from its trades and businesses with China. Or can DPP permit the government and its bureaucrats to serve its partisan agenda while criticizing the previous Kuomintang (KMT)-led government for doing so? Moreover, as many scholars have noted, can Taiwan speak against marginalization while pushing for the 'Southward Advance' policy that is marked by 'imperialist cultural imaginary' (Chen 2010: 17–64)? For many Taiwanese,[2] DPP uses transitional justice as an instrument for political ends. It is not surprising that 'during the 2018 electoral campaign, KMT candidate (and now New Taipei City mayor) Hou You-yi spoke against the commission saying it "… became a certain political party's thug" and is "confused about whether it represents the government or the party"' (Smolinske 2019: 50). What Nicole Smolinske notices is not a minority opinion voiced by a small group of people.

---

2. Note that in Taiwan's 2020 presidential election, while Tsai Ing-wen secured her second presidential term with 8.17 million votes (i.e. 57 per cent of the ballot), Han Kuo-yu, her KMT rival, had 5.52 million votes.

The difficulty to implement transitional justice in Taiwan is duly noted by scholars (Shih 2013: 40–1; Shih 2013: 285–6). For instance, in his article in the *Encyclopedia of Transitional Justice*, Christian Schafferer finds that in Taiwan, 'the political polarization has prevented a united attempt to address past atrocities' (2013: 472). The coexistence of Taipei's 228 Memorial Museum and Cihu Memorial Sculpture Park is another bitter irony. The former commemorates those oppressed and killed by the KMT regime during the 28 February 1947 massacre and the following forty years of the White Terror Period, 'a KMT-imposed period of state violence, murder and torture, mass imprisonment, and relentless censorship' (Hartnetta, Dodgeb and Keränena 2019: 239).[3] The latter honours Chiang Kai-shek whose regime was responsible for much violence and death against its dissenters. How these two memorial sites can coexist may be puzzling and even shocking to an outsider. But Liao Ping-Hui rightly notes that in Taiwan, the 'diversifying discursive positions testify to the fact that there are gaps and lags among divergent ethnic groups living on the island, who because of their different racial heritage and colonial encounters have had different senses of what constitutes Taiwanese modernity and coloniality' (1999: 199–200). In a recent book, Chin Kenpa (2016) delineates a similar dichotomy between Chinese-Mandarin-speaking churches (often tied to KMT, at least in the past) and Taiwanese-speaking churches (mainly the Presbyterian Church in Taiwan, PCT, which is more DPP friendly).

These 'different senses of what constitutes Taiwanese modernity and coloniality' cannot be overlooked. If we only focus on the KMT's past wrongs and not examine how we in the present under DPP interrogate the past, we may fetishize the past. Worse, we may even mimic and duplicate the very structure that we oppose. Consequently, the questionable structure and value system remain. Thus, transitional justice should not just hold the previous regime accountable to its past wrongs, but it should also help heal the country towards reconciliation and reconstruction, which means that the current wrongs should also be addressed. Alexander Boraine notes, 'If genuine coexistence is to take place, then the building of trust is indispensable. If trust is absent, citizens will not be prepared to invest their energies in the consolidation of democracy' (2006: 22–3). If different groups of Taiwanese cannot come to a common memory and a common goal, we must at least be willing to acknowledge the goodness of each other.

In Galatians, such acknowledgement comes to the fore in 1.22-24. Paul writes, 'And I was still unknown by sight to the churches of Judea that are in Christ; they only heard it said, "The one who formerly was persecuting us is now proclaiming the faith he once tried to destroy." And they glorified God because of me.' These verses are significant because it is incredible that the persecutor and the persecuted could work together (cf. Acts 9.13-14). What were the chances that the persecuted churches of Judea would glorify God because of Paul? Did they really forgive and trust Paul? Would they not wonder why God did not transform Paul any sooner? On the other hand, would Paul not be ashamed for having persecuted the churches

---

3. For details, see https://www.228.org.tw/en_index.php (accessed 20 February 2023).

of Judea? Of course, he would be (cf. 1 Cor. 15.8-9)! How could Paul and the churches of Judea come to terms with themselves, with each other and with God? It is in such a difficult situation that Paul wrote, 'And they glorified God because of me.' In the context of Taiwan, can different groups of Taiwanese be transformed so that we may hold each other accountable as we forgive, trust and work with one another?

Ambivalence and Freedom in Galatians

The ambivalence in Galatians is noted by biblical scholars, in particular when it comes to the issue of inheritance. For example, concerning Paul's usage of the first-person plural in Gal. 4.3 ('So with us; while we were minors, we were enslaved to the elemental spirits of the world'), Frank Matera argues that it 'can be understood in either an exclusive sense ("we Jewish Christians") or an inclusive sense ("we Jewish and Gentile Christians"). While most commentators prefer the latter interpretation,' Matera opts for the former because of 4.6 ('And because you are children, God has sent the Spirit of his Son into our hearts, crying, "Abba! Father!"') (1992: 149). This interpretation is supported by Gal. 4.5 ('in order to redeem those who were under the law, so that we might receive adoption as children'). But note the 'we' in 4.5 and the 'you' in 4.6 as well as the 'you' in 4.8 ('Formerly, when you did not know God, you were enslaved to beings that by nature are not gods'). It appears that the first-person plural can also refer to the Galatian believers, because it is unlikely that the Jews would be described as 'Formerly, when you did not know God'. Analysing Galatians from a semiotic approach, Daniel Patte calls this ambivalence manifesting a 'fragmented argumentative logic', which shows that the 'systems of convictions [are] in conflicts' (1983: 45–6). Patte further elucidates how Paul addresses six systems of convictions (that is, systems of self-evident truths which do not need to be demonstrated) in Galatians!

For instance, in the 'conversion of Paul', Paul is transformed from the conviction (1) of a Pharisaic belief system to that (2) of the gospel. Second, in the 'conversion of Peter and other Jews', there is a change of conviction from (3) Judaism to (4) Gospel with the Law (cf. Gal. 2.7). Third, in the 'conversion of Galatian believers', there is a change of conviction from (5) Hellenistic religions to (6) Gospel without the Law. Yet, as the Galatian believers were later influenced by the Judaizing troublemakers to 'another gospel' (Gal. 1.7), there is another 'hoped-for conversion of Galatians' to a 'Gospel (without the Law)' by Paul (Patte 1983: 47–8). As is also indicated by Gal. 2.7, Paul is not against the Law per se.

Now, in a manner not unlike what we see in Paul's usage of '*systoichei*' in the allegory, Patte points out that 'Pharisaism', 'Judaism' and 'Hellenistic religions' represent a state of condition *from which* Paul thinks that one should be liberated, whereas 'Gospel', 'Gospel with the Law', 'Gospel without the Law' and 'Gospel (without the Law)' refer to a state of condition *to which* one should be set free. Here, Patte is not asserting that 'Pharisaism', 'Judaism' and 'Hellenistic religions' are entirely wrong. Rather, he argues that Paul is against absolutizing any system of conviction (whether 'Pharisaism', 'Judaism' or 'Hellenistic religions') at the expense of others (Patte 1983: 57–72). A clear example is Paul enlisting the catalogue or 'list of vices' into the 'works of the flesh' in Gal. 5.19-21. Similar to Patte's argument, David A. deSilva writes,

> His [Paul's] introduction ('the works of the flesh are obvious', 5.19) suggests that this is a matter of common knowledge, and because of the work of popular philosophers, he is no doubt accurate (save for 'idolatry', a particularly Jewish innovation on vice catalogs), (2018: 459; cf. Keener 2018: 258; Patte 1983: 70)

Likewise, when it comes to the 'fruit of the spirit' or the 'list of virtues', deSilva writes,

> The importance of love as an ethical category, reflected in Gal. 5.13-14 and in the fact that love heads the list of the Spirit's fruit in Gal. 5.22, would incidentally represent one point of differentiation between Paul and the broader Hellenistic-Roman discourse on vices and virtues, as love or failures to love were not focal categories in either Greek or Latin ethics. (2018: 458; cf. Patte 1983: 70)

Here, the expression 'don't throw the baby out with the bathwater' is pertinent. Patte shows that for Paul, the systems of convictions of 'Gospel with the Law', 'Gospel without the Law' and 'Gospel (without the Law)' share the same core values and have similar features with those found in the systems of convictions of 'Judaism' and 'Hellenistic religions' (1983: 67–76). Hence, Paul does not mind calling the 'list of virtues' the 'fruit of the spirit' and the 'list of vices' the 'works of the flesh', as long as the 'fruit of the spirit' has 'love' in the list and the 'works of the flesh' include 'idolatry'. In other words, Paul is neither throwing the baby out with the bathwater nor simply promoting hybridity.

Paul is also not promoting relativism. Rather, he adjusts and reorients his understanding and interaction with 'Judaism' and 'Hellenistic religions' from the perspective of the revelation that he received from Jesus Christ and God, a perspective which cannot be objectified and fixed. As such, Paul's notion of gospel is informed and transformed by other cultures and religions that he encounters in his mission as an apostle to the Gentiles. For Patte, such dynamic mutual transformation in Paul's apocalyptic world view exemplifies 'Paul's thematic and figurative logic' that is always open to renewed and new understanding (2018: 214–332).

If 'any and all preaching on this text [Gal. 4.21–5.1] must highlight its summons to freedom' (Hays 2000: 310; cf. Betz 1979: 255), then Galatians invites us to not absolutize our own viewpoints. Thus, how do Taiwanese under constant propaganda from ideologically driven mass media see the cracks in our existing understanding and be conscientized to perceive otherwise? For a country that takes pride in freedom and democracy, we need to be empowered to see and acknowledge the goodness that other political parties have done for the people. There is no need for dogged and reified polarity. The words of Desmond Tutu come to mind, 'WHEN WE SEE others as the enemy, we risk becoming what we hate. When we oppress others, we end up oppressing ourselves. All of our humanity is dependent on recognizing the humanity in others' (2004: 139; emphasis original).

Allegory as Embodying and Unveiling Ambivalence

Allegory happens when you know you cannot represent something, but you also cannot not do it.

Jameson (1998: 376)

Since the Early Church, scholars have debated whether Paul's allegory in Galatians is an afterthought or the climax of his argument and whether it should be treated as a typology or a rhetorical trope (Riches 2008: 227–30; Di Mattei 2006: 102–4). Although Ben Witherington III argues that 'had Paul wanted us to see this text typologically, he could easily have used the appropriate terminology to signal the fact' (1998: 326), it is difficult to pinpoint the meaning of *allēgoroumena* – a *hapax legomenon* in the New Testament – in its periphrastic construction. While the meaning of *allo-agoreuō* (i.e. 'to say something else') can be taken as 'to speak allegorically' or 'to interpret allegorically', we want to highlight the ambiguity and ambivalence in Paul's allegory, which can render any interpretation necessarily inadequate. In the context of Taiwan, this essay suggests that it is precisely this lacking that causes us to pause and go beyond the surface of the allegory. As such, allegory can help clear and create space for us to think otherwise, which also befits the topic of 'freedom' in Gal. 4.21-31.

This ambivalence is not only foregrounded by the apocalyptic features of Galatians and Paul's allegory but also marked by the puzzles and gaps in Paul's allegory, which are expected, given the apocalyptic characteristics. In the event of God's intervention, who can really comprehend God's revelation? Hence, the lack of correspondence in Paul's allegory should not be a surprise. When Paul writes, 'Now Hagar is Mount Sinai in Arabia (*to de Hagar Sina oros estin en tē Arabia*) and corresponds (*systoichei*) to the present Jerusalem, for she is in slavery with her children' (Gal. 4.25), the complicated textual variants of 4.25a should signal us not to take the 'correspondence' too literally. Indeed, as Paul continues, 'But the other woman corresponds to the Jerusalem above; she is free, and she is our mother' (Gal. 4.26), the mention of 'Jerusalem above' points to that which cannot be grasped. Hence, 'the other woman' is not named, lest she is no longer free and is pigeonholed into a certain understanding only. And, of course, anything compared to that which cannot be named and grasped, even what could be the symbol of freedom in the past – that is, Jerusalem – is considered not as free. If that which cannot be grasped 'is our mother', how definable are 'we'? In a patriarchal society, it is noteworthy that 'we' are more defined by the mother than by the father in Galatians 4, even though Abraham is one of the key figures in Galatians 3.

The puzzles in Paul's allegory continue. For example, how can Abraham's son, born of the slave woman, be a slave? Elsa Tamez writes, 'In the ancient world the children of slaves were born slaves, and the children of free persons were born free. If the mother were a slave and the father free, the child would acquire the status of a free person' (2000: 267). On the other hand, while not all born of Abraham are Abraham's children (cf. Gal. 3.15-16, 29), those not born of Abraham can, however, become Abraham's children. Here, God's intervention is apparent.

Second, while Paul seems to challenge those 'who want to be under law' (Gal. 4.21) – a negative expression (Gal. 3.23; 4.4-5) – he goes on to refer to the law, albeit only in the end of 4.21-31 does he cite Gen. 21.10. Does it mean that for Paul, the problem is the interpretation of law, just as he misinterpreted, persecuted and tried to destroy the church of God (Gal. 1.13)?

Third, who are the ones born of the free woman? Those 'having started with the Spirit' (Gal. 3.3)? Those 'who believe' (*hoi ek pisteōs* in Gal. 3.7)? Those who are 'in Christ Jesus through faith' (Gal. 3.26)? Those whose hearts 'God has sent the Spirit of his Son into' (Gal. 4.6)? Those 'born of' Paul (Gal. 4.19)? Those 'born of' the Jerusalem above (Gal. 4.26)? Those who 'are children of the promise' (Gal. 4.28)? While the answer is all of the above, we note that Paul is also born of the free woman. If it was God who 'through his grace, was pleased to reveal his Son' to Paul (Gal. 1.15-16), we can say that it was also because of God's intervention that people were born of the free woman, just as the birth of Isaac (and the resurrection of Jesus Christ) (cf. Callaway 1986: 100) was the result of God's intervention.

Fourth, while 'the present Jerusalem' is under Roman subjugation in slavery, it is puzzling that the Mount Sinai that was associated with the giving and receiving of the Ten Commandments is now linked to slavery. If what was the sign of grace and liberation is now the sign of slavery, does it mean that what was considered freedom may not always be free?

Fifth, as Paul tells the Galatian believers that he is again 'in the pain of childbirth until Christ is formed in (*en*)' them (Gal. 4.19), he also cites Isa. 54.1: 'Rejoice, you childless one, you who bear no children, burst into song and shout, you who endure no birth pangs; for the children of the desolate woman are more numerous than the children of the one who is married' (Gal. 4.27). Is this repetition of 'birth pang' an intentional ambivalence? Of course, we can say that Paul's language is metaphorical and hence should not be understood literally.

Six, if Isa. 54.1, cited in Gal. 4.27, speaks of an eschatological scenario where the oppressed will be cared for, the 'descendants [of the barren and desolate woman] will possess the nations and will settle the desolate towns' (Isa. 54.3), and God will vindicate them as they inherit from God (Isa. 54.17), then the imperative in Gal. 4.30 to 'drive out the slave and her child' appears to contradict Gal. 4.27. Such a contradiction is further marked by the fact that both the imperatives in Gal. 4.27 (*euprantheti, rhexon, boeson*) and 4.30 (*ekbale*) are in second-person singular, which, for Susan Eastman, the command in 4.30 'does not speak directly to the Galatians, but to its original auditor, Abraham' (2006: 314). Now, if Gal. 4.27 does not say that the oppressed will revenge, then after 'the child who was born according to the flesh persecuted the child who was born according to the Spirit'

(Gal. 4.29), should the latter persecute the former? While biblical scholars do not take driving out as a persecution – whether driving out Judaism, non-Christian Jews or Jewish Christians – most claim that Paul indeed tells the Galatian believers to drive out the Judaizing troublemakers (Betz 1979: 251; Cole 2008: 185; de Boer 2011: 307–8; Di Mattei 2006: 121; Dunn 1993: 258–9; Fung 1988: 215; Guthrie 1992: 127; Hansen 1994: 150; Keener 2018: 227; Lightfoot 1957: 184; Luther 1939: 102; Martyn 1997: 433, 446, 450n168; Matera 1992: 177–9; Moo 2013: 311–12; Ridderbos 1953: 182; Witherington 1998: 338–9; etc.).

However, many biblical scholars are also concerned with the ethical implications of driving out the slave and her child. For instance, Pheme Perkins warns that 'one must take care not to confuse the drama of rhetoric with social realities on the ground' (2001: 93). Likewise, Carolyn Osiek writes, 'While Paul's allegory, for his own purposes, ends with Hagar still rejected, the reader of the Bible cannot forget Jesus' outreach to just such oppressed and forgotten ones' (1998: 426). Here, we can sense Osiek struggling with the text (cf. Cosgrove 1987: 233). Referring to John Bligh's comment that Gal. 4.30 'does not necessarily imply that non-Christian Judaism is doomed to extinction' and that we cannot infer Paul 'was ready to sound the death-knell of Judaism' (Bligh 1969: 407), C. K. Barrett argues that Gal. 4.30 is not 'a call to the Gentile Christians in the church of Antioch to rise up and expel their Jewish Christian brethren; it is rather the command of God to his (angelic) agents, and expresses what the fate of each party is to be' (1982: 165). And in calling Sarah's command 'uncharitable demand', F. F. Bruce thinks that the driving out imperative is 'contrary to Paul's policy elsewhere (cf. Rom. 11.13-21; 14.1-15.13) and is not a necessary inference from his language here' (1982: 224). Recently, deSilva highlights the connection between Gal. 4.30 and 4.31 and suggests that Paul

> seems to be more interested in the second half of the quotation, in which 'Scripture' declares the rival teachers and all those who remain 'under Torah' with them to be outside of the inheritance, and declares only those who have been born in the freedom of the promise and the Spirit to be God's heirs. This is the part of the quotation on which he actually comments in 4.31. (2018: 405)

Now, if Mary Callaway is right to suggest that based on Romans 4, 'the parallel which Paul draws between the barrenness of Sarah and the death of Jesus and between the conception of Isaac and the Resurrection of Jesus is presupposed in his midrash in Gal. 4.21-31' (1986: 100), then did Isaac, who according to Paul was persecuted (Gal. 4.29), retaliate and drive out the persecutor? If not, then the Galatian believers who are like Isaac (Gal. 4.28) also should not. We also should not forget that after Sarah's demand in Gen. 21.10, God told Abraham in Gen. 21.13, 'As for the son of the slave woman, I will make a nation of him also, because he is your offspring' (Gen. 21.13). Furthermore, if there is a comparison between Isaac and Jesus, then if Jesus did not retaliate, nobody should! While Richard Hays has a point when he writes, 'Lest this action [of driving out] seem too uncharitable for this interpretation to be correct, compare the anathema solemnly pronounced on the "troublemakers" in the letter's irate opening sentences (Gal. 1.6-9)'

(1989: 215n89), we need to ask who would perform the anathema, since Paul and his co-workers would be accursed if they preached a gospel contrary to what they first proclaimed to the Galatian believers (Gal. 1.8).

Seven, we see how Paul the persecutor becomes the persecuted, while those persecuted become the persecutors. If for Paul, Christ has freed us with respect to freedom (*tē eleutheria hēmas Christos ēleutherōsen* in Gal. 5.1), will Paul be free if he reacted to persecution by persecuting the persecutor in return? Moreover, how should we understand Gal. 5.14-15: 'For the whole law is summed up in a single commandment, "You shall love your neighbor as yourself." If, however, you bite and devour one another, take care that you are not consumed by one another'? Likewise, how seriously should we take Gal. 6.1-2 and 6.9-10?

One can certainly dispute and contend that we should not equate driving out 'the slave and her child' with persecuting them, but Paul's exhortation in Gal. 6.10 to 'work for the good of all, and especially for those of the family of faith' cannot be overlooked. More pertinent to the argument of this essay is that if the Galatian believers 'have received the Spirit' (Gal. 6.1; cf. 3.2, 5), and if for Paul 'the world has been crucified to me, and I to the world' (Gal. 6.14), it is unlikely that Paul would want the Galatian believers to expel the troublemakers.

Finally, as deSilva has drawn our attention to the connection between Gal. 4.30 and 4.31, we want to stress that the driving out takes place because of the matter of inheritance, which Paul stresses comes from God's promise to Abraham (Gal. 3.18, 29; cf. 4.1, 7). Indeed, as the verb 'to inherit' in Gal. 4.30 (*klēronomēsei*, future active indicative) is reiterated in 5.21 (*klēronomēsousin*, future active indicative) regarding inheriting the 'kingdom of God', the inheritance is under God's initiative, which is also tied to the guidance of the spirit (Gal. 5.18).

In the light of these ambivalences, initially highlighted by the Taiwanese transitional justice debates, this essay finds the one-to-one correspondence mode of understanding allegory inadequate. It does not consider the power dynamics and negotiation in Paul's tackling of, at least, six intertwining systems of convictions. As such, this essay agrees with Fredric Jameson's notion of allegory in describing modern Chinese literature, which Hillenbrand uses to show that 'national allegories are everywhere in 1980s and 1990s Taiwanese fiction' (2006: 647). For example, as Jameson points out that 'the allegorical spirit is profoundly discontinuous, a matter of breaks and heterogeneities, of the multiple polysemia of the dream rather than the homogeneous representation of the symbol' (1986: 73), Hillenbrand goes on to argue that 'allegory is all about duality: it is a double discourse in which the notion of a single, central, unified meaning is always potentially undone by the split-level structure of its form' (2006: 647). Note that duality does not necessarily lead to a fixed dichotomy. Hillenbrand elucidates further:

> Allegory allows for representational compromise between the two without ever finding, in any decisive way, for one side or the other. What *is* certain, however, is that allegory is divested of its autocratic and reactionary cast when the referents for its metaphoric movement are as unstable as those we find in decolonizing, multicultural, glocalist, even neo-imperialist Taiwan. Indeed, when the context to

which allegory is tied is as fluid as that of Taiwan – where so many different pasts and futures lie waiting to be claimed – allegory can become a finely modulated means of writing about questions of nation, identity, and belonging. (2006: 648)

As Brigitte Kahl has amply demonstrated the colonial context of Galatians (2010), we want to suggest that the ambivalence in Paul's allegory fits Hillenbrand's notion of 'finely modulated means of writing about questions of nation, identity, and belonging'. The 'representational compromise' fits James C. Scott's notion of hidden transcripts (1990: 1–16) as 'arts of resistance' in the face of subjugation and overpowering authority. Lest our notion of allegory seems too modern or postmodern, David Dawson's analyses of three Alexandrian allegorical traditions of Philo, Valentinus and Clement of Alexandria demonstrate that allegory 'is not so much about the meaning or lack of meaning in texts as it is a way of using texts and their meanings to situate oneself and one's community with respect to society and culture' (1992: 236). Allegory is also used to mimic, legitimate, critique, resist and reinterpret its culture and society. Here, Stephen Greenblatt's definition is also pertinent:

Allegory may dream of presenting the thing itself ... but its deeper purpose and its actual effect is to acknowledge the darkness, the arbitrariness, and the void that underlie, and paradoxically make possible, all representation of realms of light, order, and presence ... allegory arises in periods of loss, periods in which a once powerful theological, political, or familial authority is threatened with effacement. Allegory arises then from the painful absence of that which it claims to recover. (1981: vii–viii)

Both Greenblatt and Jameson have noted the discontinuity, fragmentariness and arbitrariness in allegory, but Greenblatt accentuates the psychical aspects of allegory, that is, 'the painful absence of that which it claims to recover'. Hence, what does Paul's allegory seek to recover? What contributes to the intense emotion in Galatians? In the light of Paul's deep regret and shame in having persecuted the church of God, we may say that Paul is concerned with the issue of absolutization that leads to violence and persecution. An absolutization that thinks that one is embodying and executing the law of God while one is actually against the law of God. An absolutization that fixes and objectifies one's understanding of others, leaving no space and freedom to perceive otherwise. An absolutization that even disregards the intervention of God. But instead of wanting to recover the loss and be in control again, Paul learns to let Jesus Christ, God and the spirit be in control. In Gal. 2.19-20, Paul writes, 'I have been crucified with Christ; and it is no longer I who live, but it is Christ who lives in me.'

Conclusion

While Kahl has argued that 'Paul's appeal to "drive out the slave woman" in Gal. 4.30 can be heard as a passionate outcry against Roman enslavement of Jews and nations/Gentiles alike' (2014: 267), and Tamez has similarly maintained that 'Gal. 4.30 would have to be interpreted to mean that the new life in Christ leaves no room for slavery' (2000: 269), the detrimental impacts of the 'driving out' language resonate throughout history (Trible and Russell 2006). Even if Paul himself did not tell the Galatian believers to drive out the Judaizing troublemakers, as Barrett and Eastman have propounded, Ulrich Luz's demonstration that 'the history of the interpretation and influence of the text is not an appendage but is an integral part of the interpretation' (2007: 65) teaches us that the meanings of the text are not delimited to the text itself. Fernando Segovia has further highlighted the role of the 'flesh-and-blood' interpreters by arguing that the text is a dynamic construction, resulting from how the interpreter understands and explains it, and as such, 'all recreations of meaning and all reconstructions of history are in the end regarded as constructs or representations: re-creations and re-constructions' (2000: 41).

This reminder that the text is neither a means nor a medium to meaning production is critical to our ethics of interpretation, lest we use the Scripture as a pretext to justify our agenda. Does Paul do the same thing in Gal. 4.30? From the Early Church until now, we are not content to let 'the slave and her child' only signify Hagar and Ishmael. For some, they refer to Judaism; for others, they are non-Christian Jews, or Jewish Christians, or even whoever oppose our goals and agenda. Scholars have also debated who should 'drive out the slave and her child'. The text is, indeed, a construction. The meaning we derive from the text is our construction. Therefore, it is important that we make explicit how we construct the text and its meaning.

Can Paul and his co-workers be driven out? Absolutely (Gal. 1.8; cf. 1 Cor. 9.27)! Such is the viewpoint of this essay from a Taiwanese context that wrestles with the issues of transitional justice. Given the contested modern histories of Taiwan, this essay is drawn to the apocalyptic features of Galatians that foreground God's intervention. The driving out can only be done by God since it is tied to the issue of inheritance, which is the prerogative of God. The intervention of God is important to loosen up our tight allegiance to our political party. Without divine intervention, we cannot be conscientized to perceive otherwise. The various versions of Taiwan's recent histories also help this essay to notice the ambivalences in Paul's allegory, which, contrary to scholars who take allegory as a one-to-one correspondence, seems to reveal Paul's tactic in addressing at least six intertwining systems of convictions in Galatians. These ambivalences can problematize and deconstruct any stable and fixed binary structure that aims to label and demonize the other. But just as Paul in Gal. 1.24 mentions that 'the churches of Judea that are in Christ' glorify God because of him, Taiwanese can be reminded that we are all interrelated and that we can work together for the common good of Taiwan. The constant propaganda and double standards against each other will only lead to the vicious cycle of attrition and distrust. We need God's intervention to help us be held accountable to our words and deeds so that we can move forward. The 'driving out' command should be understood in the context of inheritance, that is, the goal. As such, it can only be done by God.

References

Barrett, C. K. (1982), 'The Allegory of Abraham, Sarah, and Hagar in the Argument of Galatians', in *Essays on Paul*, 154–70, London: SPCK.

Beker, J. Christiaan (1980), *Paul the Apostle: The Triumph of God in Life and Thought*, Philadelphia: Fortress.

Betz, Hans Dieter (1979), *Galatians: A Commentary on Paul's Letter to the Churches in Galatia*, Hermeneia, Philadelphia: Fortress.

Bhabha, Homi K. (1994), 'The Other Question: Stereotype, Discrimination and the Discourse of Colonialism', in *The Location of Culture*, 66–84, London: Routledge.

Bligh, John (1969), *Galatians: A Discussion of St. Paul's Epistle*, Householder Commentaries, London: St. Paul Publications.

Boraine, Alexander L. (2006), 'Transitional Justice: A Holistic Interpretation', *Journal of International Affairs*, 60 (1): 17–27.

Boyarin, Daniel (1994), *A Radical Jew: Paul and the Politics of Identity*, Berkeley: University of California Press.

Bruce, F. F. (1982), *The Epistle to the Galatians: A Commentary on the Greek Text*, New International Greek Testament Commentary, Grand Rapids: Eerdmans.

Callaway, Mary (1986), *Sing, O Barren One: A Study in Comparative Midrash*, Atlanta: Society of Biblical Literature.

Castelli, Elizabeth A. (1994), 'Allegories of Hagar: Reading Galatians 4.21-31 with Postmodern Feminist Eyes', in Elizabeth Struthers Malbon and Edgard V. McKnight (eds), *The New Literary Criticism and the New Testament*, 228–50, Sheffield: Sheffield Academic Press.

Chen, Kuan-Hsing (2010), *Asia as Method: Toward Deimperialization*, Durham: Duke University Press.

Cole, R. Alan (2008), *Galatians: An Introduction and Commentary*, Tyndale New Testament Commentaries, Downers Grove: Inter-Varsity.

Cosgrove, Charles H. (1987), 'The Law Has Given Sarah No Children (Gal. 4.21–30)', *Novum Testamentum*, 29 (3): 219–35.

Dawson, David (1992), *Allegorical Readers and Cultural Revision in Ancient Alexandria*, Berkeley: University of California Press.

De Boer, Martinus C. (2011), *Galatians: A Commentary*, the New Testament Library, Louisville: Westminster John Knox.

DeSilva, David A. (2018), *The Letter to the Galatians*, New International Commentary on the New Testament, Grand Rapids: Eerdmans.

Di Mattei, Steven (2006), 'Paul's Allegory of the Two Covenants (Gal. 4.21-31) in Light of First-Century Hellenistic Rhetoric and Jewish Hermeneutics', *New Testament Studies*, 52 (2006): 102–22.

Dunn, James D. G. (1993), *The Epistle to the Galatians, Black's New Testament Commentaries*, London: A&C Black.

Eastman, Susan G. (2006), '"Cast Out the Slave Woman and Her Son": The Dynamics of Exclusion and Inclusion in Galatians 4:30', *Journal for the Study of the New Testament*, 28 (3): 309–36.

Fung, Ronald Y. K. (1988), *The Epistle to the Galatians, the New International Commentary on the New Testament*, Grand Rapids: Eerdmans.

Gaventa, Beverly R. (1990), 'The Maternity of Paul: An Exegetical Study of Galatians 4:19', in Robert T. Fortna and Beverly R. Gaventa (eds), *The Conversation Continues: Studies in Paul and John in Honor of J. Louis Martyn*, 189–201, Nashville: Abingdon.

Greenblatt, Stephen J. (1981), 'Preface', in Stephen J. Greenblatt (ed.), *Allegory and Representation: Selected Papers from the English Institute, 1979–80*, vii–xiii, Baltimore: Johns Hopkins University Press.

Guthrie, Donald (1992), *Galatians*, New Century Bible Commentary, Grand Rapids: Eerdmans.

Hansen, G. Walter (1994), *Galatians*, IVP New Testament Commentaries, Downers Grove: InterVarsity.

Hartnetta, Stephen J., Patrick Shaou-Whea Dodgeb and Lisa B. Keränena (2020), 'Postcolonial Remembering in Taiwan: 228 and Transitional Justice as "The End of Fear"', *Journal of International and Intercultural Communication*, 13 (3): 238–56.

Hays, Richard B. (1989), *Echoes of Scripture in the Letters of Paul*, New Haven: Yale University Press.

Hays, Richard B. (2000), 'The Letter to the Galatians: Introduction, Commentary, and Reflections', in *The New Interpreter's Bible*, vol. XI: 181–348, Nashville: Abingdon.

Hillenbrand, Margaret (2006), 'The National Allegory Revisited: Writing Private and Public in Contemporary Taiwan', *Positions*, 14 (3): 633–62.

Jameson, Fredric (1986), 'Third-World Literature in the Era of Multinational Capitalism', *Social Text*, 15: 65–88.

Kahl, Brigitte (2010), *Galatians Re-Imagined: Reading with the Eyes of the Vanquished*, Minneapolis: Fortress.

Kahl, Brigitte (2014), 'Hagar's Babylonian Captivity: A Roman Imagination of Galatians 4:21-31', *Interpretation: A Journal of Bible and Theology*, 68 (3): 257–69.

Keener, Craig S. (2018), *Galatians*, New Cambridge Bible Commentary, Cambridge: Cambridge University Press.

King, Martin Luther, Jr (2010), *Stride Toward Freedom: The Montgomery Story*, introduction by Clayborne Carson, Boston: Beacon.

Liao Ping-Hui (1999), 'Postcolonial Studies in Taiwan: Issues in Critical Debates', *Postcolonial Studies*, 2 (2): 199–211.

Lightfoot, J. B. (1957), *The Epistle of St. Paul to the Galatians, with Introductions, Notes and Dissertations*, Grand Rapids: Zondervan.

Luther, Martin (1939), *A Commentary on St. Paul's Epistle to the Galatians*, trans. Theodore Graebner, Grand Rapids: Zondervan.

Luz, Ulrich (2007), *Matthew 1–7: A Commentary*, Hermeneia, trans. James E. Crouch, Minneapolis: Fortress.

Martyn, J. Louis (1997), *Galatians: A New Translation with Introduction and Commentary*, Anchor Bible, New York: Doubleday.

Matera, Frank (1992), *Galatians*, Sacra Pagina, Collegeville: Liturgical.

Moo, Douglas J. (2013), *Galatians*, Baker Exegetical Commentary on the New Testament, Grand Rapids: Baker Academic.

Osiek, Carolyn (1998), 'Galatians', in Carol A. Newsom and Sharon H. Ringe (eds), *Women's Bible Commentary*, 423–7, expanded edition, Louisville: Westminster John Knox.

Patte, Daniel (1983), *Paul's Faith and the Power of the Gospel: A Structural Introduction to the Pauline Letters*, Philadelphia: Fortress.

Patte, Daniel (2018), *Romans: Three Exegetical Interpretations and the History of Reception, Vol. 1: Romans 1:1-32*, London: T&T Clark.
Perkins, Pheme (2001), *Abraham's Divided Children: Galatians and the Politics of Faith*, New Testament in Context, Harrisburg: Trinity Press International.
Riches, John (2008), *Galatians through Centuries*, Blackwell Bible Commentaries, Malden: Blackwell.
Ridderbos, Herman N. (1953), *The Epistle of Paul to the Churches of Galatia*, Grand Rapids: Eerdmans.
Rowen, Ian, and Jamie Rowen (2017), 'Taiwan's Truth and Reconciliation Committee: The Geopolitics of Transitional Justice in A Contested State', *International Journal of Transitional Justice*, 11: 92–112.
Schafferer, Christian (2013), 'Taiwan', in Lavinia Stan and Nadya Nedelsky (eds), *Encyclopedia of Transitional Justice*, vol. 2: 472–8, Cambridge: Cambridge University Press.
Scott, James C. (1990), *Domination and the Arts of Resistance: Hidden Transcripts*, New Haven: Yale University Press.
Segovia, Fernando (2000), *Decolonizing Biblical Studies: A View from the Margins*, Maryknoll: Orbis.
Smolinske, Nicole (2019), 'Pursuing Citizen-Centric Transitional Justice Taiwan Truth and Reconciliation Commission', in Bonnie S. Glaser and Matthew P. Funaiole (eds), *Perspectives on Taiwan: Insights from the 2018 Taiwan–U.S. Policy Program*, 48–51, Center for Strategic and International Studies (CSIS). Available online: https://www.jstor.org/stable/resrep22549 (accessed 20 February 2023).
Tamez, Elsa (2000), 'Hagar and Sarah in Galatians: A Case Study in Freedom', *Word & World*, 20 (3): 265–71.
Teitel, Ruti G. (2014), 'Human Rights in Transition: Transitional Justice Genealogy', in *Globalizing Transitional Justice: Contemporary Essays*, 49–79, Oxford: Oxford University Press.
Trible, Phyllis, and Letty M. Russell, eds (2006), *Hagar, Sarah and Their Children: Jewish, Christian, and Muslim Perspectives*, Louisville: Westminster John Knox.
Tutu, Desmond (2004), *God Has a Dream: A Vision of Hope for Our Time*, New York: Doubleday.
Witherington, Ben, III (1998), *Grace in Galatia: A Commentary on Paul's Letter to the Galatians*, Grand Rapids: Eerdmans.
Zhang, Xudong, and Fredric Jameson (1998), 'Marxism and the Historicity of Theory: An Interview with Fredric Jameson', *New Literary History*, 29 (3): 353–83.
石忠山(Shih, Chong-shan) (2013)。〈轉型社會的民主、人權與法治—關於轉型正義的若干反思（'The Democracy of Transitional Justice, Human Rights and the Rule of Law: Some Reflections on Transitional Justice'）〉。《轉型正義（*Transitional Justice*）》。施正鋒編，37–71。台北：台灣國際研究學會。
施正鋒（Shih, Cheng-feng）(2013)。〈台灣轉型正義所面對的課題（'The Issues Faced by Taiwan's Transitional Justice'）〉。《轉型正義（*Transitional Justice*）》。施正鋒編，253–91。台北：台灣國際研究學會。
曾慶豹（Chin, Kenpa）(2016)。《約瑟和他的兄弟們 護教反共、黨國基督徒與臺灣基要 派的形成（*Joseph and His Brothers: Defend the Church and Against the Communist, and the Formation of KMT-Christian and Taiwan Fundamentalist*）》。台南：臺灣基督長老教會臺灣教會公報社。

INDEX OF SCRIPTURE

Genesis	108	20.18	47, 57–8
2	89		
21.10	6, 119, 126–7	Acts	
21.13	127	1.14	56
30.13	14	9	54, 56, 56 n.26
		9.13-14	123
Psalms		9.23-25	54
1.2	14	9.25-26	54
		9.26-27	55
Isaiah		9.28-30	55
54.1	126	9.31	57 n.29, 59 n.34
54.3	126	12.12	57
54.17	126	15.23-29	23 n.10
		18.1	59
Gospel of Matthew	57	22.17-21	55
22.37	90	23.26-30	23 n.10
26.49	35	26.32	54
26.56	58	28.17	63
27.29	35	28.30	63 n.42
28.8-10	52, 57	28.30-31	63
28.9	35		
		Romans	84–5
Gospel of Mark		1-7	80
1.30	59 n.34	1.1-6	47
14.50	58	1.7	21, 21 n.4, 47
15.18	35	1.7-8	22 n.10
		1.11-12	6
Gospel of Luke		1.18–3.20	80
1.28	35	4.6-9	14
7.36	50	5.3-5	13
8.1-3	57	5.12-21	80
23.49, 55-56	56	6.12-13	89, 99
24.1-12	56	6.15-23	91
24.34	58 n.31	6.16	89
		7	5, 94–5
Gospel of John	49, 57, 60	7-8	99
12.32	60	7.5	91
19.3	35	7.5-12	91
20.1-18	52	7.5–8.13	5, 84–100
20.11-18	57, 57 n.28	7.8	92
20.17-18	59 n.33	7.10	91

7.11	92	9.27	130
7.12	91, 91 n.10	14.33b-36	50
7.13	91 n.10, 92	15	52 n.15
7.13-25	97	15.2-8	58 n. 32
7.13–8.13	97	15.3-5	52–3
7.14	89, 94	15.3-6	4
7.14-23	94–5	15.5	58 n.31
7.14-8.13	2, 88–91, 97	15.6	4, 59 n.34
7.15-8.13	85, 99	15.8	70, 75
7.16	91, 91 n.10	15.1-11	52
7.18	91 n.10	15.3-4	52
7.19	91 n.10	15.3-5	53
7.19-20	90	15.3-6	53 n.18
7.21	91 n.10	15.5	52
7.21-24	92	15.6	52
7.23	89, 94	15.7	52
7.25	94–5	15.9	52
7.25a	90	15.10	52
7.25b	90, 96		
8.1-4	92, 95	2 Corinthians	34, 60
8.1-13	97	1.2	21
8.2	92	2.2	60
8.3	92	4.7-12	13
8.5	95	5:17	60
8.6	93	6.10	13
8.18-23	80	11.5	24
8.22	70	11.16-32	13
11.13-21	127	11.23-20	75
12.12, 15	13	11.32-33	54
14-15	49	13.11	13, 34 n.33,
14.1–15.13	127		34–5, 36 n.29
14.17	13		
14.22	14	Galatians	22 n.10, 55, 108
15.16	84, 86, 99	1	56 n.26
15.23-24	54	1.1-2	119
16.3-5	59	1.3	21
16.7	59	1.6-9	127
		1.7	123
1 Corinthians		1.8	119, 128, 130
1.3	21	1.11-12	119
1.3-4	22 n.10	1.13	126
2.2	60	1.13-14	119
3.2	70, 76, 79	1.15-16	54 n.20, 119, 126
7.40	14	1.17	55, 55 n.23
8–10	49	1.18-19	55
9.1-2	46, 58	1.22-24	122–3
9.5	59, 59 n.34,	1.24	130
	59 n.34	2.1-10	55
9.16	77	2.2	119

2.7	119, 123	6.10	128	
2.7-8	55	6.14	128	
2.19-20	129			
3	125	Ephesians	88	
3.2	128	1.2	21	
3.3	126	6.12	88–9	
3.5	128			
3.7	126	Philippians	3, 24 n.13, 34	
3.15-16	126	1.1	24	
3.18	119, 128	1.2	21	
3.23	126	1.2-3	22 n.10	
3.26	126	1.4	13, 15, 23 n.12	
3.28	60	1.18	14–15, 23 n.12	
3.29	119, 125	1.18-26	23, 37, 37	
4	114, 125		n.43, 38, 40	
4.1	119, 128	1.23	38	
4.3	123	1.24-25	40	
4.4-5	126	1:24-26	38	
4.6	123, 126	1.25	15, 23 n.12	
4.7	119, 128	1.27-29	38, 40	
4.15	14	1.27-30	38	
4.17	39	2.2	15, 23 n.12	
4.19	70, 76, 79, 126	2.5-11	114	
		2.16-17	40	
4.21	126	2.17	13	
4.21-31	2, 105, 109–11, 114–16, 120, 125, 127	2.17-18	15, 23, 23 n.12, 37, 37 n.43, 38-9	
		2.18	13	
4.21–5.1	124	2.25	23 n.12	
4.21-31	5, 125–6	2.25-30	15	
4.25	125	2.28-29	23 n.12	
4.26	125–6	3	15, 23 n.12	
4.27	126	3.1	3, 13–14, 23, 23 n.12, 24, 33–6, 36 n.39, 37, 37 n.43, 38, 40	
4.28	126–7			
4.29	119, 127			
4.30	6, 119, 126–30			
4.31	127	3.1b	38	
5.1	128	3.1b–4.1	3, 38	
5.10-12	24	3.1–4.1	14–15	
5.13-14	124	3.2	24, 36, 39	
5.14-15	128	3.2-3	38–9	
5.18	128	3.2–4.1	39 n.48	
5.19	124	3.4-15	15	
5.19-21	124	3.7-8	39	
5.21	128	3.7-4.1	24, 39	
5.22	124	3.7-16	24	
6.1	128	3.8	39	
6.1-2	128	3.10	16	
6.9-10	128	4.1	14–15, 38	

4.2-3	40	5.3	70
4.4	3, 13, 23–4, 33–6, 38, 40	2.7	69–70, 75–6, 79
		2.7-8	77
4.4-7	40 n.51	5.16	13
4.4b	40		
4.4b-9	40	2 Thessalonians	
4:4-20	37 n.44	1.2	21
4.10	23 n.12, 39		
4.10-13	14	Phlm 3	21
4.10-20	24, 38–40		
4.11-13, 19-20	39	1 Pet 1.2	21
4.13	16	2 Pet 1.2	21
4.17	39		
		James	
Colossians		1.1	22 n.10, 23 n.11
1.2	21	1.2	22–3 n.10, 23 n.11
1 Thessalonians	69		
1.1	21	Revelation	
1.1-2	22 n.10	1.4	21, 21 n.4
2	69	1.4-6	22 n.10

INDEX OF ANCIENT SOURCES

Augustine 103, 105–7, 113–16

Cicero, *On Moral Ends* 13
Clement of Alexandria 129
Cyprian 114

Diodorus Siculus, *Bibiloteca histórica* 24 n.16

Gellius, *Attic Nights* 76

Homer, *The Odyssey* 33

John Chyrsostom 116

Lucian 30–1

Origen 103, 112, 116

Philo 129
Plato, *Charmides* 28–9
Plato, *Epistules* 29, 31–2
Plutarch, *Alexander* 24 n.16
  Moralia 76

Quintilian, *Institutio Oratoria* 76

Seneca, *De Providentia* 72, 79
Sophocles, *Electra* 31, 31 n.26
Soranus, *Gynecology* 71

Tacitus, *Dialogus* 76
Theocritus, *Idylls* 33

Valentinus 129

INDEX OF AUTHORS

Adam, S. A. 22 n.10
Aitchison, J. 25 n.18
Alexander, L. 34 n.33, 34 n.35, 34 n.36
Allen, Amy L. 2, 5, 86, 88 n.5
Armstrong, Robert Edward, Captain 20
Arzt-Grabner, P. 22 n.10
Aymer, Margaret 75

Bal, Mieke vii, 1–2
Bar-Ilan, Meir 59 n.34
Barrett, C. K. 127, 130
Bassler, Jouette 16
Bauckham, Richard 4, 54
Bauer, Walter 84
Beard, Alison 12
Beard, M. 24 n.15
Beare, F. W. 34 n.33
Beker, J. Christiaan 90, 119
Betz, Hans Dieter 54 n.21, 55 n.22–23, 108, 108 n.1, 124, 127
Bhabha, Homi K. 120
Bienert, Wolfgang A. 110–11
Bird, C. S. 25
Bligh, John 127
Blot, R. K. 21 n. 5
Böhm, Thomas 112
Bonhoeffer, Dietrich 15
Boraine, Alexander 122
Boyarin, Daniel 120
Bradley, Keith R. 71–2, 72 n.3
Briggs, Sheila 114
Bruce, F. F. 127
Bruns, Gerald L. 111–12
Burke, Trevor 78
Byrne, Brendan 5, 89, 91, 94–7

Cahn, Steven M. 12
Caird, G. B. 38 n.45
Callaway, Mary 126–7
Campbell, William S. 1
Carey, Greg 3, 12

Carson, D. A. ix
Castelli, Elizabeth 16, 113, 120
Charry, Ellen T. 3, 12
Chen, Kuan-Hsing 121
Chin, Kenpa 122
Clark, Elizabeth 114
Cole, R. Alan 127
Collange, J.-F. 38–9
Collins, R .F. 22 n.10
Collopy, B 19 n. 1
Corbier, Mirelle 71
Cosgrove, Charles 114, 127
Coulmas, F. 25 n.17
Cousar, Charles 34 n.33
Craddock, F. B. 34 n.33
Craven, R. 20
Crisp, Justin E. 12

Daniélou, Jean 110–11
Davis, Anne 5, 114
Dawson, David 6, 120, 129
De Boer, Martinus 127
De Lubac, Henri 5, 103, 112–13
De Saussure, Ferdinand 28
DeSilva, David A. 124
Di Mattei, Steven 125, 127
Dixon, Suzanne 71–2, 72 n.3
Dodgeb, Patrick Shaou-Whea 122
Dormeyer, Detlev 59 n.34
Ducksworth, Angela 11
Dube, Musa 51 n.14
Dunn, James D. G. 108 n.1, 109, 127
Duranti, A. 25–6, 25 n.19

Eastman, Susan G. 126, 130
Edwards, M. J. 116
Ehrenreich, Barbara 12
Ehrensperger, Kathy 1
Eisenbaum, Pamela 94 n.14
Engberg-Pedersen, Troels 13–14, 38 n.47

Exler, F. X. J. 22 n.10, 26, 29–30, 29 n.23, 30 n.24, 32, 32 n.28
Exum, Cheryl 4, 53

Fee, G. D. 21 n. 5, 23 n.12, 34, 34 n.36, 36 n.41
Findlay, Marshall 3
Fowl, S. E. 34 n.34, 39 n.49, 40 n.51
Fredricksmeyer, E. 24
French, Valerie 71 n.2
Friedrich, G. 22 n.10
Fung, Ronald Y. K. 109, 127

Gaca, Kathy L. 1
Gadamer, Hans-Georg 2, 24 n.14
Gager, John G. 28
Galindo, Florencio 59 n. 34
Gaventa, Beverly 119
Gignilliat, Mark 110–11
Goddard, C. 20
Goh, Menghun 5–6
Goodspeed, E. J. 23 n.12
Gorman, Michael J. 16
Greenblatt, Stephen 6, 120, 129
Grenholm, Cristina 1–2
Grimshaw, A. D. 25
Guthrie, Donald 127

Haidt, Jonathan 3, 11, 15, 16
Hansen, G. 127
Harris, M. J. 34 n.36, 36 n.39
Harrison, J. R. 22 n.10, 34
Hawkins, Peter S. 1
Hartnetta, Stephen J 122
Hartin, P. J. 23 n.10
Haugh, M. 20
Havea, Jione x n.2
Haybron, Daniel 12, 13, 15
Hayes, J. Daniel ix
Hays, Richard 109, 127
Heil, J. P. 34 n.33
Hengel, Martin 4, 55 n.24, 56, 58 n. 32
Hillenbrand, Margaret 6, 120–1, 128–9
Hilliard, D. 21 n.7
Holder, R. Ward 1
Hooper, R. 25
Hopkins, W. E. 25, 25 n.20

Irvine, William B. 13

Jameson, Frederic 6, 120, 125, 128–9
Jewett, Robert 91 n.11
Johnson, L. T. 23 n.10

Kahl, Brigitte 119, 129–30
Kannengiesser, Charles 111
Keck, L. E. 36
Keener, Craig S. 124, 127
Kelly, William 37
Kenpa, Chin 122
Kepple, Robert J. 116
Keränena, Lisa B. 122
Kim, Yung Suk 13
King, Martin Luther, Jr. 15, 120
Kitzberger, Ingrid R. 4, 49, 60 n.37
Koleilat-Doany, N. 25
Koskenniemi, H. 35
Kreitner, Richard 15
Kreitzer, Larry J. 48

Lampe, Geoffrey William Hugo 108
Lanham, C. D. 21, 26–27, 32 n.30
Latta, R. 36 n.40
Lau, Peter H. W. x n.2
Liao, Ping-Hui 122
Lictehnberger, Hermann 63 n. 42
Lieu, J. 22 n.10, 26, 31
Lightfoot, J. B. 23 n.12, 37, 127
Llewelyn, S. R. 23 n.10
Longenecker, Richard N. 109
Lowe, Bruce A. 3, 28
Luther, Martin 85–6, 88, 88 n.4, 90, 92, 96, 127
Luz, Ulrich 6, 130

Macbeath, A. 36 n.40
MacDonald, Margaret Y. 71
MacDonald, Neal 110
Malinowski, B. 25
Martens, Peter 110–11
Matera, Frank 123, 127
Martin, R. P. 23 n. 10, 23 n.12, 119
Martyn, J. Louis 127
McKnight, Edgar V. 64 n.45
McMahon, Darren M. 12–13
McNeel, Jennifer H. 2, 4, 9, 70 n.1
Mickelson, A. Berkeley 109
Mihoc, Vasile 1
Moloney, Francis J. 57 n.28, 59 n.33

Index of Authors

Moo, Douglas J. 127
Morrice, W. G. 40 n.51
Moschella, Mary Clark 12
Moule, H. C. G. 34 n.36, 36–7
Mussner, F. 23 n.10

Newsom, Carol A. ix
North, J. A. 24, 24 n.15

O'Brien, P. T. 36 n.41, 38 n.45
Odell-Scott, David 1
Osiek, Carolyn 71, 127

Pao, D. W. 22 n.10
Patte, Daniel ix, 1–2, 5–6, 51 n.14, 90, 92, 94–5, 123–4
Penner, Todd viii
Perkins, Pheme 127
Pesch, Rudolf 53 n.17, 63 n.44
Pereboom, Derk 13
Peskowitz, Miriam 73, 79
Peterman, G. W. 39
Pixner, Bargil 58 n.30
Polaski, Sandra Hack 81
Porter, S. E. 22 n.10
Powery, Emerson 89, 89 n.7–9
Price, S. R. F 24 n.15
Purdie, N. 20

Radcliffe-Brown, A. R. 20
Rawson, Beryl 71–2, 72 n.3
Reed, J. T. 21 n.9, 22 n.10, 23 n.12, 26–7, 27 n.21, 34 n.36, 36–7
Rhoads, David viii, x n.2
Riches, John 125
Ricoeur, Paul 6, 64
Ridderbos, Herman N. 127
Ringe, Sharon H. ix
Rollinson, Philip 108
Rosenblatt, Marie-Eloise 4, 54 n.19
Rowen, Jamie 121
Rowen, Ian 121
Russell, Letty 5, 103, 113–14, 130
Ryan, J. M. 34 n.33

Sacks, H. 25–26
Sampley, J. P. 39 n.48
Saville-Troike, M. 25

Scalise, Charles 106–7
Schaff, Philip 106
Schafferer, Christian 122
Schegloff, E. A. 25
Scheid, J. 24 n.15
Schildgen, Brenda Deen 1
Schumacher, T. 22 n.10
Schüssler Fiorenza, Elisabeth 50, 50 n.10, 53 n.18
Schweitzer, A. 24 n.14
Schwemer, Anna Maria 4, 55 n.24, 56, 58 n. 32
Scott, James C. 129
Segovia, Fernando viii, 130
Seligman, Martin E. P. 3, 11, 15
Shantz, Colleen 14–15
Shih, Cheng-feng 122
Shelley, Percy Bysshe 61
Shuster, Marguerite 91–2
Steiner, Leslie Morgan 73, 81
Smolinske, Nicole 121
Stichele, Caroline Vander viii
Stowers, S. K. 39 n.50
Strawn, Brent A. 12
Sudiacal, Sid 2, 5
Swift, R. S. 20

Tamez, Elsa 126, 130
Teitel, Ruti 120–1
Thurston, B.B. 34 n.33
Tolbert, Mary Ann viii
Tolkien, J. R. R. 19
Tough, Paul 11
Trapp, Michael 26–7, 30, 33 n.31, 35
Trible, Phyllis 130
Tulloch, Janet H. 71
Tutu, Desmond 124–5

Vaka'uta, Nasili x n.2
Van Voorst, R.E. 22 n.19
Vandenberg-Daves, Jodi 73–4, 80
Vasquez Reyes, Maritza 93 n.12
Vincent, Marvin R. 34 n.33, 37 n.42
Vitrano, Christine 12, 15
Volf, Miroslav 12
Vögtle, Anton 53 n.17
Vouga, F. 23 n.10
Von Padberg, Lutz E. 63

Waldman, Ayelet 73–4
Weima, Jeffrey 21 n.9, 27
Weiss, B. 36
Welborn, L. L. 1
West, Gerald 51 n.14
White, J. L. 21 n.8
Wierzbicka, Anna 20
Wiles, M. F. 112
Wilson, Eric G. 12

Witherington, Ben, III 125, 127
Wood, Susan K. 112–13
Woollcombe, K. J. 108
Wright, N.T. 36 n.40

Young, Frances 111–12
Youssouf, I. A. 25

Ziemann 32 n.28

www.ingramcontent.com/pod-product-compliance
Lightning Source LLC
Chambersburg PA
CBHW051527230426
43668CB00012B/1763